Military Power and
the Advance of Technology

Also of Interest

Thinking About National Security: Defense and Foreign Policy in a Dangerous World, Harold Brown

Laser Weapons in Space: Policy and Doctrine, edited by Keith B. Payne

†*U.S. Defense Planning: A Critique,* John Collins

Changing U.S. Military Manpower Realities, edited by Franklin D. Margiotta, James Brown, and Michael Collins

Nuclear Deterrence in U.S.-Soviet Relations, Keith B. Payne

Arms Control and Defense Postures in the 1980s, edited by Richard Burt

The Future of European Alliance Systems: NATO and the Warsaw Pact, edited by Arlene Idol Broadhurst

Arms Control in Transition: Proceedings of the Livermore Arms Control Conference, edited by Warren Heckrotte and George C. Smith

Strategy, Doctrine, and the Politics of Alliance: Theatre Nuclear Force Modernisation in NATO, Paul Buteux

The Evolution of U.S. Army Nuclear Doctrine, 1945–1980, John P. Rose

U.S. Military Power and Rapid Deployment Requirements in the 1980s, Sherwood S. Cordier

†*The Defense of the West: Strategic and European Security Issues Reappraised,* edited by Robert Kennedy and John M. Weinstein

†*Arms Control and International Security,* edited by Roman Kolkowicz and Neil Joeck

†*Toward Nuclear Disarmament and Global Security: A Search for Alternatives,* edited by Burns H. Weston

The Nuclear Freeze Debate: Arms Control Issues for the 1980s, edited by Paul M. Cole and William J. Taylor, Jr.

†Available in hardcover and paperback.

Westview Special Studies in Military Affairs

Military Power and the Advance of Technology: General Purpose Military Forces for the 1980s and Beyond
Seymour J. Deitchman

This new, fully revised edition of Dr. Deitchman's *New Technology and Military Power* (Westview, 1979) reflects the changes of the past five years, some of them major, in the world situation, in U.S. perceptions of national security needs, in U.S. assessments of the balance between strategic and general purpose weapons systems, and in the evolution of high technology weapons. Addressing our urgent need for multipurpose rapid deployment forces that can be sustained for fairly long periods, the book answers many important questions that have been discussed in Congress, at the Pentagon, in the White House, and, of course, in public debate: How has modern technology influenced the basic components of national security? Why must we now spend so much of our national budget to build credible general purpose forces? Is high technology running away with our military establishments and is it compatible with a large carrier force and a fleet of nuclear submarines? Why must we create an enormous arsenal of sophisticated nonnuclear weapons designed to assure victory in a battle where nuclear weapons will not be used by any of the combatants? Why do we need the potential of a preemptive presence in faraway theaters?

Dr. Deitchman also deals with the basic facts of the military-industrial complex, examining its institutional dynamics and constitutional barriers to change, its technological drive, and its societal inertia. He shows how simplistic journalistic prescriptions and trivial observations fail to do justice to the enormous complexity of an industrial economy with strong survival instincts and scientific energies.

Seymour J. Deitchman is vice-president, planning and evaluation, of the Institute for Defense Analyses, Arlington, Virginia. He spent five years with the Defense Department in various executive positions and was formerly the chairman of a NATO panel that studied some of the problems discussed in this book.

An **IDA** Book

Preparation of this book was supported
by a grant from the Central Research Program
of the Institute for Defense Analyses

Military Power and the Advance of Technology

General Purpose Military Forces for the 1980s and Beyond

Seymour J. Deitchman

Westview Press / Boulder, Colorado

Westview Special Studies in Military Affairs

This is a fully revised version of Seymour Deitchman's *New Technology and Military Power: General Purpose Military Forces for the 1980s and Beyond,* published by Westview Press in 1979.

Copyright © 1983 by Westview Press, Inc.

Published in 1983 in the United States of America by
  Westview Press, Inc.
  5500 Central Avenue
  Boulder, Colorado 80301
  Frederick A. Praeger, President and Publisher

Library of Congress Catalog Card Number 83-50434
ISBN 0-86531-573-6
ISBN 0-86531-574-4 (pbk.)

Composition for this book was provided by the author
Printed and bound in the United States of America

Before I built a wall I'd ask to know
What I was walling in or walling out . . .
—Robert Frost

Contents

List of Figures xiii
List of Tables xv
Preface to the First Edition xvii
Preface to the Second Edition xxi
List of Abbreviations xxiii

PART 1
THE GRADUAL "REVOLUTION" IN MILITARY TECHNOLOGY

1. **New Technologies** 3

2. **Tactical Nuclear Weapons** 11

   Military Effects of Tactical Nuclear Weapons 11
   The Nuclear Battlefield 14
   Problems of Escalation and Responsibility 22
   Concluding Comment: Chemical Weapons 28

3. **Tactical Air and Air Defenses** 31

   Uses of Tactical Air Power in Land Warfare 31
   Techniques of Air Attack 35
   The Problem of Hitting the Target 40
   Air Defenses 47
   Cruise Missiles: A Special Case 53
   Warfare in the Air 55
   The Consequences of Advanced Technology 59

4. **Tanks and Anti-Tank Guided Missiles** 67

   Warfare Between Armored Forces 68
   Defeating the Tank 75
   Anti-Tank Guided Missiles 77
   The Impact of ATGMs on Armored Warfare and Forces 81

ix

5.   **Ships and the Evolution of War at Sea**...................87

Background: The Purpose, the Threat, and Pressures for
    Change...87
Evolution of the Navy Since World War II................91
Modern Combat Operations at Sea......................98
Sources of Concern About the U.S. Navy...............105
The Special Problem of Vulnerability...................107
Groping for Some Ways Out...........................111

PART 2
USING THE GENERAL PURPOSE FORCES

6.   **Military Power in the Twentieth Century's Last Decades**....125

A Concise History of Warfare Since World War II.........129
Strategic Developments and Constraints.................134
On Deterrence and Escalation.........................146
Commitments and Prospects..........................150

7.   **The Soviet Union as "Threat"**.........................153

Looking East Toward the USSR........................154
Why Would the USSR Go to War?......................161
The Real Nature of the Threat.........................169

8.   **The Defense of Western Europe**.......................173

A Comparison of Military Strength......................174
Defending Germany with the New Weaponry: An
    Illustrative Scenario.................................184
Preparing the Conventional Defense.....................188
The Nuclear Deterrent................................192
Concluding Comments................................197

9.   **Rapid Deployment and the Uses of the Navy**.............199

Development of Strategy..............................199
The Prospects for Conflict............................201
Rapidly Deployable Military Capability..................206
The Navy in the Newly Developing Strategy..............211

PART 3
ABSORBING TECHNOLOGICAL CHANGE

10. **Frustrated Expectations**...............................219

Uses and Misuses of Technology........................226

11. **What Systems to Buy**.................................241

Extending the Utility of Systems........................242
Changing Institutional Patterns........................244

Notes 255
Index 269

Figures

3-1   Components of a Modern Air Attack Operation...................41

3-2   Ground-Based Air Defense Array.............................50

3-3   Interplay of Air Offense and Air Defense Capability
      Between NATO and USSR.....................................61

5-1   Comparison of Naval Formations—World War II
      and Now...93

5-2   Progression of Some Classes of Major Surface Combat
      Ships (Standard Displacement and Major Armaments
      Shown)..94

5-3   Schematic Drawing of the Air Defense of a Carrier Task
      Force..100

5-4   Elements of the Multimode Defense of the Surface Fleet
      Against Submarines.......................................104

6-1   National Expenditures in Selected Areas..................126

6-2   Ratio of Expenditures: $\dfrac{\text{Public Health and Education}}{\text{Defense}}$............128

6-3   Some "Statistics of Deadly Quarrels".....................135

7-1   Some Potentially Threatening Soviet Positions of
      Influence..159

8-1   NATO and Warsaw Pact Boundaries in Europe................174

8-2   Comparison of U.S. Military Investment Outlays with
      Estimated Dollar Cost of Soviet Military Investment
      Activities...176

8-3   Comparison of Estimated Atlantic Alliance + Japan
      Military Investment Outlays with Estimated Dollar Costs
      of Warsaw Pact Military Investment Activities.............177

8-4   NATO-Warsaw Pact Force Comparison........................178

8-5   Relative Trends in Main Battle Tanks and Artillery..............179

8-6   Defense of Northern and Central Regions......................181

9-1   Present and Potential War Areas of Concern to the
      United States...202

9-2   Restricted Soviet Access to Major Oceans.....................214

10-1 Cost-Performance Curves for Airborne Inertial
      Navigation Systems..227

10-2 Effect of Uncertainty on Advancing Technology to
      Improve Performance: A Hypothetical Case...................229

10-3 Example of Successful Performance Advance with
      Large Cost Reduction......................................230

10-4 Costs and Characteristics of Several Tanks....................235

10-5 Value of Ships Under Construction in Private
      U.S. Shipyards...238

10-6 Defense Share of the Monolithic Microcircuit Market............239

11-1 Allocation of Expenditures to Systems by the Military
      Services...247

11-2 History of Technical Manpower in a Key Defense Industry
      (Engineers and Scientists in Aerospace Research and
      Development) 252

Tables

3–1   Comparative Performance Indicators of Fighter-Bombers,
      1942-1985 42

3–2   Comparison of World War II and Current Tactical Air
      Attack Capability 46

3–3   Some Air Defense Missile Systems Available to NATO Forces 48

4–1   Comparison of U.S. and Soviet Armored Warfare
      Doctrine 72

5–1   Soviet Navy Order of Battle 89

5–2   Comparison of Aircraft Complements of Carrier Task
      Forces 95

5–3   Evolution of Fleet Firepower: 1944-1980 96

5–4   Aircraft Complement of Attack Carriers 97

5–5   Additional Aspects of Fleet Evolution 98

5–6   Hypothetical Cruise Missile Attack on a Modern Carrier
      Task Group 109

6–1   Some Military Engagements Since World War II 130

6–2   Derivations of Engagements 132

6–3   Strategic Developments and Constraints in the Modern
      World 137

6–4   Some Important Exported Soviet Capabilities 141

6–5   Situations of Apparently Effective Deterrence 146

8–1   NATO and Warsaw Pact Aircraft Strengths (Combat
      Aircraft in Place in Europe) 179

10–1 Cost-Performance Relationships for Fighter Aircraft
      Radars 228

10–2   The "Requirements Pyramid" (Based on a current major
       system acquisition)..232

10–3   An Example of Cost Growth: MARK II Avionics for the
       F-111 Aircraft..234

11–1   Acquisition Budget Allocation to Combat and Support
       Forces and Systems...246

11–2   Average Fraction of Acquisition Budgets Devoted to
       "Weapons" and "Platforms"..................................246

Preface to the First Edition

The general purpose military forces include the tanks of the Army, the airplanes of the Air Force, the ships and airplanes of the Navy, the Marines, and all that go with them. They comprise, essentially, all of our military forces other than the intercontinental nuclear forces. Under the umbrella of the balance of strategic deterrence, the general purpose forces are the ones that do the difficult work of projecting the image and the reality of American military power overseas.

These forces, together with a *pro rata* share of their essential support and the airlift and sealift needed to help them deploy overseas, absorb between 80 and 85 percent of the defense budget. They contain or occupy about 90 percent of the Defense Department's manpower. The problems they engender and the issues they raise for defense policy are legion. They can be treated in all their glory and at great length, and their various aspects have been the subject of many recent works. A comprehensive treatment of the general purpose forces was my original purpose in this book, but it did not work out that way.

As I attempted to come to grips with the problems involved in creating, sustaining, and using the general purpose forces, one underlying circumstance gradually became apparent: The advance of technology since World War II has transformed these forces, as it has transformed our society. It has changed their structure, their operations, their budgets. It has created the most serious problems they face, no matter how those problems are expressed—in terms of cost, operational capability, force size, or the value of specific systems. Yet these latter manifestations are the matters about which most of the explicit arguments on defense policy, outside the strategic force areas, revolve. Even a cursory survey of how the news media report on military matters shows that as a nation we still tend to visualize our armed forces as being similar to those that fought and won World War II. It may be that this view persists because, for most Americans, movies based on World War II are the main illustration of how the armed forces operate. Whatever the reason, it is from the clash between these outdated perceptions of our armed forces and what they have actually become that most of the cost, capability, and size arguments arise. We must exert a conscious effort to resolve these dissonances, or we will never see rational planning of the parts of our military forces that most visibly contribute to and influence our foreign policy.

The reader should know my values and biases: I believe, as I will attempt to show, that military force has a place and an importance in today's world. There will be no comfort in this book for those who want to reduce the defense budget. On the other hand, the military, political, and economic conditions affecting the use of military power today and in the forseeable future are not, in my view, well understood. In discoursing on them, I will not please those who think that strong defense forces are all we need to solve our most pressing international problems. One major area of public complaint is the high cost of the general purpose forces, as expressed in the cost of major weapon systems. These high costs are often blamed on poor management, and, surely, management difficulties contribute their share. But I make no blanket criticism of the management of the armed forces; the cost problems are at least as much structural as managerial, if not more so. However, I do not make any general call for increased defense spending. Some increase is probably necessary, but the most serious problems of the general purpose forces can be solved more readily by changing policy and force design than by throwing more money at them.

The public is of course well aware that the military technology has created capabilities that were beyond conception just a few years ago, and most of these new capabilities are embodied, as it were, in the so-called smart weapons. Such weapons have been the subjects of extensive exposition, both popular and learned. I do not believe, however, that these systems will make people obsolete on the battlefield, as do other defense experts, including some who should know better. I do believe that the new systems will drastically change the functioning and effectiveness of military forces on *both* sides of any future major conflict. We will have no monopoly on the technology, although we may have a transitory lead of a few years in implementing it, as we did in the strategic weapons area.

Finally, despite the revolutionary impact of new technology on military capabilities, I find no reason for a corresponding revolution in the composition, the structure, or the operation of the general purpose forces. We must live with our past decisions and investments in this as in any other area. But evolutionary change is essential; it must be undertaken carefully, and in many cases it will become apparent that less rather than more change may be the preferable course. I think these issues bear on the very life and death of the nation. They must be approached cautiously, with some deference to the uncertain and the unknown.

The issues of the general purpose forces are extremely complex, and I do not pretend to have complete or absolute answers to any one of those issues. Answers emerge from the day-to-day business of management by those responsible for the programs. My aim here is to increase our understanding of the directions in which our armed forces have been moving so that alternative solutions to the major issues can be evaluated. I have focused on clarifying what these trends have been in the last three decades and suggesting what they might be in the future.

*   *   *

Many acknowledgments are in order. All the analyses, interpretations, conclusions, and opinions expressed in this book are my own and I accept full responsibility for them. However, the development of ideas and learning to appreciate and understand them is the result of many years of interaction with countless colleagues. While their influences are usually difficult to trace, I am pleased to be able to mention a few individuals whose impact, through discussion and argument, was particularly direct: Douglas Andrews, Harry Davis, Bruce Erwin, Alexander Flax, Wilbur Payne, and David Signori. Chapter 5, on the problems of the Navy, was thoroughly and mercilessly reviewed by Rear Adm. Conrad Abhau, USN (Ret.), Jerome Bracken, Capt. John Coiner, USN, John Metzko, and William Schultis. Jesse Orlansky provided background information on defense manpower issues and reviewed and commented most helpfully on my treatment of those issues in Chapter 10. I am deeply grateful to Adm. Noel Gayler, USN (Ret.), and Gen. Andrew Goodpaster, USA (Ret.), for the time they took from busy schedules to read and comment on the manuscript. Their suggestions, advice, and encouragement were invaluable.

The Institute for Defense Analyses provided essential support through its Central Research Program in library services (including especially the efforts of Nick Mercury), graphics and reproduction, research assistance, and in many other virtually unnoticed ways, down to the use of the telephone. Janet Kiernan and Nita S. Schriner spent tireless hours searching out vaguely defined references and citations. Mrs. Schriner also amassed much of the historical data on the U.S. Navy, on wars since World War II, and on many other subjects that were thrown at her as I happened to think of them. James McCullough and members of his IDA Cost Analysis Group, especially James DeLang and Mark Knapp, provided most of the cost data presented here. I must hasten to add that all use of those data has been strictly on my own. The quotation from E. E. Morison, in Chapter 1, is gratefully acknowledged where it is used. Much of the foundation for Chapter 6, on military power in the last decades of the twentieth century, was laid in three talks I gave at the National War College between 1970 and 1974, and in a derivative article in *Military Review*, vol. 51, no. 7, July 1971. Chapter 3, on tactical air power, was published in an abbreviated, more technical form in the *Air University Review*, vol. 29, no. 1, November-December 1977. Similarly, a condensed version of Chapter 5 was published in *Astronautics and Aeronautics*, vol. 16, no. 11, November 1978. I am also indebted to the MIT Press for permission to quote extensively from my earlier book, as noted in the section of Chapter 2 on the nuclear battlefield.

A special debt of gratitude is due my secretary, Becky McMorrow, who typed and retyped the manuscript more times than she likes to remember and who managed the work of reproducing and assembling it each time. My wife provided some of the impetus toward starting this book, simply by being deeply involved in her own profession and working what she and I called "Pentagon hours" long after I stopped. I salute her contribution with affection.

None of the conclusions or opinions in this book should be taken as expressions of policy held or advocated by IDA or any governmental agency unless explicitly attributed as a quotation from a policy document. I must also note that, although the press of time in completing the manuscript precluded treatment of the U.S. Marine Corps' amphibious mission, that omission should not be taken as a judgment on the need for or importance of the mission. The problems facing the Marines in other aspects of land and air warfare are much the same as those described in Chapters 2, 3, 4, and 10.

S. J. Deitchman

Preface to the Second Edition

The world of defense has changed rapidly in the four years since the first edition of this book was published. The changes are mainly changes in outlook: The defense budget has increased sharply. The country has suffered a serious economic recession. The arguments now are not about whether the defense budget should increase but about whether it has increased too much or is increasing too fast. Emphasis in our global strategy has moved away from Europe and toward other parts of the world. The advancing technology of the armed forces has been attacked as being too much, too expensive, and too difficult to digest.

At the same time, the underlying technological trends that the first edition described remain, as do the basic problems of strategy, tactics, and force structure that those trends engender. Policy can be changed at the stroke of a pen, but the building of military capability takes decades and its direction is not easily shifted. That direction and its significance can, however, take on different aspects in the light of new policies.

For these reasons it appeared worthwhile to bring the data, analyses, and discussions of the first edition up to date. Some fuzziness in my thinking about the structure of the Navy has also been cleared up, and I have taken a more global view of the issues of strategy in planning and using the general purpose forces. The book has also been simplified for students of defense issues and the interested lay reader through the removal of the more complex data presentations and the discussions of management issues that were meant mainly for defense specialists. Finally, I have made a heroic attempt to simplify the complex sentence structure and technical vocabulary that marked my writing in the first edition and made it difficult for the nonexpert to read. Only you can tell me whether I have succeeded in all these aims.

The book is organized to lead the reader through the structure of the general purpose forces as it has been affected and changed by advancing technology. The evolving modes of military operation, tactics, and some elements of strategy are covered in Part 1, which stands by itself but is important for a full appreciation of the global strategy and national security problems that are covered in Part 2. Part 3, which in the earlier volume attempted to cover the whole range of management issues in creating and sustaining the general purpose forces, has been condensed here to deal with only two issues: how we use military technology to create the armed forces, and whether we have pushed that use beyond sensible limits. There are no issues of greater importance affecting our national security being argued before the public today.

Given this structure, the book can be used flexibly. Those who want to follow my logic as it develops and appreciate the full extent of the interactions among advancing technology, the weapon systems and supporting systems it creates, the form and functions of the armed forces, the issues of tactics, strategy, and policy that accompany them, and the nature of the arguments about all these things, should simply start at the beginning and read through to the end. In any case, however, I would recommend that all readers start with Chapter 1, which is brief but sets the stage for all that follows. Those who want to get right into the issues of global strategy can go directly on to Part 2, while those who want to enter the debate about whether we are pressing the frontiers of technology too hard in our defense programs can skip to Part 3 instead.

Many opinions and interpretations of data are contained in this book. I take full responsibility for all of them. Nothing in the book should be taken as necessarily representing the views of the Institute for Defense Analyses (IDA) or any agency of the U.S. government. I am grateful to IDA for the support from its Central Research Program that made the book possible and to Alexander Flax for his many helpful comments on the draft manuscript. As usual there is a lot of plain hard work in the background. I would especially thank Becky McMorrow for typing the many drafts; Ellen Bailey for helping in the same task; Evelynn Putnam for searching out obscure facts and references; and many staff members of the IDA library, graphics, and publications departments for helping in many ways to bring the final volume together. In particular, the phototypesetting efforts of Carol Evans, Margery Brighton, and Pat Lequar and the figures drawn by members of the graphics section created the text and imagery the reader will encounter in all the following pages. I must also note with gratitude the time taken by many members of the faculty and the student body of the U.S. Air Force Academy to advise me on how to make this book better than it started out to be. Especially, Major David W. Keith, USAF, helped me understand how to bridge the communication gap between specialist and student. Finally, I am indebted to the editorial staff of Westview Press for their efforts far above and beyond the call of duty to put my chapter notes and references in reasonable form for the general reader to follow.

S. J. Deitchman

Abbreviations

AA	Anti-aircraft (gun)
AAW	Anti-air warfare (usually in naval context)
APC	Armored personnel carrier
ASW	Anti-submarine warfare
ATGM	Anti-tank guided missile(s)
AWACS	Airborne warning and control system
BMP	Soviet armored infantry combat vehicle
CAP	Combat air patrol
CEP	Circular error probable (circle of dispersion, within which 50 percent of ballistic weapons will fall)
CV	Conventionally powered, multi-mission aircraft carrier (attack and ASW)
CVAN	Nuclear-powered attack carrier
CVN	Nuclear-powered multi-mission aircraft carrier (attack and ASW)
EEC	European Economic Community
FAC	Forward air controller (for close air support)
FEBA	Forward edge of the battle area (described forward defensive zone in frontal land warfare)
FRG	Federal Republic of Germany (West Germany)
GAO	General Accounting Office
GCI	Ground-controlled interception
GIUK	Greenland-Iceland-United Kingdom (refers to sea passages between them)
GLCM	Ground-launched cruise missile
GNP	Gross national product
HEAT	High-explosive anti-tank (ammunition)
ICBM	Intercontinental ballistic missile
IDA	Institute for Defense Analyses
IFF	Identification, friend or foe
IISS	International Institute for Strategic Studies

INF	Intermediate-range Nuclear Force
IR	Infrared
IRBM	Intermediate-range ballistic missile
ITV	Improved TOW vehicle
Km	Kilometers
LAW	Light anti-tank weapon
MICV	Mechanized infantry combat vehicle
mm	Millimeters
MRASM	Medium-range air-to-surface missile
MRBM	Medium-range ballistic missile
MTI	Moving target indication
MTT	Moving target tracking
NASA	National Aeronautics and Space Administration
NATO	North Atlantic Treaty Organization
nmi	Nautical miles
OMG	Operational Maneuver Groups
OPEC	Organization of Petroleum Exporting Countries
PGM	Precision-guided munition
PLO	Palestine Liberation Organization
RAF	Royal Air Force
R&D	Research and development
RDF	Rapid Deployment Force
RDT&E	Research, development, test, and evaluation
RPV	Remotely piloted vehicle (refers to unmanned aircraft piloted by radio link from the ground)
SAM	Surface-to-air missile
SLBM	Submarine-launched ballistic missile(s)
SS	Diesel-powered attack submarine
SSBN	Nuclear-powered submarine for launching strategic ballistic missiles
SSN	Nuclear-powered attack submarine
TFX	Tactical fighter-bomber (F-111) (subject of controversy in the sixties)
TOW	Acronym for U.S. long-range, wire-guided ATGM
TV	Television (missile guidance)
USSR	Union of Soviet Socialist Republics
V/STOL	Vertical or short takeoff and landing (aircraft)
WP	Warsaw Pact
WW	World War I: 1914-1918; World War II: 1939-1945

Military Power and
the Advance of Technology

Part 1
The Gradual "Revolution" in
Military Technology

1
New Technologies

From the time military forces came into being they have continually improved their weapons and tactics. But only rarely has the appearance of new kinds of weapons and tactics brought about revolutionary change in the course of warfare. The Greek phalanx, developed further by Philip of Macedon and used by Alexander the Great and the Roman legions, was one such change. The light cavalry and the archers of the Asian plains, sweeping every foe before them almost into modern times, represented another. A third derived from the breeding of plow horses capable of pulling implements through the wet, heavy north European soil and the invention of the stirrup, both of which supported the creation of heavy armored cavalry. Additional examples of this kind of military invention and its impact include the use of the English longbow, which defeated that cavalry; gunpowder, which led over the centuries to the development of artillery, powerful small arms, and the machine gun; the tank; and sea-based tactical aircraft for naval warfare.[1] Although the effect of some of these developments was immediate and drastic (as with the Greek phalanx and naval aircraft), the impact of others was more gradual, taking place over decades or even centuries. The old and the new existed side by side in differing proportions until the new completely replaced the old.

World War II was a period of sudden change in the military arts and sciences, and we have since been in the midst of another. The most recent and ongoing period is somewhat enigmatic, because the revolutionary weapons and tactics have been demonstrated only on a relatively small scale in wars peripheral to the mainstreams of history and without decisive impact. Yet the capabilities have become known from these modest demonstrations and from field tests. They are represented in the holdings of all major and many minor military powers. In a few instances they have become the property of primitive guerrillas and terrorists. Experience suggests that any future major war will be as different from World War II as that war was from World War I and all others that preceded it. However, it is difficult to separate fact and balanced assessment from the portentous anxieties, fears, and hyperbole resulting from popularization and advocacy. Thus no clear view of the current situation exists. Realistically, short of a major military conflagration, it is impossible to obtain a clear view but perhaps it is possible to clarify the points of argument and the nature of the uncertainties. The major outlines of military developments for the tactical forces that emerged from World War II are well known, but we will review them to establish a frame of reference for what follows.

Operation of land forces by the end of the war was characterized by the massive use of armor and tactical aircraft in land battles. This usage broke the stalemate in which the infantry had found itself at the end of World War I—a stalemate that had been building since the American Civil War, and that was caused by the advent of the machine gun and improvements in artillery, culminating in the evolution of huge armies facing and mauling each other from trenches on a static line. In 1939, maneuver, which had in general characterized pre-1914 warfare, again became possible, but the fields of battle and the scope of the manuevers were greatly expanded. We can appreciate the difference by comparing the decisive battle of Waterloo in 1815 with the movement of the U.S. Third Army across France in World War II.

The field of Waterloo comprised an area approximately 2.5 miles by 0.5 mile.[2] The respective armies of the Allies and the French numbered about 70,000 men, and the essential maneuvers by Napoleon, Wellington, and Blucher covered distances on the order of 12 miles. The battle, including preliminaries, took place over a period of three days, with the major action on one day. By contrast, Patton's army of about 200,000 men broke out from the Cotentin Peninsula on August 1, 1944, and in six weeks moved nearly 350 miles across France, stopping at a position roughly centered on Metz at the French-German border.[3] This was but one of the mass movements of armies using armor in World War II. Another example is that of the Soviet double envelopment of the German Sixth Army before Stalingrad. The two prongs of the envelopment were separated initially by about 125 miles, and each covered distances of 75 to 100 miles before they met at Kalach in the Sixth Army's rear.[4] Thus, in a century and a quarter, mechanization of ground forces and their support by air forces had changed the areas covered by critical battles from roughly the size of a township in the northeastern United States to the size of entire countries or more.

On the oceans, World War II saw the final demise of the gun-carrying ship of the line as the main conveyor and purveyor of naval power.[5] Instead the airplane and the submarine became key naval weapons. As tactical aircraft had limited range, the fleet provided a floating air base (the aircraft carrier) to bring the aircraft within range of their targets, and aircraft were used to attack opposing fleets and to carry firepower ashore from afar. Other ships mainly provided the carrier protection from surface fleets, enemy aircraft, and submarines; large-caliber naval gunfire came to be used primarily for shore bombardment prior to invasion.

Submarines, emerging in World War I as a scourge of the seas, were used mainly to attack shipping, but they also found a role on the periphery of naval battles that covered hundreds or thousands of square miles of ocean, picking off or dealing a death blow to an occasional warship. For example, the carrier *Yorktown* was finally sunk by a Japanese submarine after the battle of Midway. Sometimes such submarine action could be decisive, as it was in the battle of the Philippine Sea when U.S. submarines sank two major Japanese aircraft carriers, but this kind of contribution was rare. Ordinarily, submarines and small combat ships, at least by the end of World War II, could not challenge a large surface fleet.[6]

There was, in addition to surface-ship anti-submarine warfare, extensive growth of air power to defeat the submarine. Obviously airplanes, once available, would be used for any mission where their speed and range could help accomplish objectives that could not be otherwise realized. Shore-based long-range aircraft were used to search for and deliver weapons against submarines; aircraft from escort carriers (essentially, converted merchant ships) were also used for search and attack when possible. Submarines in the Atlantic proved especially vulnerable to anti-submarine operations from carriers because the submarines had to surface in order to refuel at sea and recharge their batteries for underwater operations. Although previously the Navy had been concerned mainly with forces on the sea, World War II saw major developments in the delivery and use of naval power from under as well as over the sea.

Differentiation of the tactical air forces into units having various missions and capabilities (which still exist today) actually began in World War I. Aeronautics was the area of greatest technical advance between the wars, and even the staunchest advocates of the use of aviation in warfare could hardly have conceived, in the early 1920s, of the combat missions this innovation would make possible just twenty years later. Force development included the specialization of airplanes into heavy and light bombers, fighters, and diverse utility aircraft that performed such tasks as observation and transportation. Fighters, such as the P-51 Mustang, were further specialized into interceptors, fighter-bombers, and long-range fighter escorts to accompany heavy or light bombers on their missions. Tactical aircraft were used to attack enemy forces approaching, as well as on, the battlefield, to destroy transport lines and facilities, and otherwise to inhibit military movement. They also commanded the airspace over the battlefield and over friendly territory to keep enemy aircraft from carrying out similar missions. Toward the end of World War II, the first, rather primitive versions of jet aircraft, which were ultimately to make great advances in speed, combat ceiling, and load-carrying capability, were just beginning to appear.

World War II also saw the emergence of two areas of technology that, together with aeronautics and submarines, were to revolutionize the conduct of warfare in the twentieth century: nuclear weapons and the evolution of the wireless of the 1920s into modern electronics. Keeping pace with these major technological advances during the war and since has been the development of diverse propulsion systems, including aircraft turbojets and fanjets, nuclear propulsion for submarines and surface ships, high-energy chemical fuels for rockets, and the turboshaft engines that made the helicopter a fully practical machine.

The impact of nuclear weapons on strategic war is widely recognized. With advanced delivery platforms, military forces can now deliver—at intercontinental distances with one vehicle—explosive power greater than that delivered by a 1,000-plane raid in World War II. Less commonly recognized by other than military specialists is the extent to which nuclear weapons have also changed the conditions of tactical warfare between armies, between aircraft, and between fleets. The problems of escalation and of damage to the civilian population, analogous to the problems of strategic use, are those most often cited in discussion of the use of tactical nuclear weapons. But these weapons have also made possible the delivery of enormously greater firepower in a smaller space and in a shorter time than was possible before their development. This potentiality has created as yet unsolved problems in the conceptions of maneuver and concentration of forces as well as in the management of space and time on and over the battlefield and at sea. It has also created the prospects of casualty rates and rapid destruction of ground, air, and naval forces that threaten the viability of such forces. These matters will be examined later.

Developments in electronics have given military forces other ways of "seeing"—radar, sonar, and many additional means of target detection and location, from radio direction finding to the sensing of heat-emitting radiation at infrared wavelengths. The growth of electronic technology has also led to our current ability to construct small, simple (relative to the human brain), electronic "brains," which are essentially computers and associated circuits that can integrate position and target data determined from the sensors and use these data to carry out control functions. Advances in electronics have been joined with the advances in performance made possible by parallel developments in aerodynamics and propulsion systems, and the combination has been supported by underlying technology in such areas as materials, chemistry, structures, and acoustics. This synthesis has permitted the development of guided weapons for diverse purposes varying from shooting down aircraft to attacking military vehicles or fixed installations at long range from the air or from the ground.

The combination of sensing in the electromagnetic spectrum and control through solid-state electronic devices has both captured the popular imagination and stimulated fears, which are expressed in discussions of the electronic battlefield and smart weapons, of war machines out of control.[7] On the other hand, we are told that our fascination with the advanced technology is leading to unnecessarily complex war machines that won't work at all.[8] A detailed examination of both the opportunities and constraints implied by all these technological developments and their impact on forces, tactics, and strategy is in order.

Advances in guidance as well as in vehicle performance, together with the destructive power of nuclear weapons, permitted the evolution and realization of ideas of strategic bombing that were developed in the World War II attacks on England, Germany, and Japan. On a smaller scale this conjunction of capabilities in high-speed tactical aircraft and short- to intermediate-range ballistic missiles has made it virtually impossible for military forces to escape major damage if nuclear weapons are used on the battlefield. The opportunity to incorporate such capability in the tactical air and ground forces and the need to account for their presence have, in turn, influenced the size of military units, their form, and their tactics for combat with conventional high-explosive weapons.

Development of guidance systems for weapons is, in still another evolutionary step, being reflected in new means by which military forces can exert greater conventional-weapons firepower. One of the important effects of joining sophisticated weapon guidance with more powerful high-explosive warheads has been a great increase in the destructive power of individual weapons, such as guided bombs or surface-to-air missiles. Not only does the greater explosive energy have more direct effect, it can more often be placed closer to its intended target. Now that the initial hurdles of learning how to effect this synthesis have been overcome, the rate of invention of such increasingly powerful weapons has also increased. In the cases where the sophistication of the weapons can be realized with the ruggedness and simplicity of the telephone (such as in certain anti-aircraft and anti-tank missiles), the most primitive of soldiers can use the weapons virtually as effectively as the soldiers of technologically advanced societies. The monopoly of the industrial nations over the means of modern warfare is weakening, largely through their own efforts.

At sea the development of nuclear propulsion for submarines has freed the submarines of the need to operate on the surface at all. This has eliminated a major vulnerability, and increased underwater speed, depth, and endurance have made the submarines hard to find and harder to protect against. Concurrent development of submarine-launched guided missiles has given undersea forces the ability to attack surface or underwater forces at long range and with nuclear weapons. A few weapons from a few undersea craft can be devastating to entire fleets. At the same time, the use of helicopters operating from relatively small ships to search, distribute acoustic sensors, or deliver weapons, and the use of long-endurance aircraft carrying improved electronic sensors and electronic data processors have extended the reach of antisubmarine warfare forces. Thus, in sea warfare as on or over land, space has been vastly expanded and time greatly compressed in prospective battles. Nuclear propulsion has also offered the prospect of relatively unlimited range for surface ships. However, this form of propulsion is relatively more expensive for small ships like cruisers than for large ships like carriers, thereby affecting the size and cost of a balanced fleet. The value of the application is thus more complex and its payoff less obvious than in submarine warfare. At the same time, marine gas turbines derived from aircraft engine technology offer many advantages for destroyer-size ships. Naval ship technology has thus advanced in several different directions at once.

In sum, the thirty to forty years since World War II have seen a vast array of developments in military technology. The public at large has been aware of all of them as they occurred individually, but it has been less aware of how, taken together, they have rendered essentially obsolete many aspects of the military techniques that emerged from World War II. At the same time, those techniques persist, and, because they remain effective when used in certain places, in certain ways, and in profusion, they cannot be neglected although they must be modified to meet the realities of the new weapons and sensors. The difficulties and disadvantages of the new technology, as well as the opportunities, demand attention in planning and undertaking military operations.

E. E. Morison described the state of the Navy in a similar period of rapid technological change, from about 1865 to 1890, as follows:

This was a time . . . of disordering confusion in the United States Navy. Part of this confusion . . . was produced simply by the flow of new things. It was hard to know how to use each new part and harder still, technically, to know how to fit them all together into a new structure. But the disorder was not just the product of technological change. It was caused in greater part by the fact that the naval officers did not know what to do with what they had. There was in fact a great and raging debate about the use of naval vessels in those days. Was the purpose of men-of-war to run down freighters and so starve the enemy; was it to lie off the harbors of principal cities and defend the coastline from the attacks of the enemy at sea; was it to lie in a line along a foreign coast and blockade the commerce of the enemy; was it to show the flag in an impressive way in distant ports?

To such questions, there was not, in those days, an answer. So the naval officers did the obvious thing. First, they went on building everything they could think of with the materials they had on hand. The result was a collection of ships designed to fulfill a wide variety of intentions that did not fit together in a working way as a fleet. *The hope, altogether natural, was that if the performance of the parts could be improved, the whole would fit together better.* So the officers set up boards to recommend improvements in the parts. There were boards on propellers, on boilers, on shells, on guns and engines and armor plate; there were boards on monitors and rams and commerce destroyers and cruisers and ironclads and ships of the first, second, and third rate. There were from 1865 to 1890 over one thousand boards looking at everything and, often at the same thing. . . . There was not much reduction of the prevailing confusion.

So the navy . . . sought to contain all the new machines and new forces that had produced a novel and unrecognized potential within a familiar pattern. Whatever the design and intended purpose of the new vessels, they were sent out on the old cruises and missions of the ship of the line. . . .

The situation was intensified for the naval service by several other considerations. As one thing after another dropped into the space 300 feet long by 80 broad, the members of that community came to believe that all those parts of their being that had been realized in the ship of the line were "put in the course of ultimate destruction." "Lounging through the watches of a steamer, or acting as firemen and coal heavers, will not produce in a seaman that combination of boldness, strength and skill which characterized the American sailor of an elder day." Worse still, the possibility of opening an engagement at a range of five miles "would create an indisposition to close" with the enemy, a reluctance to come into direct contact with reality.[9] [Emphasis added.]*

All of our general purpose forces are in an analogous state of uncertainty today—seeking a way through the kaleidoscopic onset of technological challenges to the known organizations, doctrines, and ways of doing things. The leaders of these forces are often reluctant to accept change, for complex reasons that we shall explore in Part 3. They are not very sure of how to proceed; and they are not being helped much by often strident and always diverse and conflicting advice from various segments of a public, each of which would like to see its money spent according to its own views.

---

*Excerpted from *From Know-How to Nowhere: The Development of American Technology,* by Elting E. Morison, © 1974 by Basic Books, Inc., Publishers, New York.

Tactical Nuclear Weapons

The advent of nuclear weapons and their diverse delivery systems has affected the armed forces of major nations more than any other technological advance. Even if nuclear weapons are not used, their presence determines much about the form of the armed forces, the design of their systems, and their tactics and strategy. The effects of such weapons must be understood if the implications of other technological changes are to be fully appreciated. Therefore we shall deal with them first.

As much has been written about tactical nuclear weapons in modern war as about any other topic in military and strategic affairs—and justifiably so. It is not my purpose here to repeat, review, or extend this literature per se. Rather, I wish to highlight some of the impact of the presence of tactical nuclear capability on so-called conventional warfare. I will begin with an examination of the battlefield implications of tactical nuclear weapons and then look at some of their broader ramifications, which will reappear in several contexts throughout this book.

Military Effects of Tactical Nuclear Weapons

Fission or fusion weapons, if they are ever used in profusion, will, to put it mildly, create a host of problems that will counterbalance their prospective military advantages. The prospect of their use visualizes quick and complete performance of what were previously difficult and lengthy tasks: destruction of large, threatening ground force units; destruction of important fixed installations, such as supply depots, airfields, or command centers; destruction of major naval units, such as aircraft carriers and submarines; and destruction of close formations of aircraft making mass raids.

Many of the problems in using these weapons lie in their ancillary effects. Nuclear explosions interfere with the operation of other systems, such as communications or aircraft that might be flying in the areas of the explosions. They can create blindness and cause fallout on friendly troops. They can contaminate with radiation the areas through which one's own forces must move or render these areas impassable because of craters and debris. Therefore, very close coordination of nuclear fire and other military activities is required if nuclear weapons are to be used over a wide area; it is not possible to allow nuclear-armed units to fire at will, even for purely military reasons. In addition, one could expect extensive collateral damage to nearby civilian populations, due to blast, heat, and fallout, since in war there is rarely a clear separation between military and civilian targets on land. Even if nuclear weapons are used exclusively at sea, there could in some circumstances remain the problem of creating fallout that can seriously affect populations on shores many miles away.

For such reasons there have been continuing efforts to reduce weapon yield to produce just enough for specific military tasks, but not enough to create extensive collateral effects, military or civilian. There have been parallel attempts to improve accuracy so that the smaller weapons will have the maximum effect by striking as closely as possible to their intended targets.[1] Enhanced-radiation weapons, the so-called neutron bomb of public controversy, resulted from this search. To illustrate the difficulties entailed in achieving the balance, consider a hypothetical example, that of trying to destroy attacking formations of tanks and other armored vehicles. We will consider "conventional" nuclear-weapons effects shown in the unclassified literature.[2]

A typical one-ton high-explosive (e.g., TNT) bomb must land within 5 to 20 feet of an armored fighting vehicle, depending on whether it is a tank or a more lightly armored personnel carrier, in order to disable it. Several aircraft loads of such bombs, under weapon delivery accuracy conditions existing prior to the advent of precision-guided munitions, might be required to destroy even one tank with certainty. With a powerful nuclear weapon— for example, 100 kilotons—and assuming that 10 pounds per square inch (psi) of overpressure* are required to do enough damage to the various weapons and vehicles to destroy the integrity of an armored fighting unit, an effective area approximately 2 kilometers (1.2 miles) in diameter could be covered. This would be enough to destroy or damage approximately 50 to 100 fighting vehicles in the typical dispersed formation adopted by modern armies. That is, one bomb of that size could knock a regiment out of action.

If the delivery were in error by even half a kilometer, it is likely that most of the desired military effect would still be achieved. But if 2 psi would hurt civilian structures seriously, the same bomb would create more general

---

*"Overpressure" is the term applied to the very rapid increase of air pressure above atmospheric pressure that is felt by the side of any object facing a nuclear explosion as the explosive wave passes over the object. This definition neglects many effects of terrain masking and other kinds of wave reflection and shielding, in the interest of simplicity.

destruction in a circle with a diameter of about 7.5 kilometers (4.5 miles). In typical Western European conditions, taken at random, a blast circle of this size would be likely to include two or three villages or towns of several thousand persons each.[3] In addition, depending on the design of the weapon, the height of the burst, and wind conditions, a much larger area could be affected by fallout for a longer period of time. The military unit wishing to use the weapons against an invader, but wanting to avoid the adverse effects on its own forces and the adjacent friendly population, might not always be able to employ the weapons when tactical conditions make such use necessary.

Suppose, therefore, that to minimize these side effects the unit uses only a 10-kiloton weapon, that is, one-tenth the yield of the original. Physics would work to its advantage: by the cube root law (which says that the radius at which a certain overpressure is created varies with the cube root of the yield), a weapon this size would still affect an area whose radius would be about half as large as that affected by the 100-kiloton weapon. Given the same dispersed formations, the smaller weapon might knock out an armored company having perhaps 15 tanks and other armored vehicles. To disable the company, the weapon would have to land within a few tens of meters of its aim point, rather than with the approximately half-kilometer accuracy tolerable with the larger weapon.

The integrity of the regiment of which the company would be a part would not be destroyed. But the blast would still affect an area over 3 kilometers (2 miles) in diameter, in which there would still probably be extensive civilian population and structures. That is, the smaller weapon would produce a much smaller military effect, but it would still create greater collateral damage than desirable or than could even be tolerated if the weapon were used on friendly territory against an invader. If such small weapons were used in greater profusion to assure the destruction of the entire regiment we are considering as an example, the side effects would be compounded and more widespread. Moreover, it might be noted that if nuclear weapons were to be relied upon heavily to destroy several prongs of an all-out armored envelopment in Central Europe, we would be dealing with, possibly, hundreds of regiments and other targets, not to mention the weapons used by the other side. It would be unlikely, in the fact of a massive attack, that just a few small weapons would be decisive in the absence of powerful conventional forces needing, perhaps, assistance at critical times and places.

Use of enhanced-radiation weapons would increase the area of military effect of each weapon by shifting much of the burden of that effect from the blast of the nuclear explosion to its emitted radiation. In the process, the area of collateral blast damage would be reduced (but not eliminated; the idea that "neutron bombs" kill people but do not damage structures is purely hyperbole).[4] It would then be possible to use smaller-yield weapons to achieve the effects described. But in my view, this would not fundamentally change the arithmetic of the scenarios outlined above: if using a few weapons will not do the military job, using many such weapons would lead to much the same overall effects as would extensive use of the weapons currently available. Although physical damage and its attending casualties would be reduced, radiation damage would be increased, and substantial numbers of people would likely be caught in the open. Also, the enemy would probably seek protection by deliberately "hugging" populated areas. One remembers vividly the streams of refugees fleeing the oncoming armies in France, Korea, Vietnam, and Lebanon. Moreover, there are problems of perception and escalation that would attend the use of any nuclear weapons, and changing the weapon type would not resolve them.

The Nuclear Battlefield

Supposing, however, that these weapons-effects problems were solved or accepted, how viable could a nuclear battlefield in the broader sense be expected to be? Since there has never been one, what we can say about it must of course be in the nature of speculation. However, there is probably no single question that has occupied the thoughts of ground warfare theorists more than this one since World War II.[5] There were, in the early years after the development of tactical nuclear weapons, many theories of how the nuclear battlefield would work, and military forces were designed to fit the theories. None of the approaches satisfactorily resolves the inherent conceptual or operational problems. All the theories and concepts of a nuclear battlefield—at least, a two-sided one—have unresolved flaws that render any possibility of successful implementation extremely doubtful.

The essential fact influencing the configuration of a nuclear battlefield conceived according to the various theories is, as suggested previously, the extreme vulnerability or large concentrations of men and materiel to small numbers of weapons. A prime principle of the application of military force has been that of concentration. Aside from the logistic concentrations necessary to supply troops in the field, the troops themselves must converge in strong groups to attack the enemy effectively with nonnuclear, or conventional, weapons. Concentrations of troops and supplies, as well as focal points of activity such as ports and airfields, are essential to conventional-weapons military activity and become most vulnerable to attack by nuclear weapons. It has been, therefore, necessary to rework the principles of concentration to rationalize battlefield operations in the face of the nuclear weapon threat. This has meant, in the new doctrines, that battle formations must in general be widely dispersed. The density of men occupying an area must be low enough that a nuclear burst will not destroy or cripple a substantial force.

Tactical aircraft are especially vulnerable when at rest on their bases and should be widely dispersed from the center of the airfield and protected by shelters able to withstand strong overpressures. When in operation against ground forces, formations of tactical aircraft using conventional weapons must mass for effect; if they are at a high enough altitude when approaching the battlefield, mass formations would be vulnerable to air defenses using nuclear warheads. To deliver nuclear weapons, only a few aircraft may be required. Thus, air tactics, tolerable levels of attrition, and the problems of anti-air defense become very different if the battle becomes nuclear.

Ideally, supplies should be dispersed among a large number of small depots that can be hidden, or moved if discovered. A substantial fraction of the supplies might then be contained within the vehicles and aircraft of the supply lines. Artillery weapons must not be massed together to protect positions and must not fire continuously on enemy concentrations, since their locations could then be easily traced. They must be dispersed and hidden, in formations designed to concentrate fire on particular targets. They may have to change position frequently. This would be especially true of dual-capable artillery and missile launchers that can fire nuclear as well as conventional weapons; they would be primary targets for enemy fire.

Even if nuclear weapons are used, conventional high-explosive weapons are still expected to play a very important role on the battlefield, at least in some part of the spectrum of escalation to all-out nuclear warfare at the strategic level. Armor will continue to be used for shock action, for mobile exploitation of breakthroughs in dispersed formations, and for protection against radiation from nuclear weapon bursts. Some concentration to achieve the full benefits of conventional-weapons firepower and to penetrate enemy positions in coordination with nuclear fire is still expected to be necessary. These combat concentrations are supposed to be brought together only when they can close so rapidly with the enemy that he cannot use nuclear weapons without hurting his own troops. This has been called the hugging tactic and has led to the replacement of the line of contact between opposing sides by the idea of a forward edge of the battle area (FEBA).

According to the theory of the FEBA in a fairly static situation, troops on both sides disperse into small, relatively independent units, each too small to be attractive as a nuclear target. They would not join together lest they become such targets as soon as they did; rather, they would remain separated and be interconnected by patrol activity, airplanes or helicopters, and radio communications. The enemy troops are expected to be similarly disposed, and the area covered by such small groups might extend for many kilometers into the territory nominally occupied by each side. Behind the FEBA, dispersed units are supposed to be deployed in great depth, so that in case of a breakthrough the defender can move to contain the enemy, trading space for time.

To break through the FEBA a sufficient concentration of men and weapons must be brought together. This may be done by infiltration into the FEBA, with the resulting concentration hugging and applying pressure against the enemy units until they are forced out of a specific defended zone. Or it can be done by concentrating conventional air and artillery fire or using nuclear weapons to reduce or remove resistance in specific parts of the forward area and to eliminate strongly defended points commanding lines of movement in the rear. The tactics of armored breakthrough offer another possibility. In any case mobile forces, armored to provide some protection from radiation hazards, must then be coalesced very rapidly to move through the gap that has been created in the opposing defenses; this movement must be followed by dispersal on the other side. Conversely, the defender may try to withdraw his forces rapidly after detecting the concentration to enable him to use a nuclear weapon against the buildup.

There is obviously a great premium on speed of movement. Concurrently, it is vital to gain intelligence of the enemy's force dispositions and movements with minimum time delay. The primary targets for nuclear weapons will now have become the rapidly appearing and disappearing concentrations of men and weapons, as well as the dangerous, elusive sources of nuclear firepower. Each side must, therefore, maintain continual surveillance of the opponent's activities and remain able to make timely strikes when suitable targets for nuclear weapons are found.

A number of severe problems of time, space, command and control are involved in this concept of the nuclear battlefield. Concentrations of troops or weapons, or individual targets such as missile batteries, will have to be discovered, identified, and related to the tactical situation; alternative actions will have to be considered and attacks or defensive maneuvers planned and carried out over large areas of landscape—perhaps thousands of square miles, involving hundreds or thousands of troops with their equipment and vehicles—all in periods of time that may be as short as a few minutes for individual units. This necessitates an acceleration of activities that would have required days or weeks under prenuclear conventional-weapons combat conditions. On the other hand, because of the risk attending discovery, many more actions of counterattack or defense, including ones that could previously have been undertaken on short notice, will have to be preceded and followed by secret troop movements that might under any circumstances be considered major undertakings.

All of this motion and the implied general tempo of battle create difficult problems of communication and control over the dispersed forces. In addition, the need for extremely rapid movement over great distances required by dispersed operations increases the logistics problem enormously. Even in World War II, where fuel was about half the total resupply requirement of an armored division, three times as much fuel could be used when the division changed from static to mobile operations. This could more than double again under the nuclear battlefield conditions described above. At the same time, vehicles and other mobile equipment, being in motion over longer distances in a shorter time, can be expected to require considerably more maintenance than in the past. More supplies will therefore be needed, but the time available to obtain them will be less. To these supplies will have to be added the greater amount of ammunition implied by possibly continuous interaction of forces along the FEBA and the attempted breakthrough operations.

With the increasing supply and maintenance problem arises a more difficult problem of distribution. A World War II army of six divisions might require about 5,000 tons of supply per day with a ten-day reserve in a single rear-area depot occupying several square miles of territory.[6] Total average load requirements could now be tripled, and the reserve supplies would have to be stored in many smaller depots miles apart. The number of vehicles needed for distribution to forward troops could double, or even quadruple if supply bases are kept movable or far to the rear. The maintenance and fuel problems would obviously be compounded still further. And the widespread use of aircraft instead of surface transport would not solve the basic problems. Aircraft require even larger amounts of fuel and maintenance, and they face further difficulties of greater detectability and of vulnerability on a nuclear battlefield. Bases of air-supply operations would have to be moved frequently with their crews and support equipment (such as major repair tools and loading devices), or else many would be required—in either case, a major logistic task in itself and one that is probably impractical.

Some of these problems are susceptible to solution, and indeed much of the research and development supporting the evolution of today's ground armies and tactical air forces has dealt with them. But a still greater difficulty is inherent in the philosophy of the conception. It is difficult to imagine that the implied frenzy of movement—perpetual motion, as it were—can take place only as a means of passive protection. It must be associated with vigorous attacks that have a goal: destruction of the enemy's forces and occupation of his territory or repulsion of his attacks. The further implication is, therefore, that a nuclear ground battle will be short and intense. This poses a contradiction. The type of force that could accommodate itself to the difficulties of logistic support would be a small one, since large forces would find it difficult to remain dispersed and mobile and to maintain the rapid shifts of disposition over the entire combat area that are needed to avoid static concentration. Yet in areas where wars like this could conceivably take place—Europe or Central and Eastern Asia—large armies would likely be needed to effect the simultaneous attacks and occupation needed to ensure rapid victory.

Despite their dispersal and continual changes of position, troops would run the risk of being struck by nuclear weapons occasionally, and maybe more than occasionally. A nuclear weapon dropped on concentrated forces in the open is certain to cause a sudden surge of casualties much greater than that expected from even heavy combat with conventional weapons. If the number of injured is more than can be treated, a severe problem of medical ethics will present itself: Should the most severely injured or the most likely to survive receive priority for treatment? However the issue is resolved, those selected will need immediate attention, and then they will have to be transferred rapidly to a large number of hospitals in rear areas. Aside from facing the difficulty of marshaling the needed doctors and ambulances in a short time, the forces in the bombed area would probably come under enemy follow-up attacks during this critical period. The shock effect of such a sequence is unknown, but it is easy to conceive of a complete halt or disintegration of organized military activity in a large area as a result. The attacking forces themselves may not be immune to the shock of a nuclear burst if it takes them by surprise and they have not been thoroughly trained beforehand—as is suggested by the events immediately after the crater was blown before Petersburg in 1864.[7]

Attempts to think logically about all these problems have led to further theories, ranging from static confrontation by dug-in-forces[8] through maneuver of small forces in a large countryside, much like ships at sea,[9] to reduction of armies to little more than well-equipped guerrillas. None of these approaches shows how the problems and contradictions might be overcome. Moreover, all of the foregoing has dealt with the area of the nuclear battle-field itself. The problem of entering the battlefield, or theater of operations, and supporting the combat forces on it through the relatively few available port and airfield facilities is a related but separate factor. These points would be as vulnerable to nuclear attack as any other concentrations. Although such facilities may be candidates for a sanctuary role in a limited war, it would probably be overly hopeful to depend on such protection for them if the war becomes nuclear. They would be tempting targets, especially if they represented part of the "outside" from which nuclear-capable forces could enter the battle.

Alternative tactics might include reliance upon completely air-supported operations, with appropriately designed aircraft using small fields in the forward areas; exclusive reliance on dispersed seaborne maneuvers "over the beach''; or some combination of these. The first alternative makes for relatively small forces simply because of the restricted tonnages that aircraft alone can furnish with any reasonable expenditure of resources. The C-5 aircraft, which was designed for just such operations, among others, illustrates another facet of this problem: to carry the necessary loads, it is large and, therefore, very expensive; consequently, it has been purchased in small numbers. Individual aircraft could easily be disabled by minor weapons, and the fleet would not last long if it entered forward areas in an intense war. The second alternative, over-the-beach shipping, would require means for exceedingly rapid transfer of cargoes from ship to shore to minimize the risk of nuclear attack. Supplies and troops would have to be loaded immediately into the vehicles and aircraft of the mobile supply system for rapid dispersal forward. Resupply requirements for a field army of six divisions (two armored and four mechanized) might call for weekly delivery by a fleet of about 10 ships able to carry 10,000 tons each. If adequately dispersed during simultaneous delivery—with, say, 5 miles between ships—they would cover a strip of beach 50 miles wide. Such lengths of shoreline with suitable beaches having access to the hinterland might, depending on the area, be difficult to find and the dispersed overland supply routes difficult to control. Spacing deliveries in time (that is, one or two shiploads each day) would lead to the need to build up reserve storage to guard against the occasional loss of a ship, which could occur even with the rapid delivery afforded by roll-on, roll-off ships or container ships, and this would increase vulnerability in another direction.

Larger fleets would be required for mass landings. Over 100,000 men landed in Normandy on D-day, 1944, from a fleet including over 2,700 ships of all kinds.[10] If such a fleet were dispersed to avoid a nuclear strike, it might be extended over hundreds of miles of coastline or over many days during successive, small-scale landings. It would be a relatively simple matter for small enemy forces to destroy such landings piecemeal, even without nuclear weapons; and if the landings were successful, the problem of coalescing the separate landing groups into a unified army for deep penetrations into enemy territory might well be insuperable.

Extending in the other direction, the potential use of nuclear weapons at sea would seriously affect the ability of marine forces to support operations ashore if a war were of sufficient duration for such support to have an impact. Unarmed merchant ships are even more vulnerable than before to the guided conventional high-explosive torpedoes of nuclear attack submarines or to submarine- or air-launched guided missiles. The potential use of nuclear weapons can make it extremely difficult for warships, such as aircraft carriers and smaller ships designed for anti-aircraft and anti-submarine warfare, to protect shipping convoys. It is also apparent that attack task forces offshore, designed to carry air power inland and to protect the terminal parts of the shipping route, could not operate in continuous and concentrated fashion as did the Seventh Fleet in the Gulf of Tonkin during the Vietnamese war, even if it could overcome determined conventional-weapons opposition. Indeed, the potential of nuclear weapons in naval warfare presents naval forces with such profound tactical problems that their entire existence in current form has been called into question.

All of these theories represent Western thought on the tactical use of nuclear weapons. Do Soviet views match them? They do, in part. In naval warfare Soviet air and submarine forces are, of course, the driving parts of the U.S. Navy problem we shall examine. In land warfare, to judge from their writings on the subject,[11] one may assume that the Soviets espouse theories of tactical nuclear warfare similar in principle to the ideas emerging from U.S. and other Western writings on the subject outlined earlier. Their approach differs in important details, mainly resulting from their concentration on warfare of continental scope across their borders. This both engenders and enhances the Soviet predilection for the use of massive forces to overwhelm any opposition and occupy territory. They describe breakthrough tactics in which they would use nuclear weapons, air strikes, and artillery to punch holes in fixed defenses. They build their offensive plans around a complex of axes of advance, planning to concentrate briefly when the opposing defenses are disorganized, to move through the holes, and then to spread out and move forward and laterally as rapidly as possible. The intent is to surround enemy forces after they have been fragmented, prevent their entering the battle effectively, and destroy them piecemeal while the main thrusts speedily occupy territory. Essentially this extends the basic conventional warfare concepts of massed offensive strategy using the speed and power of large armored forces to disorganize, surround, and destroy enemy forces and occupy their ground before Soviet forces can be hurt too badly.

Typical quotations from Soviet writings describe the tactics vividly and highlight the fact that, at least for consumption in public and military circles, they accept as a routine proposition the probable use of tactical nuclear weapons:

> Combat under the conditions of prepared enemy defenses, with the impossibility of skirting them or capturing them on the move, will begin with a breakthrough which consists in breaking the defenses by nuclear weapons and air strikes, by artillery and tank fire, and an offensive of the subunits with the subsequent development of actions in depth.
>
> The offensive starts by making nuclear strikes with tactical missiles and aviation for the purpose of destroying the means of mass destruction and defeating the basic enemy grouping on the axis of the main strike of advancing troops.
>
> After the nuclear strikes, for neutralizing and destroying the enemy which

has not been destroyed by the nuclear weapons on the front line and in the tactical depth, preparatory firing and fire support of the advancing subunits will be carried out. . . .

In modern combat, superiority over the enemy is achieved primarily by concentrating the fire efforts of the forces and mainly the nuclear strikes. The concentration of the troops on the main axis should be carried out on the basis of strict and detailed calculations so that their grouping and number make it possible primarily to utilize the results of the nuclear strikes, to successfully pierce the enemy defenses, and rapidly complete the destruction of the forces which have remained after the nuclear strikes. It is extremely important to concentrate the necessary forces and means on the direction of the main strike in a rapid and covert manner, from different directions and only for the time necessary for making the strike. As soon as such necessity is passed, the troops must be immediately dispersed. This is caused by the constant threat of the enemy's use of nuclear weapons. The dispersion of the troops on the battlefield at the same time should provide for carrying out the mission, it should not obstruct a new concentration of the units and subunits for making a strong strike against the enemy, and at the same time should exclude the possibility of the simultaneous destruction of several subunits by a medium-powered nuclear explosion. . . .

Dispersion is not the only means for protecting the troops. In this regard of enormous significance is, primarily, a rapid closing with the enemy and the making of powerful strikes against him, the careful camouflaging of the troops, the construction of fieldworks and the use of the protective properties of the terrain, as well as the able and prompt use of mobility and maneuverability of the motorized rifle and tank subunits.[12]

Attention is given in the Soviet writings to the need to disperse and operate in small units when under threat of nuclear weapon attack, and also to the need to find and destroy the sources of nuclear firepower. The Soviets consider that tanks, armored personnel carriers, and other armored fighting vehicles will protect troops against radiation when they move through contaminated areas. However, their theories are as susceptible as our own to the conflicts and contradictions among the tactics suited to either nuclear- or conventional-weapons fighting. They are vulnerable to nuclear strikes from the air or from fast-reacting surface-to-surface systems when they concentrate for breakthrough, though even when concentrated a division is planned to occupy several times the area it occupied in World War II.[13] The artillery concentrations they talk about as being essential to the breakthrough would be as vulnerable.[14] They stress the need for rapid resupply, greatly increased usage of fuel and ammunition, pickup and repair of damaged vehicles and weapons, and the ready availability, in echelons to the rear, of units to replace those that might be badly hurt, destroyed, or played out in forward areas. All of this would force them into concentration patterns when they are working with very large forces, in which the vulnerability to nuclear weapons would increase and threaten the destruction of the integrity of their forces.

All of the theories of the nuclear battlefield, combined with the problems of entering the battle area, lead to the conclusion that a battlefield where nuclear weapons can be used freely and as needed works against massive forces. Moreover, the uncertainties and logical contradictions in all these theories raise the question of whether the idea of nuclear weapons on a battlefield is tenable at all, except as a desperate, all-or-nothing measure. The attempt to come to grips with such problems in the NATO situation, where both sides have many tactical nuclear weapons and the possibility that such weapons would be used in a military conflict is real, has been a continuing source of concern to governments and military commanders alike. Consideration has been given to means for reducing decision-making time for weapon release, using the weapons only in special ways or under particular circumstances, and avoiding or deterring unintended escalation. The situation is obviously difficult when both sides perceive a deterrent value in keeping their intentions ambiguous and their plans secret. This arises as a major issue in connection with the proposal by former Secretary of Defense Robert McNamara and others that the United States and NATO renounce first use of nuclear weapons,[15] as we shall explore later.

There would probably, in actuality, be many compromises with the theoretical concepts, even if the use of nuclear weapons were accepted as a possibility. For example, it is likely that ports and major air terminals will be used, that there will be concentration of supplies and troops, and that for a variety of reasons having to do with cost and interaction with the civilian environment the locations of tactical airfields will be fixed. Since neither side could long survive as a cohesive military force if nuclear weapons were to be used indiscriminately, purely military inhibitions against their use may well be as strong as the countervailing pressures in their favor. Moreover, if there is any doubt that nuclear weapons will be used or hope that the battle can be won before a decision is made to use them, the advantages of force concentration accruing to the more audacious side will demand that the other side also take risks, or lose.

Problems of Escalation and Responsibility

One gathers from Soviet writings that if the planning were left to the military alone, they would intend to open the battle with nuclear weapons to destroy the sources of nuclear fire, such as airfields and known nuclear-weapon storage sites, as well as to prepare for breakthrough. But this might be inconsistent with Soviet political purposes in going to war. Political considerations aside, however, all these speculations about the nuclear battlefield highlight the difficulty of keeping tactical nuclear warfare in bounds. As we have seen, the purposes of using nuclear weapons in a major war covering a large area may not be served unless they are used in large numbers. If they are, the destruction, both civilian and military, could then be expected to be enormous, with no certainty for either side that the outcome could be controlled in its favor. Further, the use of tactical nuclear weapons cannot be considered without also considering the escalation problem.

Suppose it is argued that some necessary number of nuclear weapons, not extremely large, would be used only against obvious military targets. These weapons would be of a tactical type, perhaps of the newer kind that would cause less collateral damage and would have only local effects on the military forces and installations hit. (As we have seen, this might be difficult, but let us pursue the argument.) Suppose, even, that they were small enough to use against only a single tank with certainty or only at sea against naval forces—perhaps an unambiguous example of how it might be possible to eliminate substantial damage to the civilian population. Assume the accuracy is the best that can be achieved with precision guidance and that the weapons are clean, thus eliminating secondary fallout effects.

There would still be difficulties. Limitations in war are in general tacit, not known precisely to either side during its ongoing military and political operations. Neither side can be sure of the future actions the enemy will take; both must attempt to predict intentions from past and current observations. This fact had led the Soviets to encourage the belief that they think nuclear war cannot be kept limited. They stated that U.S. planning for *tactical* nuclear weapons was merely a stratagem to hobble the Soviets in case of war. In the early days of the nuclear-weapon double monologue they stated that if we were to use *any* nuclear weapons, they would feel free to use any size weapon in their arsenal that would bring a military advantage.[16] Although their views have evolved through the years, as ours have, they have not publicly withdrawn the basic precept, and their writings still stress the importance of nuclear weapons in a major war (i.e., war against the "imperialists"). It would be speculative to think that they have come to agree with U.S. theorists.[17]

However, the theme stressing the importance of maintaining a clear separation between nuclear and nonnuclear war persists. This is evidenced by the late Party Chairman Leonid Brezhnev's remarks in a 1977 pre-Christmas press interview, when he warned that the neutron bomb, if adopted by NATO, would threaten this distinction. Of course, his warning may have been a simple attempt to exploit the many well-known views in the West about the importance of maintaining such a distinction. Indeed, there were many statements by opponents of the neutron bomb in the West that were essentially identical to Brezhnev's remark and made well before his.

Such statements thus have some obvious deterrent and propaganda value, but they have some clear logic as well. If tactical losses, potentially translatable into vital strategic losses, are suffered through nuclear weapons, it is most likely that the military setback will be much more obvious and sudden than a defeat inflicted by nonnuclear weapons would be. The dimensions of the latter might take some time to become apparent. In such a situation emotional factors, such as loss of prestige and commitment to winning regardless of the consequences, could well outweigh objective consideration of the wisdom of expanding the military conflict and its objectives. Commanders, from those in the field to those in the topmost levels of government, might try to recoup their loses or regain the tactical and strategic initiative by using more, and more effective, weapons rather than accepting the consequences of defeat. In other words, this is a question of stability of limited conflict in the face of unlimited power of weapons. Neither we nor the USSR can know for sure whether tactical nuclear war can be limited, because *truth* in such matters depends on human conception of the alternatives and imminent consequences at the time rather than on any objective measures. At a time when others may also feel free to make nuclear decisions (e.g., England, France, China), the uncertainty is even greater all around.

We are faced, then, with a problem of drawing clear boundaries between stable and unstable situations. It is undoubtedly true that, even if there were no nuclear weapons in existence, as long as neither side applied the maximum force available, there would be a danger of escalation to higher levels of force. But the difference between nuclear and nonnuclear weapons in such a situation is one of kind rather than degree. Escalation to higher levels of force within a nonnuclear, conventional-weapons conflict is inherently limited by the ultimate level, however high, of resources that can be applied. Such limits clearly were reached by both sides in World War II. (Chemical warfare *could* have been used but was not for reasons similar to those that might inhibit nuclear war today. Clearly, however, this was not a case of tacitly *limiting* its use; there was *no* use. Presumably, then, deterrence, if not human kindness, worked.) If nuclear weapons are used, however, it is possible that no limits of force application will be reached until the entire population of both sides is exterminated by a series of blows and counterblows. The only clear boundary, without shades of difference between small steps of escalation, is that between nonnuclear and nuclear weapons. The tacit limitation of nuclear weapon use is certainly possible and might occur, since the enemy would be no more desirous of being wiped out than we would; but there can be no certainty. Therefore, before crossing the threshold each side must assess not only the risks it would undertake by making an incorrect estimate of possible enemy response, but the stability of the ensuing situation as well.

Aside from the possibility of uncontrolled escalation, a very large element of risk exists in the military uncertainty of tactical nuclear exchange. This is exacerbated by the difficulty local commanders would have in anticipating whether nuclear weapon use might be imminent. The many and varied potential uses of nuclear weapons on the battlefield, as well as against fixed installations in a theater of war, have led to the evolution of diverse types of delivery systems. Each has different characteristic range and accuracy and is suited for delivery of warheads having a particular range of yields. These systems include cannon that can fire nuclear shells;[18] battlefield missiles like the U.S. Army's Lance;[19] and various tactical aircraft. In the next few years they may come to include relatively short-range land-based cruise missiles as well. The Soviet Union has a similar mix of nuclear delivery systems, although different in detail.[20] In addition, the USSR has deployed large numbers of medium- and intermediate-range ballistic missiles (MRBMs and IRBMs)[21] that play a role vis-a-vis Western Europe (and China) similar to that played by the strategic intercontinental ballistic missiles (ICBMs) deployed to threaten the United States. It is the enlargement of this MRBM/IRBM force by addition of the mobile, 5,000-km range, three-warhead SS-20 missile that has led the United States and some of its NATO allies to agree on deployment of a "long-range theater nuclear force" composed of Pershing II ballistic missiles and ground-launched cruise missiles, both able to reach targets in the USSR. When these missiles are deployed the European theater analogy to the U.S.-Soviet strategic nuclear confrontation of forces will be complete.

Except for the longer-range missiles obviously and specifically designed for nuclear delivery, most of these systems are dual capable (for example, the cannon, battlefield missiles, and aircraft); they can deliver conventional (and in many cases chemical), as well as nuclear, warheads. With these dual-capable systems a subtle appreciation of operational factors—where they are, their formations, whether and how they are being massed—is required to predict which type of warhead they may deliver. These factors may be difficult to observe in the heat and uncertainty of battle. Especially in situations whose outcome is thought to be critical for either side—for example, a major war in Western Europe or on the Soviet-Chinese border—the presumption may have to be that they *will* be used to deliver nuclear weapons unless there is a specific announcement of intention not to use them that way. Such an announcement would be improbable when both sides are seeking maximum deterrent advantage.

In the presence of these ambiguities and all the unresolved contradictions in the military theory of tactical nuclear war, it could not be said beforehand that on initiation of nuclear attacks the military situation could be controlled. There is simply no experience on which to base such a conclusion. Introduction of nuclear weapons would thus throw the tactical situation into a realm where military commanders could have no clear idea of the possible outcome or even of whether they could win at all. As in prenuclear wars, an audacious commander may be willing to risk the uncertainty, believing he can improvise well enough and rapidly enough to win. But in view of the attending risks of escalation into major strategic war, the question is whether the *nation* can afford to let any military commander undertake such risks to win a war whose objectives did not originally warrant the initiation of a strategic war. (What might warrant initiation of such a war we can only speculate about. It might be safe to say that, short of this kind of accidental escalation, a strategic attack by each side might only be made in response to a strategic attack by the other. Therefore, between the United States and the USSR alone there would seem to be *no* such objectives. The matter is different in the European context, as we shall see in Chapter 8.)

Where will the potential need for nuclear weapons on the battlefield be so great that there is a strong probability they will be used? It is difficult to imagine an adversary, other than the USSR or the People's Republic of China, that might threaten our vital interests in such a way that we would feel we must use nuclear weapons to win at all costs. The recent improvement of U.S. relations with China would seem to remove it from this category; but the international situation could change again, as it has twice before. During the Korean War we found it politic not to use nuclear weapons, even though we had a virtual monopoly and even though our troops were almost pushed to the sea at Pusan. A new attack by North Korea on South Korea might invite their use, but the situation would be very cloudy. Part of the reason for resisting such an attack would involve the security of Japan, but Japan would almost certainly object to the use of nuclear weapons. The U.S. public might also object to assuming the attendant risks of escalation in defense of a Korean regime they view as oppressive.

In the current situation, we are faced, if engaged with either major Communist power, by a strong probability that nuclear initiation would elicit a nuclear response. Outside Europe our vital strategic interests—that is our *immediate* survival—would not be involved in a conventional-weapons limited war, whereas the danger of escalation after nuclear initiation would immediately involve those interests. By using nuclear weapons, we might needlessly create a situation of maximum danger out of keeping with limited, local objectives. And we cannot forget the constraints of working with allies whose own survival would be at stake in such a war. Not only is it unlikely that the use of nuclear weapons would seem imperative at the start of such a war, but given the complex political dynamics within the United States that such a peripheral war might engender, it seems that the longer and less conclusive the war, the less politically feasible (or necessary) the use of nuclear weapons would appear to be. That is, the longer a war went on in these areas outside of Europe, the less likely it is that nuclear weapons would be used. All of these factors make it appear highly unlikely that such weapons would be used in areas outside the most vital.

Thus, although a nuclear response to major aggression anywhere should not be ruled out, the question of using nuclear weapons in limited war resolves, for us and for now, primarily to war in Europe. (The situation is not symmetrical for the USSR, which is concerned about warfare on two fronts, Europe and China. But the general reasoning would be the same for it in either area.) The possibility of nuclear limited war in Europe is intimately related to the question of whether limited war in Europe is possible at all (see discussion in Chapters 7 and 8). We can anticipate the conclusion that if an appropriate deterrent posture has been maintained the potential for *limited* war in Europe is uncertain and that if such a conflict were to develop in an ambiguous way it would be unlikely that nuclear weapons would be used at the outset. The likelihood of their use would then decrease if the developing situation increasingly appeared limited and limitable. Thus, the only case in which the use of tactical nuclear weapons may be likely would be that of a massive and sudden attack in Europe (i.e., what has come to be known as a "Eurostrategic" attack) and one that appeared immediately to threaten our own vital strategic interests. Then, tactical nuclear weapons and our own strategic intercontinental weapons might be coupled into a single response. This possibility itself reduces the chance of such war occuring which, as discussed in Chapters 7 and 8, can be made very small by the appropriate defense policies and forces.

Despite the remoteness of this possibility, however, we find that the very presence of tactical nuclear weapons has revolutionized tactical warfare— warfare by the general purpose forces—and how those forces might operate. The directions of evolution of the general purpose forces are influenced not only by the potential presence of tactical nuclear weapons but also by the increasingly obvious dilemmas and uncertainties attending their potential use. Therefore, just as we might note with respect to the *use* of the general purpose forces in the field, efforts in *creating* such forces are coming to concentrate more and more on conventional-weapons combat. But that is being revolutionized by the advent of advanced platforms and weapon-guidance systems, which will be examined in the next three chapters.

Concluding Comment: Chemical Weapons

The end of a chapter on tactical nuclear warfare may appear to be an odd place to put a discussion of chemical weapons. However, the two kinds of weapons have been linked, mainly by the USSR in its tactical war fighting doctrine. Almost all the Soviet battlefield weapons, including rockets, missiles, and aircraft, can deliver chemical as well as nuclear weapons.[22] Chemical warfare elements are an integral part of Soviet division and army structures. All Soviet equipment includes provision for the protection of troops against chemical agents. In their writings the Soviets describe chemical attacks virtually in the same sentences they use to describe nuclear attacks. They view chemical and nuclear weapons along with conventional high-explosive weapons as part of a weapon continuum that will allow their forces to prevail on the battlefield. Growing Western awareness of this Soviet concentration on chemical weapons has been stimulated by reports from Afghanistan and Southeast Asia describing the use of biologically derived toxic agents in a chemical warfare mode against unprotected tribesmen and guerrilla troops.

Although the two types of weapons are considered together in Soviet discussions of the "art of war," chemical weapon effects are different in kind from those of nuclear weapons. Their effects are more limited and specialized and they don't have the potential, as nuclear weapons do, to eliminate virtually the entire populations of countries having enormous geographic areas. However, used against unprotected forces they can create large numbers of casualties, rendering those forces incapable of carrying out useful military functions. They can deny terrain and they can make buildings, tanks, ships, and other "structures" not equipped to resist absorbing them impossible to occupy and to operate. Thus chemical weapons could be decisive in battle if one side uses them when the other is not ready.

We noted previously that in World War II chemical weapons were not used by either side because neither cared to risk retaliation from the large arsenal of chemical weapons known to be held by the other. Today the feeling has grown that the USSR has moved ahead of the West in the extent and diversity of its chemical arsenal and in the readiness of its forces to fight in a chemical environment. Therefore, potential deterrence by Western (largely U.S.) holdings in chemical weapons has not been as certain. This situation has resulted in part from the heightened pressure to reduce research and development in chemical weapons that attended the agreement of 1971 on control of biological weapons.[23] In this atmosphere the attempt to modernize the chemical arsenal by replacing existing weapons with binary munitions—that is, munitions loaded with two chemicals that are innocuous by themselves but become lethal when they are mixed by explosive impact—has met resistance. This resistance has joined with the resistance to nuclear weapons in the popular movements that wish to eliminate both from warfare. The problem is, of course, that although these popular movements in the West can affect Western weapon development and procurement plans they have no effect on Soviet plans, so the delays they impose on weapon modernization have the perverse effect of reducing deterrence when many of the resisters would wish to increase it.

After many years of debate the Congress has still refused to authorize the acquisition of the binary munitions that would replace the obsolescing earlier generation of chemical bombs and shells. At the same time, however, increasing attention is being given to protection of U.S. and NATO forces against chemical weapons. This protection includes such steps as provision of protective clothing for troops that have to operate in the open after chemical weapons have been used, design of ventilation systems to prevent the penetration of chemical vapors and aerosols, and incorporation of automatic water flushing systems for the surfaces of ships. In addition, the medical corps must be ready for rapid treatment of troops that may have been exposed to toxic chemicals.

These defensive measures by themselves must be considered an inadequate deterrent, however. Aggressive use of chemical weapons by the USSR against targets where they are not exposed to the potential weapons effects (e.g., against NATO airfields) can cause NATO's forces to suffer the degradations attending "suiting up" and other defensive measures while Soviet forces can operate relatively unhampered by the need for similar steps. Only the likelihood of a chemical counterattack can force them to pay the same penalties. Balanced protection and weapons are needed for effective chemical deterrence.

It is clear, however, that the Soviet concentration on chemical warfare and the Western response that is being stimulated are, just like the presence of nuclear weapons on both sides, imposing a price on the design and function of the conventional general purpose forces in terms of requirements for equipment and potential operating difficulties.

Tactical Air and Air Defenses

Uses of Tactical Air Power in Land Warfare

Use of aircraft over the battlefield began in World War I with their application as observation platforms. Aircraft were then crude and light and could not carry much payload; their role as attack bombers was therefore of no great importance. During and following World War II, however, tactical aircraft had great impact as deliverers of massed firepower on troops in the field and on the installations and logistic lines supporting them. The main uses of tactical air power in combat have thus become (1) observation of enemy positions and movements and (2) delivery of massed firepower against targets at locations ranging from the immediate battle area to great depths in the rear of the engaged combat forces.

In part because of the rather sweeping claims of some proponents of air power, there has been a tendency to expect that it can, by itself, win key battles and wars.[1] Experience has shown that this expectation is seldom realized. Air forces occupy no territory and by themselves have defeated no armies. But they can have a powerful impact on battles. Thus, it has always been true, from World War II to Vietnam, that the unopposed ability of aircraft to deliver weapons in immediate support of one side in a ground battle has made it difficult, if not impossible, for the opposite side to operate. U.S. forces at Anzio in World War II had trouble establishing their beachhead until German aircraft were driven from the battle area.[2] A massive air bombardment of the German armored division facing U.S. forces near St. Lô paved the way for the Third Army's breakout from Normandy in August 1944.[3] In the battle of the Ardennes, it was difficult for the Allies to exert immediate strong resistance while moving their ground forces to meet the German attack because the weather was poor and their aircraft could not operate.[4] In the 1967 Middle East War, Israel defeated the Jordanian forces by first pounding them from the air and then attacking on the ground while they were still reeling from the air attack.[5] In Vietnam, the Viet Cong and North Vietnamese tended to break off a battle on the ground when U.S. or

South Vietnamese forces received direct air support. The strong use of air power was largely responsible for preventing besieged Khe Sanh from becoming a little Dien Bien Phu.[6] According to contemporary news accounts, Israeli moves into the densely populated parts of Beirut that were heavily defended by Palestinian irregulars in the 1982 war were preceded by air bombardment of defensive positions to avoid Israeli Army casualties. This was apparently a successful military tactic, considerations of collateral civilian casualties aside.

The advantage of providing direct fire support from the air is, of course, that commanders do not always know where the heaviest firepower may be needed. When they find out, they may not have ground firepower—artillery, missiles, and tanks—available where it is needed most. Air power can be massed on short notice and at essentially arbitrary locations, as long as the aircraft are available. Use of air power in this manner is, however, controversial among the air forces of the non-Communist world. The controversy arises from the difficulty of achieving the necessary close coordination between ground and air forces, especially in highly mobile war if air tactics dictate very low-altitude flight to evade defenses. Under those conditions it is extremely difficult for pilots to make certain that they attack only enemy forces. Less concrete, but nevertheless important, each air force has its style and plans for combat under particular conditions consistent with that style. An Israeli Air Force colonel remarked to me after the 1967 war that the Israeli armed forces at that time did not believe in using precious and expensive aircraft as cannon. But, in fact, they have used them that way when the problems of economy of force—the need to use the least military resources to achieve given objectives—together with the opportunities for rapid agglomeration of heavy fire have indicated an advantage in doing so. In the U.S. armed forces response to such problems has reinforced the trend toward less use of artillery and more use of aircraft for close support of engaged forces.

Although the desirability and means of providing close air support may be controversial, no disagreement has existed about the advantages of using air power to attack the enemy beyond the immediate area of conflict between the ground forces, the zone just past artillery range and beyond. Here, targets and missions have been many. They range from destruction of command posts and communication centers; disorganization and attrition of units moving to the battle; elimination of long-range weapons, such as opposing aircraft and surface-to-surface missile systems; to disruption of the supporting transportation system—roads, railroads, bridges, tunnels, junctions—to delay or prevent the forward movement of troops and supplies.

The effects of tactical air attacks in the enemy's rear tend to be more ambiguous and difficult to establish, however, than the effects of direct support of "troops in contact." The Germans felt that the Luftwaffe in 1940 had protected the flanks of their advancing columns against French counterattacks.[7] The allied air attacks against German installations and communication lines in France succeeded in cordoning off a large area around the invasion zone in 1944, making it difficult for the Germans to shift their forces to meet the invasion and requiring them to incur the delays attending their ability to move only at night.[8] This mode of using tactical air power drew considerably on the lessons of Operation Strangle, which had taken place earlier in 1944 in Italy. This operation was supposed to prevent resupply of the German defensive Gustav line south of Rome. It did not succeed in doing that. Yet it was found afterward, when the records on both sides were examined, that the extensive bombing of the supply and transport routes had prevented the German commander Albert Kesselring from shifting units to and across the front in the face of the Allied offensive. The air operations thereby made a critically important contribution to the success of the drive to push the Germans out of Italy. (Even during the battle Sir John Slessor, the deputy air commander in Italy, noted that "supply denial could not be achieved without the need for ground action that would impose heavy comsumption on the enemy." He also became aware that "air power could make a possibly more important contribution by denying the enemy armies their power of movement while under attack, when mobility would be at a premium."[9]) The principles he enunciated are reflected in current U.S. Air Force doctrine, which states that "continued pressure by friendly ground forces is required to cause the enemy to use up resources as they arrive in the battle area. . . . When the advantage has been attained it must be exploited."[10]

A similar attempt at supply denial in Korea (also called Operation Strangle) in the summer of 1951 failed to prevent resupply by the Chinese and North Koreans. But it did force them to move troops and supplies at night with extensive efforts to camouflage those movements, at a cost we cannot know.[11] In Vietnam the air campaign had quasi-strategic aspects. It was variously said to be designed to persuade the North Vietnamese that they did not want to pay the price for continuing the war or to be designed to act as a bargaining chip in negotiations.[12] From the immediate tactical point of view, just as Strangle failed in its primary objective in Korea, air attacks in North Vietnam and Laos failed to keep the North Vietnamese from supporting the war and resupplying their own and Viet Cong forces in the South. But this support clearly required a large effort and extensive losses on their part to keep adequate supplies moving into South Vietnam along the Ho Chi Minh Trail through Laos.

There were far more important long-run effects of the air attacks in Laos that were not commonly recognized, however. Communist operations in

Vietnam were undertaken mainly in the dry season of each year, since the heavy tropical rains severely inhibited mobility and combat at other times. The incessant bombing of the road net in Laos prevented rapid reinforcement of North Vietnamese forces in the South in the course of a single campaign season. In order to avoid heavy casualties, troops moving from North Vietnam to the battlefields in the South had to make a three-month march on foot along jungle trails instead of taking a week's ride in trucks along roads that had been built for moving supplies. The impact was illustrated dramatically in the spring of 1975 when this restraint no longer obtained because the United States had withdrawn its forces. Then, the North Vietnamese could take advantage of the confusion of the South Vietnamese withdrawal from the Central Highlands, and they brought the war decisively to Saigon's environs in a few weeks with massive troop movements along good roads that they had built through South Vietnam proper.[13]

Thus, it can be seen that, although on the battlefield "victory through air power" alone is illusory, tactical air power operating as part of a concerted air-ground campaign can have a powerful and direct effect on the outcome of battles through close support of troops in contact with the enemy. It can have more subtle and indirect, but no less important, effects on sequences of battles by attacking the communications zone behind the front. In the most successful of such campaigns the direct effect of limiting logistic support, which was avowedly sought, was seldom achieved. But the often unintended effect of inhibiting maneuver at critical times affected the outcome of the campaigns.

In conflicts between two sides, both of which have extensive and effective air forces, the drive to gain air superiority by destroying the other side's aircraft has come to symbolize the struggle between air forces. However, it is clear that this drive is ancillary. Air superiority or supremacy is needed to allow one side's own air force to have the desired effect on the ground battle and to prevent the air force of the other side from doing the same.

There have been, since the mass use of air power in World War II, many arguments about priority in the air-to-ground war. Until recently these arguments generally took the approach that air superiority must be gained first with subsequent attacks against the ground. The following quotation from a World War II field manual is typical, and although it dates from 1943 it expresses views still widely held:

Missions.—a. The mission of the tactical air force consists of three phases of operations in the following order of priority:

(1) First priority.—To gain the necessary degree of air superiority. This will be accomplished by attacks against aircraft in the air and on the ground, and against those enemy installations which he requires for the application of air power.

(2) Second priority.—To prevent the movement of hostile troops and supplies into the theater of operations or within the theater.

(3) Third priority.—To participate in a combined effort of the air and ground forces, in the battle area, to gain objectives on the immediate front of the ground forces.

* * *

Airplanes destroyed on an enemy airdrome and in the air can never attack our troops. The advance of ground troops often makes available new airdromes needed by the air force. Massed air action on the immediate front will pave the way for an advance. *However, in the zone of contact, missions against hostile units are most difficult to control, are most expensive, and are, in general, least effective.* Targets are small, well-dispersed, and difficult to locate. In addition, there is always a considerable chance of striking friendly forces due to errors in target designation, errors in navigation, or to the fluidity of the situation. Such missions must be against targets readily identified from the air, and must be controlled by phase lines, or bomb safety lines which are set up and rigidly adhered to by both ground and air units. *Only at critical times are contact zone missions profitable.*[14] [Emphasis added.]

However, such views are currently changing because of the recognition that wars in which both sides can use their air forces may not last long enough for the sequence to be enforceable. Thus, it has been recognized that, particularly against superior forces, it may be necessary to undertake air-to-ground warfare and attempt to gain air superiority simultaneously. Current U.S. Air Force doctrine states that

To defeat an enemy attack, tactical aircraft perform counter air, close air support, and interdiction. [These missions] are—in practice—inseparable in their effect on the air-land battle. . . . The mobility, flexibility, and responsiveness of tactical air forces enable them to perform multiple, diverse combat tasks. . . . The joint force commander apportions air resources to meet the overall objective.[15]

But all these air operations have the same tactical end in view: creating the greatest possible number of opportunities for observing the enemy's disposition and movements and carrying firepower against his ability to wage war on the ground.

Techniques of Air Attack

Since World War II there has been considerable evolution of the techniques of air warfare, in keeping with the changing capabilities of both the aircraft and the defenses against them. Air attacks against ground targets on and beyond the battlefield are complex operations requiring extensive communication, theaterwide coordination, and massive support. Such attacks must be explored in detail if the impact of the new weapon technologies is to be appreciated.

To provide direct support of troops under fire it is necessary to be in close and continuous radio contact with one's own troops. This is to make certain that they are not inadvertently attacked but that weapons *are* delivered against specific, imminently threatening enemy units against which the friendly troops need help. Air targets include concentrations of infantry that have friendly troops under fire; artillery pieces firing on them; tanks and other armored vehicles moving into the immediate battle area; or a forward-observer position calling fire down on them. It was difficult enough to be able to tell friendly forces and enemy forces apart from the relatively slow fighter or bomber aircraft of World War II; it is much more difficult to do so from modern high-speed jets. Therefore, to avoid mistaken identity and consequent deadly accidents, the individual targets for air attack must be explicitly designated by friendly forces. In the last years of World War II, and in Korea and Vietnam, where close support aircraft did not face significant air- or surface-based opposition over the battlefield, light, slow aircraft flying at fairly low altitudes came to fulfill this role.

The pilots of these spotter planes—or as they are currently known, FACs (forward air controller aircraft)—are told by the troops on the ground where the enemy units of concern seem to be. They then must see the targets themselves and describe them and their location to attack aircraft whose arrival in the attack area is precisely timed. Alternatively, they can mark the targets with such munitions as rockets, placing smoke grenades next to them or at check points from which the direction and distance to the target can be estimated. The FAC must then vector the fast attack aircraft to the point where, with the aid of the target description, the attack pilots can "acquire" the targets themselves and aim and release weapons against them. Sometimes two FACs work together, one acting as "briefer" and the other acting as "spotter."

The designation of targets for close support can be and is also performed from the ground, just as spotting for artillery is. A ground observer (or ground FAC) is likely to be much more restricted in how far he can see than an airborne FAC—perhaps 2 to 4 kilometers in open country. But he is in intimate contact with the battle, and in any case he may be required to act because the airborne FAC is not available.[16] For example, enemy fire may force the airborne FAC away from his required observation position. In the future, forward observers or FACs on the ground (or in the air, if they are not driven away by the defenses) are likely to be equipped with laser designators. These are hand-held or tripod-mounted devices that can point a narrow beam of light (perhaps infrared light) at the target. The attack aircraft would have TV-like displays showing the ground scene, on which the spot of laser light illuminating the target would be highlighted. The pilot could then convert to visual attack or to attack using electronic bombing aids. Further communication with the FAC would be unnecessary, thereby greatly increasing the rapidity and efficiency of the attack sequence.

The growing power of the ground-based air defenses, which we shall deal with shortly, is throwing into question the viability of the airborne FAC, whether in a slow or in a fast aircraft. For operation much beyond the FEBA the ground FAC needs to extend the scope and range of his observations. For this reason there is experimentation on the part of the ground forces with small, hard-to-detect remotely piloted vehicles (RPVs).[17] These are small airplanes controlled from the ground and carrying various sensors and laser designators. It is anticipated that such devices will in time be able to replace the vulnerable airborne FAC in the close air support system.

The provision of close air support in the manner described calls for continuing and extensive efforts to solve the problems posed by ever-evolving weaponry and tactics. Interservice coordination on the battlefield, the determination of target priority in the presence of limits on the numbers and availability of close support aircraft, and procedures to determine whether and when air power is to be called in are all problems requiring continuous attention. The controversies of the mid-1960s and early 1970s regarding the choice between Air Force fixed-wing aircraft and Army helicopters for close support, arose from these adjustments.[18] When the Air Force followed the philosophy expressed in the World War II field manual (which it did until quite recently), the Army felt an obvious need to see to its own provision of highly mobile air fire support on the battlefield. The helicopter, which could operate organically with the ground forces without the need for fixed, elaborate air bases, was its chosen instrument. However, the Air Force's commitment to providing close air support was confirmed in the crucible of war, during the years of Vietnam, as it had been in Korea. With the adoption, in 1974, of the A-10 aircraft specifically for the purpose, these arguments came to a close, at least for a while. Vietnam also proved the value of the armed helicopter, which was able to operate in ways not available to the fixed-wing aircraft; today the controversies are muted, and the two types of aircraft are filling complementary roles. The search for solutions to the operational problems continues, however, driven by the vastly improved effectiveness of air defenses.

The selection of targets for attacks well beyond the FEBA, as well as the tactics, depends on the nature of the opposition. The targets are not visible to the ground forces and, especially when deep in the enemy's rear, are not in an obvious position to affect them imminently. The air forces are thus required to obtain and evaluate target information in these areas without assistance from front-line ground combat units. This requires aircraft with various sensors—"eyeballs," cameras, radar, radio location devices—to observe enemy-occupied areas. The resulting data must be processed and combined with other intelligence to produce information on the enemy, his weapons, and his movements in sufficient detail for the planning of air attacks. The rapidity of maneuver expected in war between armored forces requires great effort in research and development and operational training programs in order to improve the timeliness of the information obtained. For example, a unit 50 miles to the rear of the FEBA might enter the battle in a few hours, or a missile launcher even farther back might fire at any time. The problem, of course, is that the cost of acquiring targets increases dramatically as the time from sensing to presenting processed data for use decreases.

For example, an aircraft with a relatively inexpensive camera can fly over enemy territory, photograph targets, and then fly home. The film is developed, analyzed by photointerpreters, and the information sent to the staff of the tactical air commander (or higher-level combined arms commander) who must decide on target allocations. The entire process can take from one to six hours, in which time the armored unit in question can have entered the battle, achieving surprise and perhaps decision. If it is desirable to have the information within a few minutes from the time the aircraft flies over the armored unit (which may or may not be disposed so that it is visible to the pilot*), automatic developing equipment can be added to the camera on the aircraft or an all-electronic imaging system using magnetic tape but not needing chemical processing can be used. The finished "photo," whatever its form, can be scanned electronically and the information then transmitted electronically by a radio data link to the command center. The data link would of course have to be resistant to enemy jamming. All of this equipment would cost several times the price of the camera itself, and the photointerpreters and equipment on the ground would still be necessary. In addition, different units from those who must use the information, perhaps even Army aircraft or sensors, obtain it by reconnaissance. It must be transferred to the attack forces and integrated with operational plans in order to be used at all, leading to additional

---

*During the planning for the Market-Garden attack aimed at the Ruhr industrial area in World War II, two German armored divisions moved, unknown to the Allies, into the vicinity of Arnhem. The few observations and isolated tank photographs by reconnaissance pilots were not persuasive enough to affect the plans for the operation, which failed to achieve its objectives. C. Ryan, *A Bridge Too Far* ,(New York: Popular Library, 1974), pp. 158–163.

command, control, and communication delays. The provision of computers for information processing, synthesis, and display, as well as jam-proof communications links to transfer the data rapidly, all add to the cost, increasingly so as their capacity and timeliness increase.

The subsequent attacks are themselves highly complex affairs requiring elaborate (and also costly) command, control, and communication mechanisms. A group of aircraft cannot simply be sent out over enemy territory to make attacks on whatever targets it may happen to see. The aircraft are too few, and modern antiaircraft defenses are too effective to permit such a procedure. Whereas in World War II there were thousands of fighters and light bombers available for tactical air-to-ground fighting, the number now is in the hundreds. Although it is true that current aircraft carry much more weaponry, it is more difficult to distribute the load as needed, since the weapons are on fewer platforms.

As an illustrative analogy, we might imagine the scheduling problem that would ensue if an airline that served a network with a fleet of four 90-passenger DC-9s suddenly found it had to do the same job with a single, 360-passenger 747 transport. The total number of sorties (a sortie is one flight of one aircraft from takeoff to landing) is limited, and the loss of a single aircraft removes a significant part of the available capability. Thus, for example, a local corps commander may be assigned one or two hundred tactical support sorties in a day when he knows of hundreds of targets to be struck— and he is but one of many calling for the help. The tactical air command center, therefore, not only must receive target information and requests from the ground forces for support, it must also decide target priorities and aircraft assignments. To help the aircraft cope with enemy defenses, it must also vector the planes to the target areas, where local control can take over. In addition the center must bring other aircraft, intended to suppress defenses and provide protection against enemy interceptors, over the target area with the main attack at the appropriate time. There may be two to four times as many aircraft engaged in a strike operation as the number actually delivering weapons against enemy ground forces.

To facilitate the necessary integration of information and close coordination of air operations, what might be called a command pyramid has evolved; it includes, from higher headquarters to the field level, one or two Tactical Air Control Centers; two or three times as many Direct Air Support Centers; and, for close support, many Forward Air Control Parties. All must have interconnecting communications among themselves and communications to all the aircraft. The attending centralization and close interconnection among functions also increases the vulnerability of the entire system to degradation or elimination by enemy attack.

The components of this complex attack system are illustrated schematically in Figure 3-1.

The Problem of Hitting the Target

Once all this complex mechanism has been established, it would be desirable if it indeed had the intended effect of reducing enemy fighting capability. Aircraft speed, range, load capacities, and other operating characteristics have continued to improve since World War II, as shown in Table 3-1. However, a persistent limitation on the effectiveness of tactical air power has been the accuracy of weapon delivery. The circular error probable (CEP) of a group of bombs defines a circle within which half of a load of bombs from an aircraft will drop at random. The other half of the load will land outside the circle. The error in bombing is caused by ballistic dispersion, aiming errors, errors in accounting for winds on the way down, and the difference between intended and actual location and velocity of the aircraft when the release button is pressed. Although the CEP can be 100 feet or less in practice or test sessions on a bombing range, experience shows that in combat, with the uncertainty of target location and the stress of a pilot under fire, typical accuracies are likely to be several times that. These statistics are true for release of bombs. In some cases, such as strafing vehicles on roads, weapon accuracies can be better, but these cases are specialized and do not typify the effectiveness of attack aircraft.

Night and bad weather have created additional problems for weapon delivery from the air. Although aircraft today can take off, fly, and land at night or in almost zero visibility, with the clouds as low as 200–300 feet, they need assistance in finding and seeing targets when conditions approach such limits. Elaborate technology has been developed to provide this assistance, but it is expensive and has enough limitations that attack aircraft performance is severely constrained under such conditions.

Problems of operating at night and in clouds are different. For fairly clear nighttime conditions it has been possible, although difficult, to make ground attacks by parachuting flares to light the battlefield for a time. Now, advances in electronic devices and solid-state circuitry make possible the use of image intensifiers or infrared (heat-sensing) devices that, under appropriate atmospheric conditions, can show targets such as tanks, trucks, or structures that stand out from the terrain. Although these devices now open up the night to visual attack on targets, the distances they can "see" and their image quality under many conditions, especially if the enemy uses countermeasures such as smoke or the creation of false "heat" targets, are sufficiently limited that pilots cannot use them for random searching as they would their eyes in the daytime. Rather, they must know where they are going and what they

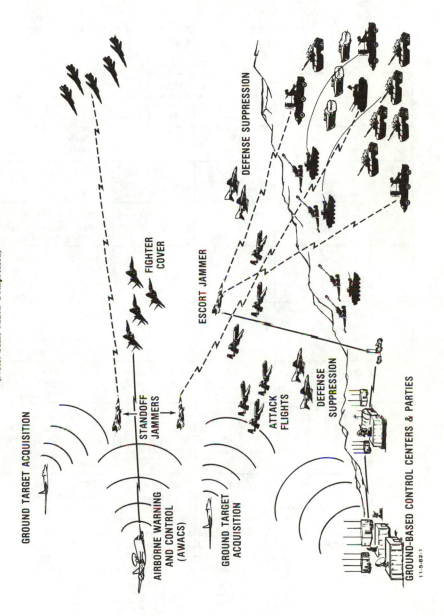

FIGURE 3-1: Components of a Modern Air Attack Operation
(Note: Scale Much Compressed)

GROUND TARGET ACQUISITION

AIRBORNE WARNING AND CONTROL (AWACS)

GROUND TARGET ACQUISITION

STANDOFF JAMMERS

FIGHTER COVER

ESCORT JAMMER

ATTACK FLIGHTS

DEFENSE SUPPRESSION

DEFENSE SUPPRESSION

GROUND-BASED CONTROL CENTERS & PARTIES

11-5-82-1

Table 3–1: COMPARATIVE PERFORMANCE INDICATORS OF FIGHTER-BOMBERS, 1942–1985

		Approximate Performance[a]		
Year	Aircraft	Combat Speed Knots	Radius Nautical Miles	Weapon Load (typical)
1942	A-36 Invader (version of P-51A)	280	150–200	4 .50-cal. guns 2 500-lb. bombs
1944	P-51H (fighter-bomber version)	350	400	6 .50-cal. guns 2 1,000-lb. bombs
1955	A4-C[b]	500	600–800	2 20-mm cannon 3 store stations capable of 5,000-lb. bomb load
1960	F4-B[b]	500[c]	850	16,000 lb. of payload (e.g., ll 1,000-lb. bombs or bombs plus gun pods and rockets)
1964	F-111A[d] (Mach 1.2 at sea level)	700[c]	Over 1,300	45,000 lb. of fuel + weapons 8 store stations + internal bomb bay
1975	A-10A	390	250 + 2.2 hrs. "loiter" over battlefield	30-mm, 6-barrel Gatling gun + 16,000 lb. payload on 11 store stations
1980	F-16A	500[c]	500	1 20-mm cannon 7 store stations capable of total load up to 20,000 lb. + 2 wingtip air-to-air missile stations
1985 (est.)	AV-8B Vertical or short takeoff & landing	500	150 + 1 hr. loiter	9,200 lb. (bombs, gun pods, or missiles) on 9 store stations

a. These are simply indicators of performance that do not especially go together. Speed is less than maximum; radius with heavy weapon load would be less than shown.
b. These aircraft (as later versions) still active in the forces.
c. Arbitrary ground attack speed: aircraft capable of Mach 2 performance.
d. Data as of 1976.

are looking for, and they must be able to navigate accurately (with or without outside assistance) to a point from which target acquisition is possible—not over 6 or 7 kilometers (about 4 miles) from the target, and usually less. All this requires a system of radar and other electronic surveillance and target location devices in addition to the navigation systems aboard the aircraft themselves.

If the weather is closed in—that is, with low clouds—air-to-ground attacks must depend on radar. In general, except for a few, very advanced "synthetic aperture" systems carried by specialized reconnaissance aircraft, attack aircraft radar does not give a pictorial image except for large, clearly defined structures such as bridges or areas of distinctive shape and signature such as railroad yards. Small, individual targets like vehicles on roads or in fields show as small blobs of light on a TV-like screen marked so that the pilots can estimate distance and direction to the targets. Seeing targets on the screen is made more difficult by extraneous radar returns, or clutter. The pilots need external assistance in flying to the target locations and in identifying the blobs of light as the targets they are seeking. This aid can be provided by systems that, once general target locations are known from external sources of battlefield surveillance and intelligence, can vector aircraft by radar to the location for target acquisition and weapon release. The targets may have been marked by a radio beacon delivered to their area by other aircraft or artillery, or onboard radars can assist in the final acquisition. If desired, the more certain, elaborate, and expensive moving target indication (MTI) and moving target tracking (MTT) can be added to the onboard radars. (The A-6E and F-111D have such radars.) Then the aircraft would be able to attack such targets as vehicles moving on roads (above a certain minimum velocity) by seeing them from in or above the clouds and attacking in what might be called an armed reconnaisance mode. Guidance to the general target areas and assistance in identifying the blobs as the targets to be attacked would still be necessary. Navigation to known road locations in enemy territory may be sufficient if friendly ground forces are not nearby.

Radar target information is subject to degradation by various means of electronic warfare. "Noise" jammers can mask or lose the targets on the screen in large blotches of light. "Deception" jammers can affect the output of the radar circuitry so that target locations shown on the screens are offset from the targets' true locations, degrading or destroying useful bombing accuracies. False targets can be shown on the screens. Communications that convey "cueing" or identification information can also be jammed. Both radar and communications can be made resistant to jamming; their cost would increase correspondingly, sometimes to such high levels that the systems can no longer be purchased.

The problem with all these schemes, including radar and infrared sensors even when they work well, is that they tend to be no more accurate than visual bombing and in most cases less so—sometimes very much less. The utility of the achievable accuracies (in either visual or radar bombing) depends on the weapons and the targets. The accuracies cited might, at an earlier time, have been considered satisfactory for delivery of nuclear weapons. But as we noted in the previous chapter, CEPs of several hundred feet might not be compatible with the desire for combining smaller yield with higher accuracy to reduce collateral damage. Conventional high-explosive weapons would be devastating to troops in the open or in unprotected vehicles, and they could also destroy large, fixed targets such as buildings or arrays of stored supplies. But troops on a modern battlefield are likely to be either well dug in or in armored vehicles. Against such hard targets the effect would be most likely to come from the mass of weapons delivered, not from each one's hitting a target. This would be a random effect and could not be relied upon to be effective. Similarly, there would be little assurance that structures such as bridges could be destroyed or even seriously damaged.

These terminal effectiveness problems existed until the mid-1960s when a number of technological advances appeared. One was the development of cluster weapons, such as the Rockeye anti-armor munition, which have distributed terminal effects over an area greater than the typical weapon delivery CEP. Against hard targets their effectiveness depends very much on the disposition of the targets in relation to the submunition pattern. If armor is closely spaced on a road or concentrated for an assault, such weapons can be very effective, even in blind or radar-assisted release modes. Against widely dispersed targets (and the effective use of such weapons will doubtless encourage dispersion when ground units come under air attack), the weapon effectiveness falls off rapidly as their CEP increases.

Two other approaches have concentrated on increasing the accuracy of weapon delivery by the aircraft or of the weapon itself. The first was made possible by the development of accurate navigation and bombing systems. One type of system uses an inertial navigator (such as those used by the airlines to fly across the oceans) and a solid-state bombing computer. These are combined in such a manner that once the pilot feeds target location coordinates to the computer, the system follows the flight of the aircraft, calculates the proper bomb release point as the pilot flies over the target area, and automatically releases the bombs at the appropriate time. In the future, the navigation and positioning task might be done using data from a satellite navigation system such as the Navstar, but the principle would be the same. Such systems can reduce bombing errors to about one-third of their previous value.[19] But they are expensive, and because they are complex their reliability has not been as high as might be desired. However, even if the combined systems are superseded, the parts of the systems that aid accurate navigation will remain essential to the air-to-ground attack function.

The other new approach to accurate weapon delivery is weapon guidance. There have been guided air-to-ground weapons since World War II. The Germans made use of crude radio-guided bombs against Allied ships at Anzio,[20] and the United States was experimenting with the Azon, Razon, and Tarzon manually command-guided bombs at the end of the war.[21] The V-1, a guided flying bomb, was nevertheless very crude—it had only to hit a very large city from two or three hundred miles away. The Japanese kamikazes were, in effect, a particularly brutal form of guided weapon. The struggle, since those early uses of weapon guidance, has been to build the capability of the kamikaze into a small machine that would seek its target as effectively.

Practical success was first achieved with air-to-air missiles, where the weapon could be designed to seek and fly itself to the heat from an aircraft engine or to fly to the source of radar reflections from an aircraft. It was easiest (but not trivial) in this case to separate the hot target from the complex "noise" of the background sky. The advent of the coherent, fine light beam of the laser permitted a conventional bomb to be fitted with seeker and control system that could fly the bomb to a laser spot held on a target by a designator in the same or in a separate airplane. Similarly, successful self-contained TV systems could see and fly a bomb or a missile to a particular characteristic of a target, such as the contrast edge between the light and dark parts of the target. These advances led to the first practical air-to-ground weapons (known as precision-guided munitions, or PGMs) that could attack small, hard targets with accuracies of a few feet. A single aircraft could, with a very few such weapons, destroy tanks or bridge abutments, for example, that would previously have required dozens, and in some cases hundreds, of bombs for the attacker to be certain of the necessary direct hit.

Of course, each new kind of equipment brings its own complexities. In this case they include such requirements as a two-part team to use some weapons, weapon release within the "guidance envelope" (or the fairly small location from which the weapon has enough control power to maneuver to the target, similar to the need for a precise release point for ballistic bombs), high reliability in the guidance system, and appropriate atmospheric conditions or a lack of smoke on the battlefield for accurate guidance. Nevertheless, even accounting for such problems, these weapons, combined with the load-carrying capability of modern jet aircraft, have drastically changed the nature of tactical air power's potential impact. Table 3-2 sums up the implications of the combination by comparing statistics for Operation Strangle in World War II with the results of performance calculations for current aircraft. The table shows the relative capabilities of tactical attack

**Table 3-2: COMPARISON OF WORLD WAR II AND CURRENT
TACTICAL AIR ATTACK CAPABILITY**

Category	World War II[a]	Current[b]
Number of aircraft	About 2,500 (P-47, P-51, Hurricane, B-25, B-26)	100 (F-4, A-7, A-10)
Sorties per day per aircraft	0.61	1–3
Average bomb load	2 500-lb. bombs or equiv.	8–18 500-lb. bombs or 3–6 PGMs[c]
Tank equivalents Damaged or Destroyed by force, per day	60–70[d]	300–800[e] (using PGMs)
Sorties to destroy bridge over minor river	20–30	1 (using PGMs)

Notes: [a] Statistics from: Sallager, F. M., "Operation 'STRANGLE' (Italy, Spring 1944): A Case Study of Tactical Air Interdiction," Project RAND Report R-851-PR. Prepared for the U.S. Air Force, February 1972.
[b] Estimated.
[c] Depends on number of pylons, weight each can hold, and type of PGM (precision-guided munition).
[d] Based on estimated effectiveness of weapons, typical accuracy, and average bomb load per sortie.
[e] Depending on type of aircraft and combat conditions.

aircraft forces in the two periods in terms of an arbitrary but meaningful measure: the potential to destroy tanks or bridges. It is clear that although modern aircaft are much larger and more expensive (by perhaps a factor of twenty), a much smaller force can now do much more than was possible in World War II.

Even aside from the doctrinal differences about usage and the sometimes disappointing expectations for tactical air effectiveness that we have discussed, these advances have not yet led to the unequivocal impact on modern land warfare that the numbers shown in Table 3-2 suggest they might have. Nor did the use of such weapons in Vietnam and the 1973 Middle East war result in such an impact. Why?

First, the uses of air-delivered precision-guided munitions in recent wars were too limited to be decisive, and the awareness of the current shortcomings remains keen. Second, as we have noted, since the high costs of the aircraft limit their numbers, even with the best performance the available air force will run out of sorties long before it runs out of vitally important targets and day-to-day missions. For this reason alone, tactical air power is unlikely to be decisive on the battlefield even though its collaboration with the ground forces is indispensable. Third, tactical air power will not always work as planned in terms of expected sortie rates or in delivering weapons under the good conditions usually incorporated in battle plans, because the enemy and the weather are not likely to cooperate. Currently available PGMs need clear weather and an unobstructed view of the target, and the enemy will take great pains with camouflage. Moreover, there will be purposefully distributed or incidental smoke and dust in the target area. Aircraft will be damaged and airfields attacked, which will reduce sortie rates. Thus, the theoretical performance is unlikely to be achieved in actual operations. The fourth and most important reason for the potential failure of tactical air power in meeting current expectations is that ground-based air defenses (which have also capitalized on guidance technology) have advanced to match the air attack capability. Not only will attack aircraft have less than a free ride, in some scenarios their viability against a dense air defense system will also be in doubt.

Air Defenses

The use of radar for anti-aircraft gun direction was initiated in World War II, and it made a big difference.[22] Before the use of radar a hit on an aircraft by flak was rare, although if there were very many guns they could fill the space near aircraft with enough flying metal to shoot down many of them. The new radar-directed guns finally permitted consistently effective anti-aircraft gun performance. They could, for example, shoot down up to one-third of the aircraft attacking a major ship. With the introduction of modern, fast, high-flying aircraft, the guns themselves could not keep up with the airplanes. The aiming errors of the radar and the ballistic dispersion of the shells degraded accuracy against airplanes at high altitude and high speed. Yet the possibility of the aircraft's carrying nuclear weapons made an increase in kill probability essential.

The technological advances that made missiles and guidance possible in many other applications also contributed to the gradual evolution of surface-to-air missile (SAM) defenses to their current form. Guidance schemes may use infrared heat seekers in missiles that can be carried and launched by one person against close-in aircraft. They may also use radar guidance at long range and high altitudes, with missiles homing on the reflected energy from a radar-illuminated target. Or they may use command guidance to the target by means of a radio link from the ground, with the radar providing aircraft

Table 3-3: SOME AIR DEFENSE MISSILE SYSTEMS
AVAILABLE TO NATO FORCES

Type	Guidance	Mobility	Operating Range
Nike Hercules	Radar	Fixed	Medium to high altitude
Hawk and Improved Hawk	Radar	Movable	Low to medium altitude
Patriot	Radar	Mobile	Low, medium, and high altitude
Rapier, Roland, Crotale	Radar	Mobile	Low altitude
Chaparral	Infrared	Mobile	Low altitude
Redeye, Stinger	Infrared	Man-portable	Close-in

Source: *Jane's Weapon Systems,* (New York: Franklin Watts, 1981-82) pages according to index.

and missile positions. There are various types and sizes of missile systems that can operate from fixed sites, that are movable, or that are mobile. They can be used in various situations with overlapping coverage to protect mobile forces and fixed installations from air attack. Table 3-3 lists some of the systems available to NATO forces. Radar-directed, rapid-fire guns can cover very low altitudes and make it uncomfortable for airplanes operating down where ground returns of radar energy (clutter) may interfere with missile guidance. In some SAM systems the radar is made elaborate enough to reject the ground clutter; thus, low-altitude SAMs with radar guidance, infrared-guided SAMs, and radar-directed guns can complement each other. Figure 3-2 shows a diagram of the type of overlapping coverage that can be obtained by a complete, multistage air defense system. In Vietnam the presence of the relatively crude SA-2 induced our aircraft to operate at low altitude in some circumstances where they were vulnerable to fire from simple guns with optical sights. A defense array like the one shown in Figure 3-2 would be far more difficult to withstand and would require a great diversity of countermeasures. The Israeli Air Force was surprised and lost many aircraft to such defenses in the early stages of the 1973 war. By 1982 it demonstrated in Lebanon that it could defeat such an array operated by Syrian forces in a small geographic area. Whether such performance is possible against a much larger set of defenses operated by a technically sophisticated force is very much an open question. It depends on the reliability and degree of integration of the defense units, on the attacker's knowledge of the systems, and the effectiveness of the attacker's countermeasures and suppression attacks.

Although technical developments in the air defense area have been paced by the West, the Soviets have given special attention to such systems. U.S. and general Western reliance on tactical ground-attack aircraft has been obvious, and the capability of the planes was well demonstrated in the Middle East and in Vietnam. SAM defenses have had important implications for the use of tactical aviation everywhere. Their broader implications will be considered in another context; for now, let us look at their implications in a contest between the two main military alliances, NATO and the Warsaw Pact.

If it should come to armed conflict, U.S. and other NATO aircraft attempting to attack Warsaw Pact armed forces on the ground would face the kind of dense network of ground-based air defenses shown in Figure 3–2. Long-range search radars would see the aircraft coming toward the ground forces' operational areas and would alert both fixed defenses at key locations and mobile defenses moving with the ground forces (as well as interceptors). At whatever altitude aircraft attempt to attack the defended ground forces, they can be engaged by heavy anti-aircraft fire from overlapping defensive systems. This was the problem that the Israeli Air Force encountered in the 1973 Middle East war.[23]

All SAM systems do have weaknesses, however. Like all systems based on radar (including guns), or on electro-optical devices like infrared seekers, they are susceptible to jamming and deception by electronic warfare;[24] they are also vulnerable (after exacting a penalty) to multiple-aircraft attacks specifically designed to destroy them. The missiles themselves are large, expensive, and complex to transport and to load on launchers for sequential firings in large quantities on the battlefield. At some point a massive attack against the SAM defenses could saturate their target acquisition and tracking capability and run them out of ammunition. The combination of all these factors undoubtedly contributed to the Israeli defeat of the Syrian SAM system in the Bekaa Valley of Lebanon in 1982.[25]

In the European arena the Soviet Union has made up for the West's more technically advanced systems—better guidance and a higher kill probability, with more resistance to countermeasures—by sheer weight of numbers. Individual systems might be countermeasured and might have to fire more missiles to hit an airplane. However, calculations show that the great volume of fire that the Soviet multiplicity of systems could put up would, unless tactics are changed to account for the defenses, cause so much attrition of NATO aircraft that NATO's air force would be left with insufficient strength to be useful. Here, then, we see the obverse of the capability shown in Table 3–2.

What can be done in this situation? Clearly, for tactical air power to do its work against attacking ground forces, the defenses must first be defeated. In Vietnam, defense-suppression tactics were developed that assigned a

50

FIGURE 3-2: Ground-Based Air Defense Array

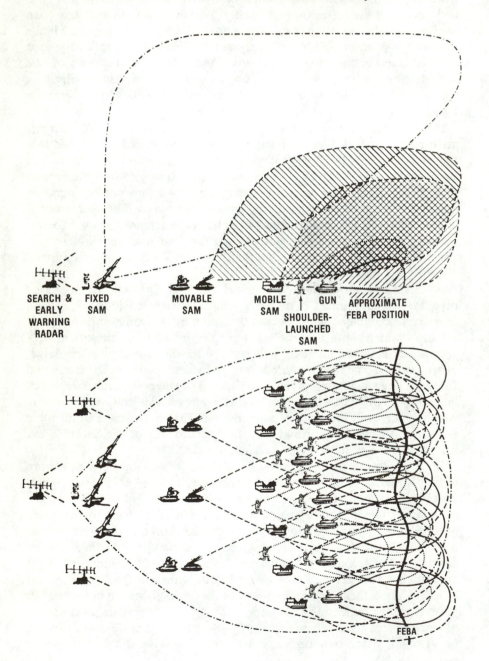

SEARCH & FIXED   MOVABLE   MOBILE   GUN   APPROXIMATE
EARLY   SAM   SAM   SAM   SHOULDER-   FEBA POSITION
WARNING   LAUNCHED
RADAR   SAM

significant fraction of the attacking aircraft to countering and attacking the North Vietnamese defenses. Precision-guided munitions were used in these efforts, too, including missiles such as the Shrike, which could home on signals from the emitting SAM radar

An obvious countermeasure to radar homing is to shut the equipment off; but without it, of course, the SAM systems could not fire. In addition, early warning radar is needed to track incoming aircraft so the local defenses can be ready for them. This problem can be alleviated by extensive use of radar decoys and by interconnecting the defense radars in a practice called netting. With such a system any radar station can feed target information by radio or wire links to appropriate defense sites. Netting also implies some central control over the priority and passage of information. Thus, the entire defense network can, even if degraded, react and support opposition to penetration at particular locations. Over North Vietnam, even with suppression, the defenses took their toll of both the attack and the suppression aircraft.

However, electronic technology is advancing now, and it will soon be possible, by listening to the enemy's radar signals from several remote sites behind our own lines, to process those signals in a computer and obtain the radar locations. Such a system would probably use receivers elevated on aircraft that fly in a known geometric relationship to each other and whose location can always be determined. It will then be possible to launch long-range guided missiles or guided glide bombs against the radar stations from standoff positions—that is, from positions beyond the reach of the air defense systems being attacked. Losses during defense suppression would be reduced, fewer defenses would remain to oppose the attack aircrcft, and more aircraft would become available to attack primary targets instead of having to fly support missions.

In the more distant future such guidance technology might be applied against the targets themselves. Currently, the problems of acquiring targets that do not emit characteristic electronic signals, limitations on the number of weapons that can be launched and remotely controlled, and the projected high costs of the standoff missile systems inhibit the development of the standoff capability for use against massed targets. The new systems may first be able to attack the relatively few SAM systems that can reach to high altitudes and long distances. Then they could attack other forces with less expensive weapons from altitudes above the range of the forward air defense systems shown in Figure 3–2, in the process reducing the number of defense systems that would present a danger and have to be suppressed. Current experimentation is seeking a generation of missiles, known collectively under the term Assault Breaker, that can deliver many guided submunitions from considerable standoff distances. The munitions are released over the target area and then must find and home on individual targets. This capability is probably many years in the future, and it may not be achieved at a cost that allows such weapons to be proliferated. In the meantime standoff missiles with unguided cluster warheads might be designed to attack not only SAMs but exposed troops in rear areas and trucks or lightly armored vehicles attempting to move forward, and to sow mines to make movement more difficult, dangerous, and time-consuming.

Suppression of defenses remains necessary, but it will have to be done in concert with the air-to-ground attacks that are the reason for it all. This will lead to complex tactics and intricate and costly command, control, and communications systems. Even so, if the defenses are mobile and numerous, they will not all be taken out or evaded, and those struck might be repaired. Defenses may be designed to defeat standoff missile systems, also. Thus, even advanced technology is unlikely to defeat all the defenses at once, and the outcome will not be certain for either side. What *is* certain is the growing cost of advanced technology for both sides.

We could, as the British say, "do the sums"—add up the total cost of the attack, including the remote, or standoff, defense suppression and attack systems; the complex target acquisition, command, and control systems; and the guided weapons. We can then divide that cost by the number of targets that could be destroyed, including the effect of losing aircraft to the defenses. We could also add up the costs of the defenses (including their search and tracking radars and the netted command and control system) required to destroy some number of attacking aircraft so as to save targets on the ground from being destroyed by them. The resulting cost trend as sophisticated attack and defense systems proliferate is such that destroying a target like a tank or an artillery piece or saving it from destruction may come to cost more than the target itself.[26] Thus, both sides must increasingly justify the expenditures, not on an individual-system cost-effectiveness basis, but in terms of the value of winning the battle or the war, which is not quantifiable in any practical sense.

Among the alternatives difficult to quantify are the tactics and objectives for air-to-ground warfare. The evolution of PGMs, in addition to the consciousness of the massive armored threat that has accompanied our concentration on NATO problems since the late 1970s, has encouraged a trend toward air support concepts that stress one-on-one dueling between attack aircraft and armored fighting vehicles at critical locations. This general concept is embodied even in such multiple-weapon concepts as Assault Breaker—each submunition is supposed to find and home on its individual target. But the cost trends noted, as well as the difficulties of doing the job, suggest caution about excessive reliance on this approach. Analyses show that in the environment of armored warfare, the air component may well pay for itself better by attacking supporting arms such as artillery or by interdiction beyond the battlefield to delay and weaken the entry of follow-on forces with their logistic support trains into the battle than by destruction of armor *per se*. As noted, weapons of mass destruction, including cluster bomb units on the noses of standoff missiles that can be guided accurately to release points, would probably be much less expensive and might be equally effective in such roles. However, destruction of armored fighting vehicles will be necessary at times. It might best be undertaken at locations near the FEBA, where the ground forces can help suppress the close-in mobile defenses, or against units attempting to exploit a breakthrough, when they may outrun many of their covering defenses. Attacking aircraft could then use shorter-range and less expensive PGMs whose effect is more certain. All this speaks for a variety of weapons and tactics, extensive and effective coordination with the ground forces, and great flexibility and responsiveness to local and strategic developments in prosecuting the air war. All of this complicates the tactical air system and certainly does not reduce its cost.

Cruise Missiles: A Special Case

Another potential attack system is appearing that, by extending one of the capabilities we described earlier, will again challenge some of the precepts of air warfare even before the new doctrines we have been talking about here, which represent radical changes from those of a decade ago, have been absorbed. This system is built around the cruise missile, which represents the ultimate in standoff. The tactical version can be launched from the ground or water without requiring an airplane to carry it to a launch point, and it can reach targets several hundred kilometers away. Even greater flexibility can be achieved by launching such weapons in large numbers from transport-type aircraft such as the C-130 Hercules or from large bombers such as the B-52.

Modern cruise missiles emerged from the synthesis of several new technologies that were developed for various other reasons, including small jet engines, advanced guidance equipment (possible because of solid-state electronics of the kind used in modern microcomputers), and advanced structures and aerodynamics. These small, pilotless airplanes can fly at extremely low altitudes (thereby making it more difficult for the defenses to shoot them down) and reach their targets with precision characterizing PGMs in general.[27]

Since, just as with other modern systems, these capabilities do not come cheaply, wholesale substitution of cruise missiles for airplanes is not likely to be in the cards early. Rather, the U.S. armed forces—and others, if they achieve or acquire the capability—will have still another level of complexity to deal with. Projected acquisition costs of cruise missiles in modest quantities (a few hundred) may be as much as $2 million each. Allowing for some cruise missile losses "on the way in," if manned aircraft can be supported as described earlier to keep their attrition down, it would be considerably cheaper per warhead-on-target to use manned aircraft to deliver PGMs on specific targets than to launch cruise missiles with conventional warheads. The reason is, of course, that the airplane is reusable, and the cruise missile, unless it can be designed as a recoverable RPV that delivers weapons to a target like an airplane, is not; thus the cost structures for the two systems are very different. However, cruise missiles with appropriate guidance and warheads could be used against fixed targets such as bridges, tunnel entrances, and important buildings. They could also serve as the standoff weapons used to destroy high-altitude SAM sites to enable attacks by conventional aircraft.

In all such applications the value of the target must be high to justify using such an expensive weapon. If cruise missiles are acquired in much larger quantities, however, the cost relationships will change, making a wider spectrum of targets worthwhile for attack by such means. For example, procurements on the order of tens of thousands would reduce the missile costs substantially as a result of the greater efficiency of large-quantity production. The costs per warhead-on-target might become comparable for cruise missiles and PGMs delivered by airplanes. But the numbers of cruise missiles we are now talking about are so large that the entire structure of the ground attack forces would have to change: There would be enough cruise missiles to displace a significant number of missions previously planned for airplanes.

A cruise missile is unlikely to be very useful against mobile or moving targets such as groups of armored combat vehicles because in its relatively long flight time the targets may have moved and the expensive weapon will have been wasted. (Future generations of such missiles may have the capability to be retargeted in flight, which would again change their utility; at present that seems a long way off.) In this respect cruise missiles are different from the currently more conventional standoff weapons launched by airplanes, which have shorter ranges and therefore shorter flight times. But there are many fixed targets, including bridges, terminals, depots, and fixed command centers, that are currently considered targets for airplanes. Airplane losses from attacking such targets, even after enemy defenses are suppressed, tend to be high because the targets are usually deep in enemy territory and consequently require long exposure to remaining ground-based defenses and also to air-defense interceptors. Thus, the cruise missile–airplane cost relationships, as well as operational *desiderata* like minimizing losses of expensive airplanes and pilots, might come to favor the use of cruise missiles in this type of mission. This would, if it happened, suggest changes in the air-to-ground warfare force structure, simplifying or deleting some of the most expensive tactical air-warfare systems.

Again, however, things are not so simple. As we noted with respect to the battlefield use of nuclear delivery systems, there is enormous political sensitivity involved in the presence and planned use of cruise missiles. This is because they can carry either conventional or nuclear warheads. In this respect they would not be different from airplanes but for the proliferation aspects. Nuclear-capable tactical airplanes exist in the few hundreds or very low thousands; they can penetrate modern defenses only with difficulty, and their bases are vulnerable to counterattack. Cruise missiles can exist in the tens of thousands; they may be much more difficult to shoot down, and since they do not need elaborate fixed bases, it may be impossible to destroy many of them before launch. Thus, the presence of large enough numbers of cruise missiles to affect the airplane part of the air-power structure significantly would also seriously affect the nuclear deterrent posture, since even though they may be *said* to have conventional warheads they *might* have nuclear warheads. Such a development may have either a stabilizing or a destabilizing impact on deterrence of war, especially in Europe. If the perception that emerges suggests that great proliferation of tactical cruise missiles would be destabilizing or would accelerate the nuclear arms race (and this will not be independent of Soviet and European views and the pressures of U.S.-Soviet strategic arms limitation agreements), large numbers of these missiles may not be acquired. Moreover, if uncertainty remains and causes them to be acquired at low rates (a few tens or hundreds per year), their costs will remain high. Their acquisition might thus be limited largely to those needed for avowedly nuclear forces alone. Currently (in 1982) there are tentative steps toward acquiring conventionally armed cruise missiles for land warfare— e.g., the medium-range air-to-surface missile (MRASM)—in modest quantities. But the value of the acquisition remains in contention among Congress and the Services. It will be many years before we know how these decisions will finally be made, and longer still before the extent of their impact on the tactical air forces becomes apparent, is understood, and is absorbed.

Warfare in the Air

In all this, we have considered neither the air-to-air warfare that proceeds concurrently nor the use of interceptors and fighter aircraft to escort and protect or to intercept and destroy the ground attack aircraft. Here the relationship between the major players is the same, with added complexity. While the United States and other Western countries have developed fighters and air-to-air missiles to a higher level of technology and capability than the Soviet Union,[28] the USSR has acquired greater numbers of fighters. Until recently (the late 1960s), they appeared to concentrate on short-range interceptors, such as the MiG-21 in various versions, to supplement and back up their ground-based air defenses. NATO also has extensive ground-based air defenses (as shown earlier) and is creating new ones, like the U.S. Patriot air-defense system and the French/German/British family of short-range SAM systems (the Roland, Crotale, and Rapier). Nevertheless, NATO has tended to rely more on use of high-performance fighter aircraft to guard against Soviet air attacks on airfields and ground forces than on ground-based defenses. These aircraft have included versions of the French Mirage fighter, the well-known F-4 Phantom, and the new U.S. F-15 and F-16 fighters.

Such aircraft on either side are guided to intercept incoming aircraft by radar operators on the ground—ground-controlled intercept, or GCI. GCI and modern interceptor aircraft can be used in any weather, firing missiles guided by the onboard radar when incoming enemy aircraft are in range but still on the order of some tens of miles away, unless they are inhibited by rules of engagement requiring visual identification of opponents. Even then, telescopes can permit engagement at ranges measured in miles. Such air warfare is very different from the dogfights that took place in World Wars I and II. If the weather permits aircraft to close to visual range (where they might find each other with the combined assistance of GCI and their onboard radars), their speed and large turning radii (over 1.75 miles for a fighter in a tight "5-g" turn at 500 knots) would still lead to separation on the order of several miles between opposing maneuvering aircraft. The aircraft would in such circumstances use shorter-range, infrared guided missiles such as those in the well-known Sidewinder family, and they would use guns only if they could close to very short visual range. Because the number of missiles carried is limited (two to eight) compared with gun ammunition available and because of the high fuel consumption of jet aircraft, such battles cannot last as long as those that took place between aircraft in World War II—a few minutes might be typical for a modern air engagement.

The public is aware of many arguments about the design of such airplanes. Since greater maneuverability than that of the opponent can help an aircraft achieve a better firing position, it is desired by fighter pilots. However, long range is the key to the U.S. Air Force philosophy of carrying the war to the enemy, and obtaining it has led to relatively large and heavy aircraft. This design requirement reduced maneuverability; and until recently we have tended, as a result, to build missiles to compensate for this loss by engaging at long range. New advances in aerodynamics and propulsion have permitted a change in this trend; the F-15 and F-16 are much more maneuverable than the F-4 (and more maneuverable than comparable Soviet aircraft) but still have the necessary range and speed.

This reversal of the trend toward larger and heavier tactical aircraft has been accelerated by a decisive change in the required doctrine and tactics for defeating an opposing air force. It will be remembered that in the 1967

Middle East war, the Israelis took the Arab air forces out of action at the beginning of the war by attacking them on the ground and destroying most of the aircraft. The Japanese did this to us at Pearl Harbor and at March Field in the Philippines in World War II; we did it to the Japanese in the Western Pacific campaigns; and Hitler tried to destroy the RAF by bombing their bases, although for various reasons he shifted his campaign to terror bombing before it succeeded in grounding the RAF. Thus, over many years the standard doctrine for gaining air supremacy was the destruction of the enemy air force on the ground. This philosophy lay behind the design of aircraft such as the F-111 (the TFX of notoriety in the 1960s) and the U.S. Air Force version of the F-4.

However, in recent years a new view of this approach is being enforced by the proliferation of shelters. Shelters are built to protect individual aircraft, even against some nuclear bursts; they are situated around an airfield so that each shelter is far from the next one. This design makes it extremely difficult to destroy an air force on the ground, as the 1973 Middle East war demonstrated.[29] Both sides in Europe have extensive shelter programs to protect their aircraft from ordinary bombing. Unless large numbers of nuclear or persistent chemical weapons are used or runways and key facilities can be destroyed beyond hope of repair by specially designed munitions that can be accurately delivered in the face of strong anti-aircraft defenses, there is little hope of success for the old doctrine. Although airfields might be closed temporarily, it is in the long run cheaper to pour a lot of concrete for more runways or to repair bombing damage than to destroy airfields from the air using aircraft or missile systems with high-explosive warheads. Hence there must be more reliance on air-to-air combat and effective ground-based defense systems to gain air superiority or supremacy. This doesn't mean attacks against airfields will never be undertaken. It means, rather, that such attacks are no longer the best means for grounding and destroying an enemy air force. This new view of how "counterair" can best be performed is not yet fully accepted by U.S. and NATO air forces. I believe, however, that the adverse economics of exchanging concrete for weapon systems will, in time, enforce it.

At the same time these trends have affected U.S. and other Western air forces, the Soviet Union appears to have changed its tactical aviation policy. Originally its Air Force concentrated on short-range interceptors and light to medium bombers, but during the 1970s we saw the appearance of increasingly heavy attack aircraft with long-range strike capability. The newer Soviet tactical aircraft, such as the Fitter-C (SU-17), the ground attack version of the Flogger (MiG-23 D), and the Fencer (SU-24), approach U.S. aircraft like the F-4, the F-16, and in some respects the F-111A in weight and attack capability much more closely than the Soviets' earlier aircraft.[30] These developments foreshadow the growth of an offensive tactical air capability patterned on or similar to ours. The current intensification of interest and effort on the part of the United States and NATO in ground-based air defenses is being driven in part by the realization of the growing Soviet ground attack capability. Thus, the variation of technology on both sides imposes its own cyclic logic and convergence on both sides' capabilities, tactics, and doctrine.

The simultaneous presence of very effective ground-based air defenses and fighters for air defense, together with both sides' offensive air-to-ground operations, obviously complicates the command and control problem. Each side must know the locations of all its own aircraft as well as the enemy's. It must allocate the diverse individual defensive weapon systems among the various attackers so as to avoid total confusion in the conduct of the battle, the waste of precious resources such as air-defense missiles, and the inadvertent destruction of its own aircraft. Command and control in this context depends primarily on information obtained from radar. One means for attackers to degrade the opposing SAMs and GCI is to fly very low. The opposing radar, which sees in a straight line over a curved earth and is blocked by hills and terrain irregularities, simply cannot see the low planes until it is too late for effective counteraction. There are two ways to defeat this tactic, and the major opponents use some of each method to different degrees.

The first approach is to proliferate radars and mount units on advantageously high terrain; in this manner, even though their range against low fliers may be short, all low-altitude gaps are filled. This obviously demands considerably more men and money than are needed for the fewer radar units that can provide high-altitude coverage alone. On the Soviet side the proliferation of mobile SAM defenses helps to do part of this job for them—each SAM battery has its own acquisition radar.

The other way to fill the low-altitude gaps is to raise the radars up very high to enable them to look for low-flying aircraft crossing a much more distant horizon. The obvious way to do this is to mount long-range radar on aircraft flying at high altitudes behind the combat area where friendly fighters can give them a measure of protection. How much protection can be provided is, of course, a subject of extensive argument. All systems, including ground-based radars, are vulnerable to attack. The radar-carrying aircraft, which would see incoming fighters, could also carry out the equivalent of the GCI function from the air. In doing this they would become airborne command centers controlling the battle. Thus, the presence of airborne radar and associated combat control systems can lead to much more effective and efficient use of the ground and air-defense resources than would be possible otherwise, as long as the airborne system survives. Its importance obviously makes it a prime target and can serve to focus the air battle, at least initially.

To use the airborne radar and control scheme, it is necessary to improve greatly the technical quality of the radar so that it can see low-flying aircraft from on high by eliminating the effect of ground clutter. It must be made resistant to electronic countermeasures, and appropriate integration of target information and communications must be provided in the aircraft. In analogous fashion, if a multiplicity of so-called gap-filler radars is provided on the ground, low-altitude SAM defenses must be proliferated if the information the radar provides is to be used. Otherwise, the combat information and control system must be made more complex to control fighters after integrating data from a multiplicity of sources. Or both must be done. Thus, either means of detection and protection against low-flying attackers causes costs to increase. The airborne system, which we have come to know as AWACS (airborne warning and control system), will cost on the order of $85 million (in 1982 dollars) per aircraft for as many as 30 to 40 aircraft.[31] The large numbers are required to make certain that some number—for example, 3, to cover the 600-mile European central front—can be airborne at all times when needed. This high cost, in combination with the uncertain survivability, made the acquisition of the aircraft and its potential effectiveness subjects of intense controversy, both in the U.S. Congress and among our NATO allies who have agreed to purchase it.

The Consequences of Advanced Technology

Now that we have laid out the main directions of the evolution of tactical air warfare, we must take stock of their meaning. In part, this depends on the comparisons we have made between trends in Western and Soviet forces and doctrines. To summarize, the West has relied heavily on offensive air against ground forces to carry a large share of the load in warfare, although the main mission of its military forces as a whole has been considered defensive. The practical development of precision-guidance systems for weapons has promised to close the gap between effectiveness desired and that achieved, caused by the inherent inaccuracies of ballistic weapons ("iron bombs") interacting with the uncertainties of flight dynamics. The Soviet Union has countered by proliferating ground-based air defenses that have also seen great improvements in accuracy, deriving from the advance of electronic technology. These defenses have made the task of using offensive air power more difficult, despite the presence of air-launched PGMs, and they have forced the West to design for the problem of overcoming those defenses. This interplay has brought to center stage, as never before in this context, the conflict between air offense and ground-based defense.

In the air, the Soviet Union initially concentrated on short-range interceptors, but it is currently acquiring an offensive tactical air capability analogous to that developed much earlier by the West. The United States and other NATO countries have also developed highly advanced ground-based SAM defenses; although these defenses have not yet been deployed in the profusion (and therefore with the potential effect) evidenced by Soviet force development, there is an intensification of effort on such systems. The new Western fighter aircraft, such as the F-15, the F-16 and the latest versions of the French Mirage fighters, are being specialized more for air combat. In parallel, a change is being required in the basic approach to achieving air superiority, brought about by extensive air defenses and shelter programs on both sides. Complex and expensive systems are also evolving to gather combat information rapidly and to control the actions of attack and defense systems in a tactical air war. Thus, both sides, while capitalizing on the general trends toward vastly improved performance of weapons systems, have displayed almost cyclic weapon and tactical system design changes that can be taken to represent a response to capabilities developed by the other. These trends are illustrated in Figure 3–3.

Although Western technology continues to be more advanced, the Soviets are advancing also; hence, *differences* in technology evolving over the years may remain about the same, on the average. What the Soviets lack in quality they make up in quantity, and the big question is whether the better quality of U.S. and other Western weapons compensates for the greater Soviet quantity. Although we will not attempt an answer to this question for the time being, it is convenient to explore the question's significance in terms of exchange ratio. This is the ratio, for one side, of targets (whether tanks on the ground, SAM sites, or fighter aircraft) destroyed by its aircraft to aircraft lost in the process. Suppose, for some form of engagement, the exchange ratio favored one side—say, for example, that U.S. fighter aircraft could shoot down 3 to 5 Soviet aircraft for every one of ours shot down in air-to-air combat. We could also consider analogous numbers for air attacks against ground targets—for example, 100 tanks destroyed or damaged for each attack aircraft lost. Suppose, also, that we retain the technological edge, at least to the extent of keeping the exchange ratio the same even as both sides' systems improve. (The ratio would not remain the same if one side improved while the other did not.) Even if the exchange ratio, signifying *relative* loss rates, doesn't change, the increasingly greater destructive capacity attending the weapon system improvements will cause the absolute loss rates on both sides to be much higher unless they adjust rapidly to the new realities and engage each other only at selected locations or times at which each will have a decisive advantage. With both sides fully engaged, such times and places may be rare. As a consequence, either both sides will run out of aircraft and targets on the ground very quickly or they will act conservatively to avoid severe attrition and will therefore not use their forces very effectively.

FIGURE 3–3: Interplay of Air Offense and Air Defense Capability
Between NATO and USSR

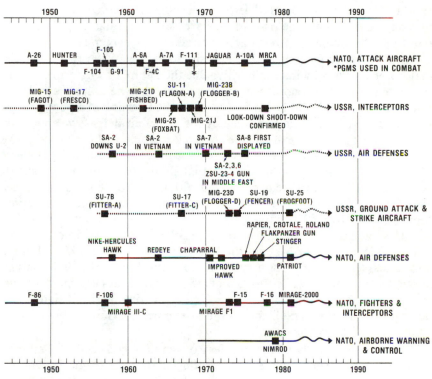

NOTE: All systems are not shown, and dates are approximate.
SOURCES: Janes, All the World's Aircraft; Aviation Week & Space Technology - various issues.
1-19-83-8

The significance of these changes can be illustrated by a few simple quantitative examples. In World War II, Korea, and Vietnam the average attrition of aircraft was on the order of a few tenths of a percent per sortie. At this loss rate the "half-life" of an aircraft force (that is, the time to reduce the force by half if losses aren't replaced) would be between one and two years. If under modern conditions the average attrition per sortie increases to 4 or 5 percent, the half-life of the aircraft force would be reduced to a week or so. On the other hand, as we have seen earlier, it might have taken 100 aircraft a month or more to destroy a thousand military vehicles during World War II. The same level of destruction could be achieved by 100 aircraft in a day or two now. The pace of warfare has accelerated rapidly during the "quiet" technological revolution described in Chapter 1.

All of this describes the anticipated situation should the two strongest nations or alliances interact militarily. But the nature of the technology is such that this kind of denouement can take place elsewhere. It occurred, for example, in the 1973 Middle East war, where the Israelis had a powerful air force and Egypt and Syria had some of the Soviet air-defense weapons. In 1982 in Lebanon nearly half of the Syrian Air Force and the dense SAM array in the Bekaa Valley were each reportedly destroyed in a day or less of fighting. We also found, in Vietnam, that although the North Vietnamese Air Force itself was very weak compared with that of the United States, we were far from having a free ride. The early warning sytems and air defenses supplied to the North Vietnamese by the Soviet Union accounted for many lost U.S. aircraft—and there were none of the SA-6s and few of the low-altitude infrared SAMs that the Israelis encountered in 1973. Modern attack missiles accounted for a number of British ships in the 1982 conflict in the South Atlantic, while SAMs and air-to-air missiles eliminated a large fraction of the Argentine Air Force. Hence, in some perhaps significant degree, the conditions and high loss rates described for the worst case must be anticipated everywhere.

This brings us finally to the problem of developing a tactical air force structure within a budget while incorporating all the technological advances that are driving tactical air power today: advanced aircraft, new navigation and target acquisition capabilities, PGMs, standoff defense suppression and other countermeasures, and AWACS. The cost of tactical combat aircraft has, on the average over the past thirty years, increased about ten times faster than the U.S. Air Force budget. New kinds of support aircraft programs, such as the AWACS or various target acquisition systems, are coming to cost in the billions, whereas earlier there were few separate programs for this purpose and they might amount to a few radars or reconnaissance versions of existing combat aircraft. Attack and defense missiles are costing tens or hundreds of thousands of dollars each (with some costing over $1 million), whereas previously ammunition and bombs could be purchased at about a dollar a pound. Thus, not only for aircraft but for the entire combat force individual system costs are increasing much faster than the overall budget. This uncomfortable relationship has led to a search for *lebensraum* within the available resources, and that in turn led to the concept of the high-low force mix.

This has commonly been interpreted to mean that we would reserve relatively small numbers of the most sophisticated systems for use against the most capable enemy (e.g, in Europe) while acquiring large numbers of simple and therefore cheap systems for use elsewhere. The problem with this conception is that "elsewhere" may not be different from Europe in terms of opposing capability, and consequently the elements of a successful tactical air system are not separable in terms of scenario. Moreover, it neglects the higher manpower, operating, and support costs that would attend this dual force concept. As soon as we proliferate aircraft we need more pilots, maintenance crews, and bases; all of this would be added to the "high" part of the force that must be bought in enough quantity to meet the large European threat in any case. Finally, the argument for proliferation of "low-technology," "simple" systems suggest that the sophisticated systems are too difficult to maintain and so are not often enough able to fly when needed. The simpler systems would, in this view, require much less maintenance and support and so would be cheaper even in a larger force. This view greatly oversimplifies current trends in aircraft system technology. Followed to their long-term conclusion those technical trends don't lead to the results described here at all, as will be seen in Chapter 10.

The high-low idea has merit if it is reinterpreted in terms of an integrated force structure. It does not take sophisticated and expensive aircraft to launch sophisticated and expensive standoff weapons or to carry receivers used for radio or radar location or to deliver either PGMs or close-in weapons once defenses have been effectively suppressed and targets acquired. The simple and slow A-10 close-support aircraft, for example, could serve just as well as an F-4, F-111, or F-16 in these roles—its large payload would be an advantage. Similarly, if air-to-air weapons are capable of reaching targets many miles away, the delivery aircraft needs only load capacity and the ability to reach the launch point while using its radar. High dogfight maneuverability, which is very costly, becomes much less important although some degree of maneuverability is needed for evasion of missiles if electronic countermeasures can't defeat them. For capabilities now coming into being, the sophistication lies in data processing on the ground; in countermeasures-resistant command, control, and communications; in countermeasures-resistant weapon guidance; and in such aids to target acquisition and weapon delivery as forward-looking infrared sensors and laser target designators.

A force mix combining these elements in appropriate proportion would reduce the present (and currently preferred) reliance on a force of all fully self-sufficient aircraft, each of which can perform all of the tasks in air warfare. It would increase reliance on integrated and coordinated subsystems, some in the air and some on the ground, each performing an essential part of the task. For example, all aircraft could launch weapons, but only some would have complex target acquisition systems. They would designate release points for the others. Other functions would be similarly distributed. This would complete trends already begun, in which some aircraft are designed to carry special airborne radar, some are designed for defense suppression, and so forth. Redundancy—i.e., several available subsystems—would be required to cover loss of critical elements within such a force. Even so, as a whole it would be a less expensive and more effective force than one that attempts to incorporate all high-technology features in one set of aircraft to be used exclusively for one scenario (but too small as a result) and to use low technology exclusively for another force designed for a different scenario (a force that is consequently both overlarge and ineffective). In fact, although such integration and distribution of functions tend to be resisted by the peacetime Air Force, when pressed to it by the exigencies of combat in Vietnam, the U.S. Air Force adopted such an approach in the field by devising "strike packages" for various missions, as illustrated in Figure 3-1. I believe that the constraints of budget must inevitably encourage the evolution of tactical air power in this direction during peacetime prepartion for the tactical air mission, in view of the trends in evolving technology and its costs.

Thus we see the uncomfortable reality of advanced technology in modern war. In the popular view the new smart weapons should allow our forces to stand back and take fatal potshots at the enemy, dealing death and destruction by means of a science fiction war machine until he is defeated.[32] In fact, those weapons will not substitute machines for people at all but will actually make air warfare vastly more costly, difficult, and complex and will place serious constraints on its flexibility and viability. The same effect occurs in ground warfare, which we will examine in the next chapter.

Before proceeding, we should give some attention to an important philosophical aspect of this unexpected outcome of the march of military technology: If the effectiveness of tactical air power and all its accouterments has been placed in doubt by the power of the defenses and if the price keeps rising until it may come to cost more to destroy a target by means of tactical air power than the target is worth, why pay the price?

Tactical aircraft are still the most flexible means to amass heavy firepower on short notice and bring it where it is desperately needed; to carry firepower deep into enemy territory when that is appropriate; to shift attacks rapidly from one form of target to another and from one location to another as the situation demands; and to observe what is happening beyond sight of the land forces to permit rapid *ad hoc* action to be taken to meet shifting military needs. Surface-to-surface missiles can be used for all these purposes, but it can be shown that they cannot be used nearly as effectively for the same cost unless they use nuclear weapons.[33] They may have a role in striking fixed targets and in destroying some air defenses, as we discussed for cruise missiles. But unless the remote target acquisition and homing capability exbodied in the massed, terminally guided submunition concept can be realized at reasonable cost—and that may be many years off if it can be achieved at all—tactical combat aircraft armed with close-in precision- guided munitions will remain the least costly means for exercising very mobile combat power from remote locations, wherever the defenses can be overcome by direct attack, or by electronic warfare, or both.

It is also clear that, since the anticipated effectiveness of ground-based air defenses rests, as does that of tactical air power, on many uncertainties and suppositions, the side that has tactical air power available might still be able to use it to help impose its will at critical times in a conventional military conflict. It would be difficult or impossible to win such a war without tactical air power, even though tactical air power cannot win it alone. (The outcome in Vietnam might seem to some to belie this; but without arguing that war here, we might remember the observation made earlier, that the North Vietnamese did not win until the absence of U.S. tactical air power gave them greatly increased freedom of movement on the ground.)

Thus, the necessity of maintaining military preparedness among the foremost military powers demands that the price for effective tactical combat aviation continue to be paid by all if it is paid by one. It is, moreover, not a trivial matter that about 40 percent of the investment in our general purpose forces is in tactical air power. This is not to be written off lightly, if its presence is demanded for other reasons, and if ways can be found, as they can, to mitigate the most seriously adverse effects of the current trends to greater complexity, higher costs, and consequently shrinking forces.

SOME OF THE GUIDED MISSILES THAT ARE
CHANGING THE NATURE OF MODERN WARFARE*

Roland Low-Altitude SAM System

Shrike Radar-Seeking Missile Being Fired from A-4F Skyhawk Attack Aircraft

*Photographs, Courtesy U.S. Government, Various Sources.

Sidewinder Air-to-Air Heat-Seeking Missile

Tomahawk Cruise Missile

Harpoon Anti-Ship Cruise Missile

Harpoon Anti-Ship Cruise Missile Being Launched from P-3C Orion Maritime Patrol Aircraft

TV-Guided Maverick Air-to-Ground Anti-Tank Missile Being Loaded on A-10 Attack Aircraft

Maverick Anti-Tank Missile Just Before Impact

TOW Anti-Tank Guided Missile Emerging from Launch Tube on a Jeep

TOW Anti-Tank Missile Leaving Armored Launcher on Bradley Fighting Vehicle *

*Photograph Courtesy Hughes Aircraft Company, Electro-Optical and Data Systems Group, El Segundo, Calif.

Tanks and Anti-Tank Guided Missiles

The tank is a mobile, heavily armored platform carrying a trainable cannon and one or more smaller anti-personnel weapons. It can move cross-country at relatively high speeds. En masse, tanks compose the battle fleet of the ground forces, and they impose their own kind and pace of warfare. Because of the relative invulnerability to most kinds of fire afforded by their armor, tanks have been used in the past fifty years for every military purpose. They have guarded presidential palaces against coups, provided the traditional cavalry functions of screening and scouting for a main force, and acted as the basic striking power of main forces for attacks through and behind opposing armies to destroy them and their bases of support and resistance.

Since the introduction of the tank, weapons have been developed to defeat it.[1] In the ground forces they have included the guns of other tanks, self-propelled anti-tank rockets, and land mines capable of blowing off a tank's treads or fatally damaging its armored hull. The anti-tank guided missile (ATGM) is the most recent development in this direction. It takes advantage of the new guidance technology for accuracy and of the new propulsion technology to project a shaped-charge warhead larger than can be fired from most tank guns or anti-tank artillery. ATGMs fired against tanks standing or moving slowly in the open will score fatal or near-fatal hits more than five times out of ten. Therefore, there seems to have come about another of the major changes in relationships among weapons, such as that between the battleship and the airplane, and, as a result, the tank is becoming obsolete. For some, at least, that has become the "conventional wisdom."[2]

But perhaps it is not so. To examine the question in some depth we must examine armored warfare as a whole in the light of this new development. We will begin with a description of armored warfare and will then assess where ATGMs fit in the general scheme of things and what effect they may have.

Warfare Between Armored Forces

The tank was invented by the British during World War I in an attempt to break the trench warfare stalemate that had been brought about by the effectiveness of the machine gun and the artillery. As often happens with new military inventions, the British tanks were used in small numbers and without what today's military would call a clearcut concept of operations suited to the potential of the weapon. These early tanks were mechanically clumsy and armed with machine guns, and they had no decisive effect. During the period between the wars, tanks and more suitable concepts of operations were developed much further—ironically, mostly by the French. The opening of World War II showed that the Germans had learned the lessons best, however, and their Panzer divisions swept all before them on the battlefield.

Their tanks had cannon, which were quite effective. Although relative to the larger conventional artillery pieces they were small and short-range, they could fire more accurately than conventional artillery in direct fire—that is, with their flat-trajectory weapons the gunners could see their targets and correct for misses without the assistance of forward observers required by long-range artillery. Their mobility permitted them to travel on roads or cross-country if necessary, to places where defending troops were sparse or were not armed to defeat tanks and, therefore, could be overrun. Subsequently, they could move beyond the local defenses into the enemy rear, placing supplies and rear-area support forces and reserves in jeopardy. This would force withdrawal of defending troops from other forward positions to prevent those troops from being cut off and surrounded. If these withdrawal maneuvers were undertaken in haste, they could easily become a rout. This was especially true in 1940, in the Low Countries and France, where roads were clogged by refugees, and the withdrawing forces, dependent on the roads, were slowed to a crawl. The armored forces, moving cross-country, were able to surround and destroy any organized resistance piecemeal. They then reached deep into the territory they were attacking to seize and control key points in the transportation and supply systems, rendering the defending armies incapable of operating as a coherent force. Thus, the tank joined the mobility of a tracked vehicle with the firepower of the cannon and provided protection for that firepower. The full development of the tanks' military potential by one side before the other gave birth to the blitzkrieg—the lightning war—and revolutionized warfare.

However, the other side—the Western Allies and the USSR—also learned the techniques and improved on them. In the North African desert, armored formations maneuvered against each other at high speed, magnifying the movements of earlier footborne armies of limited size in analogous forms of war of maneuver. More massive armored conflicts in Europe led to breakthroughs, envelopments (turning movements in which attacking columns move behind defending forces and attack them from the rear), and pursuits of defeated armies over hundred of miles of territory. Since World War II, this form of mobile armored warfare has been practiced only in the Middle East in successive Israeli victories over Arab armies.

But armor has also been used in other areas less suited to maneuver over large terrain distances. Tanks were included in the North Korean attack on South Korea in 1950. The French, and later U.S. and South Vietnamese forces, used them in Vietnam to protect movement of large convoys along roads and in the few open areas suitable for tanks' maneuver. The North Vietnamese used them on a small scale, but often with the decisive effect of surprise because they weren't expected to materialize out of terrain heavily covered by vegetation. India and Pakistan used armored forces in their 1965 border war. The Soviet forces in Afghanistan have used them together with armed helicopters against opposing guerillas, but with indifferent success in the rugged, mountainous terrain. Only the India-Pakistan war resulted in a stalemate between armored forces. It is clear, however, that despite the vagaries of some adverse situations armored warfare has become a permanent feature of the organization and operation of armed forces. In the deserts of the Middle East, in the open areas of Europe, and in the vast spaces of Central and Eastern Asia along the Soviet-Chinese and Mongolian-Chinese borders, where there is room and suitable terrain for maneuver, the potential use of armor completely shapes the form of warfare that might be anticipated.

When we talk of armored forces today we mean just that: not simply a group of tanks, but a whole congeries of weapons and vehicles, all designed to work together in a particular way. Most of these systems are built around the tractorlike endless track or tread, which permits the vehicle to move across open terrain. Infantry moves with the tanks in armored personnel carriers (APCs) that, although lightly armored, afford protection from small-arms and machine-gun fire and from most artillery fragments. APCs, now coming to be more heavily armed, can fight with each other and with unarmored infantry. Some artillery—especially that which is intended to move with tanks in assault of strongly defended positions and then in exploitation of breakthroughs—is also self-propelled, using tracked, lightly armored vehicles. Air-defense weapons, anti-tank weapons, and many logistic vehicles use tracked suspensions or they use wheels having tires, suspensions, and drives suitable for some degree of cross-country movements, similar to those of four-wheel-drive jeeps or of road construction machinery. Some artillery is still towed and must be deployed to firing positions off roads, but even then it is usually mobile enough to keep up with armor (tanks and armored personnel carriers) that is moving rapidly along roads to exploit an initial battlefield success. Thus, all the ground-force weapons are designed to have mobility compatible with that of the tank, enabling an entire force to move and fight as a unit. Moreover, other systems such as armed helicopters are being designed with the idea that destruction of opposing tanks is one of their main missions.

Thus, the tank has become the centerpiece of a modern army. That army does fight as a unit, however; all its weapons are used to support each other. It is important to appreciate what this mutual support means. No single weapon or weapon system can be considered to operate in isolation, nor can any one system be decisive on the battlefield (except for nuclear weapons used unilaterally in sufficient numbers and sizes or chemical weapons used in profusion against unprotected troops). Let us consider the stages of an armored conflict and, in the process, the nature of the interactions among the various weapon systems.

We have already noted what experience in modern warfare shows about the broad sweep of armor tactics. If the opposing lines of resistance are not continuous and uniform in strength, tanks can be used as the spearhead of an attack, to pass between the strong segments of defense and envelop them from one or two directions in their rear. This was the tactic used to defeat the German Sixth Army before Stalingrad and attempted by the Germans in the Ardennes in 1944. If resistance is strong and distributed along a more or less continous line, it is necessary to penetrate the solid front of defenses. Although tanks may make the penetration, the opposing defensive positions must first be softened up by air and artillery bombardment. The remaining defense may still be too strong for tanks and APC-mounted infantry to take it by storm because, for example, extensive, protected anti-tank barriers and weapon emplacements may remain. Then the infantry may have to press through first, dismantling the defenses with artillery fire on call; mortar, grenade, and small-arms fire; and hand-emplaced demolitions, taking each position and going on to the next until the following armor can rush through from behind and strike into the enemy rear. This was the pattern of movement through the hedgerows of Normandy before Patton's Third Army broke out and raced east toward Paris in August 1944.

Once through the forward defenses, the armor comes into its own. It undertakes flank attacks and attacks to the rear, rushing for objectives far behind the front with the intent of breaking up the enemy's forces, surrounding and destroying or capturing large groups of men, and generally attempting to end organized resistance. The collapse of the German defenses after Patton's breakthrough, or the Israeli encirclement of the Egyptian Third Army in the 1973 war, are examples of the technique. The other side may make counterattacks against these penetrating columns, whose flanks are exposed, and then disaster can result. It did at Bastogne, for example, for the German forces driving toward the Meuse River through the Ardennes in 1944.

In these battles, again, combined arms are the rule, although the combinations are different. The operations include air attacks to create shock and disruption, to pin retreating forces in place, and to pave the way for the onrushing armored columns; they also include tank attacks out of column formations when resistance threatens, the use of self-propelled artillery to help tanks and APC-mounted infantry storm strong points that cannot be bypassed, armed helicopters and heliborne or airborne troops to act as cavalry by advancing past main defenses to disrupt enemy resistance before the main ground forces arrive, and air defenses to fend off enemy aircraft trying to slow the columns. All the systems collaborate with and complement each other at every stage.

It has often happened in such battles, especially in the desert, that tanks meet tanks and shoot it out as fleets moving against each other. Preferably, however, tanks are used against soft targets that cannot resist very easily—it is better to leave the opposition behind and unsupported, picking it off when it has no place to go and little fight left, than to meet it head on if that can be avoided.

The nature and theory of armored warfare, as it has evolved among the nations equipped to employ it, is illustrated in Table 4–1, which shows side by side excerpts from U.S. and Soviet descriptions of armored tactics and doctrine.[3] Despite the fact that the U.S. example is an extract from a terse instruction manual and the Soviet example is taken from essentially philosophical works on the nature of modern war, it can be seen that, in addition to describing graphically the philosophy and sequence of armored conflict, the two accounts are essentially similar. The nature of the weapon drives and makes possible the modes of its use.

Now, despite the correctly conveyed impression of the power of an armored attack, armored forces could not long sustain a battle without a steady stream of supplies—fuel, ammunition, spare parts. Armored forces are vast consumers of fuel when they are moving and of ammunition when they are engaged. Tanks can withstand extensive artillery fire and aerial bombardment, but they can be shaken apart by rough ground. A unit of 100 tanks starting out on a mission may be down to 50 because of mechanical breakdowns by the time it has gone 100 miles across rough country.[4]

Tanks moving over normally rough ground cannot move faster than 2 to 5 miles per hour, since to go faster would be beyond the endurance of the crews, subject to the shaking caused by the terrain. One of the improvements sought in designing new generations of tanks (e.g., the M-1 Abrams tank that succeeds the M-60) is a better suspension that will allow higher speed over rough terrain. Tanks might go about 30 miles per hour for short stretches

Table 4-1: COMPARISON OF U.S. AND SOVIET ARMORED WARFARE DOCTRINE

Phase or Characteristic of Operation	U.S.—From FM 17-1[a]	USSR—From Sidorenko, Savkin[b]
Basic Philosophy	Armor operations are conducted by fire and maneuver . . . to create a preponderance of combat power that culminates in a powerful and violent action at the decisive time and place . . . calculated to obtain decisive results.	War experience has shown that greatest success in the offensive [is] achieved when the main attack [is] delivered on an axis which provide[s] for a swift breakthrough of the enemy defense and development of the offensive at high rates . . . with the aim of encircling and destroying defensive enemy groupings.
Command Flexibility	Commanders must avoid rigid adherence to the original plan in the face of significant changes in the situation that provide opportunities to destroy the enemy. . . .	The increased significance of combat actions in operational depth . . . require[s] the corresponding training of . . . command personnel and their manifestation of broad initiative and independence. . . . The goal of the operation of battle must fully conform to the conditions of the actual . . . situation. . . .
Deception	. . . all forms of deception, cover, dispersion concealment . . . [are] of importance.	. . . surprise may be achieved by leading the enemy astray with regard to one's intentions, by secrecy in preparation and swiftness of troop operations . . . by delivering a forceful attack when and where the enemy does not expect it. . . . In defense, great attention is devoted to camouflage and the use of measures to deceive the enemy.
Breakthrough tactics (use of armor)	Whenever possible, tanks lead the attacking formation. . . . It is desirable that the infantry remain mounted as long as possible so that . . . movements can be conducted at the speed of tanks to rapidly close with and destroy the enemy. . . .	In all cases the [information] . . . must ensure . . . the delivery of a coordinated attack by tank and motorized rifle [units] against the forward edge.

(Cont'd)

Table 4-1: COMPARISON OF U.S. AND SOVIET ARMORED WARFARE DOCTRINE (Cont'd)

Phase or Characteristic of Operation	U.S.—From FM 17-1[a]	USSR—From Sidorenko, Savkin[b]
Fire support	The mission of the base of fire is to minimize the enemy's capability to interfere with the movement of the maneuver force and, within its capabilities, to destroy the enemy. . . .	. . . the period of the fire preparation by direct fire [is] the most effective method of destroying observed enemy weapons as well as destroying defensive works on the FEBA and in the immediate depth.
Exploitation and Pursuit	In the exploitation, the attacker seeks to follow up the gains of a successful penetration or envelopment. The attacker drives deep into the enemy's rear to destroy his means to reconstitute an organized defense or to initiate an orderly withdrawal. . . . The pursuit is the final phase of the exploitation. Its goal is annihilation of the enemy force. . . . Enemy forces encountered are not engaged unless they can interfere with the accomplishment of the mission. . . . The attacks continue day and night. When conditions permit, elements of the enemy force are enveloped or cut off. . . . In the exploitation, nuclear, conventional, and chemical weapons may be used principally on targets of opportunity.	Pursuit represents an attack on a withdrawing enemy for the purpose of final destruction (or capture) of his forces . . . only parallel pursuit will ensure high rates of advance and permit outstripping the enemy . . . moving to his flanks and rear . . . cutting off routes of withdrawal for the main body. . . . The pursuit is conducted continuously day and night . . . under any weather conditions . . . consists of hitting a withdrawing enemy with nuclear weapons, air strikes, and artillery fire . . . of dismembering and destroying him piecemeal or taking him prisoner.

[a] *Armor Operations;* Department of the Army Field Manual FM 17-1, Headquarters, Department of the Army, Washington, D.C., October 1966.
[b] Sidorenko, A. A., *The Offensive,* Moscow, and Savkin, V. Ye., *The Basic Principles of Operational Art and Tactics,* both translated and published under the auspices of the U.S. Air Force. (Quotations taken from scattered locations in these works)

over hard, relatively smooth ground, as on the desert or in rolling farm country, but to exploit a breakthrough over long periods they must move along roads. High speed makes for more wear and tear on the machine. Forces on the move must avoid or surmount terrain obstacles, cross streams and rivers on bridges (which probably have to be erected by combat engineers), or ford them. All the combined arms must stay together in some reasonable order related to their combat functions in order to defend the forces if they are attacked or to overcome centers of resistance. Withal, the fuel, supplies, and ammunition that go into battle with the unit will last only a few days. These items must be replenished, or other units must be passed through to carry on while those previously in the lead rest and are reloaded. Tanks and other major equipment must be brought within a few miles of the battlefield on tank transporters or railroad flatcars. Delicate items like air-defense missiles have to be brought up on special vehicles and loaded for combat. The whole moves rather ponderously.

Thus, although in armored warfare mobility and high speed are the watchwords, they are relative terms. The mobility of an army on wheels and tracks is nothing like the personal mobility that allows us to drive to a city hundreds of miles away in a day, nor does it correspond to the speed of a tank running freely along a road at its top speed of 35 to 40 miles per hour. Patton's army, pursuing the Germans across France, averaged 15 miles per day and did 30 miles on its best day, covering a distance of almost 350 miles before it ran out of supplies.[5] Soviet writers claim that their forces have moved at about twice the average speed achieved by the Western Allies,[6] but they had much more open space and greater distances to cover, with smaller density of populated areas to slow them. Advanced elements of armored forces could indeed go 100 miles in a day against no opposition. Moving the entire army and maintaining its fighting integrity, even without opposition, would not permit such rapid movement. But we cannot fail to note, of course, that 15 to 30 miles per day means that if, after a breakthrough, penetrating forces can move that fast and sustain the motion, all of Western Europe from the East German border to the Bay of Biscay could be overrun in about a month. An invading army would move more slowly against determined opposition—the two world wars illustrated the extremes.

In defensive armored warfare, also, the various arms must collaborate with and complement each other. Air defenses and defending interceptor aircraft must fend off attacking aircraft. Artillery, fixed-wing aircraft and helicopters with anti-armor munitions and missiles, and infantry with anti-tank weapons in well protected positions must attempt to slow the attacking armor as it tries to penetrate to and beyond those positions. Tanks in this role can be used simply as mobile guns moved into defensive emplacements, but this is not the way an armor commander prefers if he can avoid doing so.[7] If he could use his resources as he wished, the defending commander would again take advantage of his tanks' mobility. He would hold them in reserve and bring them into action with speed and shock once the penetrating enemy's forward forces were engaged and pinned. Or, if the enemy had moved through the defensive positions, the defender would attack the flanks of the penetrating columns and attempt to cut and destroy them piecemeal.

We will examine some important details of these interactions among armored forces later, as part of our exploration of the function of the new anti-tank guided missiles. Suffice it to be noted in summary that, first, warfare with armored forces can take place over vast areas of territory; but, second, the weapon coordination and supply problems call for complex design of forces and operations that go well beyond simply driving tanks into enemy territory and letting following infantry occupy it, if any organized resistance is expected. It is important to keep this in mind when considering the context in which anti-tank weapons are used.

Defeating the Tank

Despite the power of a properly executed armored attack, it has, of course, been possible to defeat such attacks. As suggested by the previous discussion, many of the means for doing so involve tactics, including judicious disposition of defending forces and intelligent use of terrain and built-up areas. However this is done, one of the chief tasks of defensive forces is to disable or destroy the armored vehicles that make up the main strike force of the attack. The most difficult of these is the tank itself, since it is at once the most heavily armored and the most heavily armed. There are, however, many ways to defeat tanks, and all of them have been demonstrated in recent warfare.

Among the first is to rob tanks of the advantage of their mobility by forcing or enticing the battle onto unfavorable terrain with natural obstacles such as steep slopes, dense trees, or soft ground that cannot support tanks or that impedes their progress. The difficulty that can be caused by poor terrain was illustrated by Montgomerey's move toward the bridge at Arnhem, Holland, in 1944, in Operation Market-Garden.[8] There, he allowed the forces of the British XXX Corps to be caught by anti-tank gun emplacements on dike roads twenty feet above the surrounding farmland. The following tanks could not leave the road when the lead tanks were knocked out, and even if they could have they would have bogged down in the soft Dutch soil. Built-up areas such as villages, cities, or towns are, of course, even more deadly for armored forces. If attacking tanks can be forced into such areas, where every house can harbor infantry with anti-tank weapons, they are much easier to defeat. Supposedly "mobile" warfare can be slowed to a painstaking, house-to-house firing match, as happened for months during the battle of Stalingrad, and as the Israeli forces feared as they entered Beirut in 1982.

The artificial analog to natural and urban barriers is the field of concrete tank traps consisting of closely spaced tall posts and tetrahedrons shaped like children's jacks. These can be blown up by artillery or demolition teams, as the Allies demonstrated on the Normandy beaches. Again, however, the need for such efforts slows the attack and exposes the armor to anti-tank fire for longer periods.

Another method to defeat tanks was illustrated when the Viet Minh destroyed the heavily armored Groupement Mobile 100 on Route 19 in the Vietnamese Highlands in 1954. In that part of Indochina, tanks and other vehicles were forced to move on the roads. The Viet Minh several times ambushed columns moving in the vicinity of An Khe and put armored vehicles out of action by swarming all over them. They came so close in a rush from ambush that the guns of the armored vehicles often could not fire on them for fear of hurting their own forces. The attacking infantry climbed on the vehicles, including tanks, firing through the crews' viewing slits and dropping grenades through hatches if the suddenness of the ambush caught them with their hatches open.[9] The Hungarians used exactly the same tactics to defeat Soviet tanks, including the use of Molotov cocktails, in Budapest at the start of the 1956 rebellion.

A tank can also be immobilized or seriously damaged by mines, which, depending on their size, may blow off treads, punch a hole in the bottom, or even turn a tank over. Thus, part of every prepared defense against armored attack is a minefield. Even though the attacker may know the mines are there, time and trouble must be taken to move through with mine-clearing infantry or leading armored vehicles designed to detonate the mines (for example, with heavy rollers attached to their front ends) and make a path along which other armored fighting vehicles and tanks can follow. Even if the armor gets through, the attack will be slowed and channelized, again making the tanks more vulnerable to anti-tank fire. Techniques to emplace minefields rapidly during the battle are currently emerging, including mines that can be delivered suddenly and in large numbers by artillery, helicopters, and airplanes. If tanks are caught in a minefield unaware and then brought under fire when they are stopped, the resulting casualties and confusion can be devastating unless they are able to push through despite the mine damage and unless other forces can follow through the opening.

Perhaps the main work of defeating tanks is done by direct-fire anti-tank weapons of various kinds. These weapons must be able to penetrate the heavy frontal armor of the tank, and there are two main mechanisms by which this can be done. The first is a very high-velocity, solid projectile made of hardened steel or heavier metals, which penetrates the armor and expends its remaining energy destroying the "soft" inside of the tank (a kinetic-energy round). The second is a high-explosive round with a shaped charge that focuses the explosive energy to penetrate the armor (HEAT, or high-explosive anti-tank, round). Although any anti-tank weapon can deliver a shaped-charge warhead, only a cannon projectile can develop the muzzle velocity necessary for a kinetic-energy round to penetrate the heavy frontal hull or turret armor of a tank. The combination of flexibility in choice of weapon, maneuverability, and armor protection of the tank against all but specially designed anti-tank weapons leads many armored-warfare specialists to consider tanks as the preferred anti-tank system. However, as we have noted, tanks and their accompanying more lightly armored APCs and infantry fighting vehicles are likely to seek combat against other, "softer" types of forces, especially the infantry. There has consequently been a proliferation of other weapons that such forces can use against tanks.

The first to appear, before and during World War II, were flat-trajectory cannon such as the much-feared German "88"; and such weapons remain the only ones other than tanks that can fire kinetic-energy rounds. These are essentially short-range weapons (effective up to a few thousand meters) because the kinetic-energy round loses much of the velocity necessary to penetrate in a relatively short distance. Such cannon were supplanted in U.S. forces largely for reasons of cost, mobility, and flexibility, by jeep-mounted or man-portable recoilless rifles (which launch a rocket-assisted shell out of a tube). These weapons, equally short range, are not as accurate as a cannon and can fire only HEAT rounds.

Another part of the family of anti-tank weapons was the bazooka of World War II fame. A small, fin-stabilized rocket with a shaped-charge warhead and an effective range of a few hundred feet, it could be aimed and fired by one man from a shoulder-held tube. Although each individual weapon had a very low probability of hitting its target, if enough of them were fired, the tanks would clearly be in danger of sustaining at least a few hits. With many such weapons in the infantry a tank crew could never be sure that any nearby ruins, ditches, or shell holes did not harbor an infantryman or two with bazookas. Thus, these weapons not only helped to protect the infantry itself, they constrained tank tactics as well. The descendants of the bazooka are more modern versions, including the U.S. LAW (light anti-tank weapon), the Viper that is to replace it, and the Soviet RPG-7 rocket. The latter was used with devastating effect by the Viet Cong and North Vietnamese against South Vietnamese and U.S. vehicles and by the PLO against tanks in Lebanon in 1976.[10]

Anti-Tank Guided Missiles

To appreciate the role played by the subsequent development of anti-tank guided missiles or ATGMs, one must recognize the complex interplay between range and accuracy in anti-tank warfare. The typical small errors in aim and the ballistic dispersion of free-flying projectiles mean that miss distance tends to increase as the distance between the firing point and target increases. Thus, useful anti-tank weapon accuracy falls off sharply at distances beyond about a thousand meters. The development of missile guidance permitted the achievement of essentially constant accuracy (miss distance) out to the limits of a weapon's range. Limitations on the utility of range in direct fire arise because in real terrain with hills, gradual slopes and undulations, and vegetation, a moving tank target more than three to four kilometers away cannot be kept in view long enough for the missile to reach it at readily achievable flying speeds. Moreover, long range and high speed make for a large missile, and consequently unwieldy systems with fewer shots available. Thus, ATGMs have tended to be designed for ranges of a few kilometers, reaching well beyond the accurate fire capability of the tank gun and yet within the relatively short range at which terrain (and often the weather) will in general force most tank/anti-tank engagements to take place. Longer-range ATGMs have been designed to be fired from helicopters, where the weight and viewing problems are less constraining. There are still limits, however, resulting from both missile design and the desire to minimize the time during which the helicopter is exposed to hostile fire while the gunner guides the missile to the target. At the other end of the scale, some ATGMs have been designed for ranges of a kilometer or so, permitting them to be small enough to be handled and fired by an individaul infantryman. These serve the special purpose of allowing bazookalike fire with much greater accuracy at much longer effective ranges than those of a bazooka. Such weapons are heavier than bazookas, and they have more blast effect on launching, so that handling is more difficult. (As always in weapon system design one doesn't get something for nothing, as these examples show.)

ATGMs have tended to use guidance systems very different from those used in missiles designed for launching from fixed-wing aircraft or from SAMs. Because electronic countermeasures need to be foiled and because the "signals" from a distant tank are difficult to capture and to distinguish from the "noise" of the surroundings, command guidance toward a visually observed target has been favored. Control commands are sent to the missile by the gunner over a fine wire that reels off the back of the missile, just like a fishing line off a spinning reel, while the gunner keeps the tank in the cross hairs and flies the missile to it. The missile is usually made visible to him by a flare in its tail. Early versions of such missiles had a small joy stick so that "flying" them was as literal as flying a model airplane. Since current ATGMs have semiautomatic flight control, the gunner has only to keep the cross hairs on the target and let the guidance system do the rest. Modern attempts to eliminate even this physical connection between the missile and its director are centering on laser-aided guidance schemes, some of them similar to those used in air-launched laser-guided bombs wherein the weapon seeker homes on a laser spot kept on the target. The helicopter-launched Hellfire missile is of this character. The gunner (whether on the ground or in a helicopter) can then fire and forget; but someone (perhaps elsewhere on the immediate battlefield) would still have to use a laser designator to keep the spot of laser light on the target for missile guidance.

The firing errors and flight disturbances common to all projected weapons cause a distribution of fire around the target, such that the probability of hitting it exactly and destroying it is less than unity. In general, from such distributions, we would find that all anti-tank weapons prior to ATGMs would have a single-shot probability of damaging or destroying a tank well toward the lower end of the zero-to-one range of probability. The accuracy afforded by the guidance system and the large warheads of the ATGM have raised this probability well into the upper half of the range. The ATGM's essentially constant accuracy throughout its firing range permits effective engagement of the tank at long range where the tank's gun is least effective in counterfire. These ATGM characteristics have brought about what mathematicians would call a step-function improvement of anti-tank capability, at least in one-on-one engagements—one ATGM system against one tank.

But in weapons design one rarely gains such an advantage without also incurring some countervailing disadvantages. These arise from the size and weight of the ATGM, its softness, its relatively slow flight speed, which is much less than that of a cannon projectile, and its susceptibility to countermeasures.[11] If a tank crew detects the launching of an ATGM at long range, for example by the flash or smoke emitted when the rocket motor is ignited, they may well have time to deploy masking smoke. If the tank is very maneuverable and the terrain favorable, it might move behind a terrain feature such as a hillock or clump of vegetation (or, if one is available, a manmade structure) before the ATGM arrives. The smoke and dust of battle can have a similar masking effect. If there is no clear target at which to aim for the entire ATGM flight, the chance of its hitting the tank becomes essentially zero. In addition, because of the time required for the missile to accelerate to high enough velocity to respond to guidance commands, a minimum distance is required between the launch point and the missile for the latter to work at all. Of course, a tank hiding is not a tank charging.

The softness of the ATGM, its launcher, and its crew, which in the early versions were jeep-mounted (and which for the shoulder-fired weapons are exposed during launch even if crews ride into combat in armored personnel carriers), means they are vulnerable to artillery fire. Massive artillery fire is almost always used to prepare for an assault on a defended position, and the general locations of many ATGM launchers in such positions might be surmised from knowledge of their typical firing range (and would be confirmed once they fired). The ATGM crews would thus be highly vulnerable to the artillery fire in the combined arms engagement even before the tank/anti-tank duel begins. This problem is solvable in part by digging in, but mainly the trend is to mount ATGM launchers on armored vehicles to protect the crew from artillery fragments. This approach also has the advantage that the resulting system has at least as much maneuverability on the battlefield as a tank, and perhaps more. However, an armored fighting vehicle having a multiple ATGM launcher that can be reloaded from inside is likely to cost nearly as much as a tank. And because the ATGM-launching vehicle is likely to have much thinner armor and a slower rate of fire, it cannot stand and slug it out with a tank as other tanks might do in some circumstances. (Note that this comparison of costs among fighting systems is the appropriate one in evaluating ATGMs against tanks, not the comparison, which is sometimes used, of the cost of a single missile, perhaps $5–10,000, against a tank costing $1–2 million.)

The United States has made one attempt to integrate ATGMs with a tank, in the M-60A2 version of our M-60 main battle tank. This tank has a dual-purpose gun that can fire a HEAT artillery round or the Shillelagh ATGM; but the system costs about twice as much as a conventional tank and still does not solve the problem of exposure to a counterfire kinetic-energy round during the flight of the missile.[12] The Sheridan armored reconnaissance vehicle, which could fire the same weapons, was a more lightly armored, more agile vehicle, designed to use with armored cavalry. It didn't perform well in Vietnam and is being phased out of service. Systems like these can serve critically important roles in combat, but they are not the means to proliferate ATGMs on the battlefield.

We have alluded to still another critical difference between ATGMs, even on armored vehicles, and tanks; namely, rate of fire. The difference here arises from the difference in flight time and loading time of the two weapons. A tank might fire ten to twelve rounds per minute, while an ATGM crew might fire one or two—perhaps three or four if missile flight time is small and the crew has a multiple launcher with several rounds already mounted and ready to fire. In addition, the size of the ATGM round dictates that there will be far fewer of them with the vehicle than there will be tank rounds. Therefore, if the tank is not knocked out early in a multiple-shot exchange, it can keep fighting while the ATGM vehicle must depart, if it can, or be destroyed. Thus, we see that although ATGMs have added greatly to the anti-tank capability of the defense, they pose the problems, for both sides, of having two distinctly different types of weapons fighting each other and, therefore, of designing tactics whereby each can take advantage of the weaknesses of the other in order to apply its strengths to win. To examine this problem let us depart from the one-on-one comparison and examine the actions where an armored assault is trying to overcome a defense incorporating ATGMs.

The Impact of ATGMs on Armored Warfare and Forces

If the defensive positions were such that hidden ATGM emplacements could take an advancing armored column by surprise and fire on it from its flank, the initial impact could be devastating to the tanks and other vehicles in the column. The attacking armor commander would have to stop the column or deploy immediately into assault formation and attempt to overcome the defenses. Then the situation would come to resemble that of a breakthrough attempt against a defensive line, and this is the most interesting situation to examine from the viewpoint of the comparison we have been discussing here.

The *line* is, of course, not actually a line, but the zone of distributed defenses, including minefields, anti-tank positions, artillery, and tanks, to a depth of many kilometers, that was described in Chapter 2 for the region of the FEBA. Consider for the sake of illustration that this defensive zone is continuous in either lateral direction for an indefinite distance. The problem for the offensive (in nonnuclear warfare) is to punch a hole through this defensive zone to permit it to pour its armor through and destroy the remainder of the defenses by spreading out and attacking them from the rear. The commander of the offensive can choose the point at which he will attack. This selection depends on his assessment of the balance among interacting considerations, including the distribution of opposing strength, terrain advantageous for movement, and the advantages of using less probable terrain to achieve surprise. The defending commander also takes these terrain considerations into account; but unless he has large reserves to the rear to move against a penetration, he cannot afford to leave any part of his defenses extremely weak. He is, therefore, required to distribute his forces roughly uniformly along the defended area. Depending on terrain, roads, buildings, etc., he may let his defenses vary so that they are perhaps twice as strong in one place as in another. The defender has the advantage of prepared positions, and it has been traditional to say the attacker needs about a three-to-one force advantage to overcome such positions. Even if the attacker has a lesser numerical advantage overall, he can concentrate forces for the breakthrough to achieve a force advantage up to six to one or eight to one locally while using forces of nominal strength to pin the defense down elsewhere and keep it from moving to meet the attack.

To visualize the nature of this advantage, consider two forces distributed along a front 50 kilometers wide, which is defended by a two-division corps acting as part of a longer frontal-defense array. Suppose the defender has 1,000 antitank weapons, including tanks, and 100 of the tanks have been withdrawn to act as a mobile reserve. Now suppose that an attacking army has some 2,500 tanks and APCs. According to the rule of thumb, the attacker does not have the 3 to 1 superiority across the front that is needed to overcome a strongly defended position. But suppose the attacking commander decides to concentrate his assault on a 15-kilometer-wide sector of the front. If the defender's forces are distributed uniformly, he will have 270 defensive weapons in the critical 15-kilometer sector, with 630 elsewhere and 100 in reserve. If the attacker uses 500 of his tanks and APCs in diversionary attacks elsewhere, he can throw 2,000 of them into the critical battle—achieving a force ratio of nearly 7.5 to 1, or about 5.5 to 1 if all the defender's reserve tanks enter at the right place. Even if initially the defender had correctly estimated the likely attack position and doubled his strength there, he would still be outnumbered over 3 to 1, after commiting his reserves.

The actual battle would take place as a series of small-unit actions, with forces varying from company to regimental size.[13] It would involve artillery fire by both sides against defending and attacking weapons, to attempt to fix them in place or destroy them, and the attacker's artillery fire would be followed by a tank assault with accompanying armored infantry against the defenses. Here the rate-of-fire advantage of the tank over the ATGM, the tank's greater ammunition load, and the ATGM's lesser ability to exchange fire with a tank at close range would work to the advantage of the tanks if the attacking commander were willing to take some losses, perhaps heavy, in his first assault wave. The anti-tank positions would eventually be overrun. Even if on the average the defender's weapons could achieve a 5 to 1 exchange ratio—destroying five attacking tanks or APCs for each weapon lost—it is clear that there would eventually be an assault wave, in the numerical example given above, that would face weak enough opposition that it could not be stopped. (The Soviets demonstrated many times during World War II that they were willing to fight this way.) And of course the attackers would have the option of concentrating on an even narrower front, thereby saving casualties by increasing the local force ratio, even while taking greater risk of damage in case of a nuclear response.

Now, even this complex description of the battle for a breakthrough oversimplifies the dynamics of the conflict. The defending ATGMs can be protected by short-range anti-tank weapons. Minefields, perhaps consisting of "scatterable" mines emplaced during the battle by artillery and aircraft, would slow the attacking armor and make it more vulnerable to attack by anti-tank weapons in addition to the direct casualties the mines would cause. Defending tanks can maneuver and strike the attackers from unexpected directions, breaking up their rush and giving the ATGM gunners more time to do their work. On the other side, the attackers will also have ATGMs, specifically to guard against the use of tanks in mobile defense and also to attack pillboxes or well-dug-in defensive positions. In addition, there can be a powerful impact of both sides' tactical air on this battle; and ATGM-firing helicopters' ability to move to critical locations rapidly to achieve surprise can tip the balance locally—if they are not shot down by the attacker's mobile air defenses. Thus, the actual battle involves such complex interactions among diverse weapons systems that, even with the exaggerated local force ratios in favor of the offense that we have been considering, the outcome in the presence of modern weapons is by no means certain. The simplified examples can only illustrate the likely trends and the means by which armored forces acting in concert can overcome the advantage given the defense by the ATGM.

If the offense can break through in only a few places on a long front of adjacent divisions, corps, or armies, its initial strength advantage can work for it in other ways. Once he has broken through, the attacker can maintain large force ratios locally by judicious choice of attack location. By maneuvering, he can bring his forces where the defending side is weak. Even though there may be many defending forces, most of them may not be able to enter the battle, and they face the prospect of fighting surrounded until they run out of supplies. This is the sort of situation that leads to panic and surrender and one that has permitted forces of inferior numbers to win—as the Germans did in France in 1940.[14] But staunch local defense is possible, and against inferior forces it will ultimately tell. Against an offensive that is superior in numbers overall, there is also a chance that if the defense is deployed in sufficient depth the attacker may never break through but can only move in deeper, suffering attrition all the way. He must also count his losses and measure the apparent success of his campaign, or lack of it, against his plans.

Thus, it appears that a defending force, built around ATGMs and tanks and appropriately supported by other arms, can put up a stalwart defense against conventional armored tactics. (Such a defense was also possible in World War II.) The impact of ATGMs has been to change the quantitative relationships—the potential of relative losses—very much in favor of the defense; and they have changed the factors of time and space on the battlefield. They inhibit the free run of a battlefield by unsupported tanks (as the Israelis found to their distress in the early days of the 1973 Middle East war).[15] They can be used decisively against armor that is committed in small numbers and piecemeal, as might be done by smaller powers not equipped with enormous resources and perhaps not well trained in the use of armor. They can make it possible for relatively unsophisticated troops and guerrillas to fight effectively against occasional groups of tanks. They also contribute to the phenomenon, for ground warfare, that was described for air warfare:

If technological differences between two sides remain roughly in a similar relationship and *relative* ability to destroy each others' weapons remains the same, the increase of destructive power of individual weapons implies that military resources will be used up at increasingly higher rates in combat.

The discussion thus far does not arrive at any conclusion about the ability of possibly inferior forces using ATGMs to defeat a major attack by superior forces on a theaterwide scale. (This question goes to the heart of the problem of defending Western Europe or of meeting massive attacks on the Eurasian periphery with expeditionary forces, and we will reserve detailed discussion of it for later.) The conclusion for the viability or armored warfare as we have known it in the past is pertinent here. Consider all other aspects (training, morale, and such intangibles) as equal. Consider also that the attacking side is willing to pay the price of proliferating attack systems with strict attention to the mutually reinforcing effects of combined arms, to achieve an overall weapon superiority of two or three to one in balanced forces. Finally, assume that that side is willing to take heavy initial losses as well as the risks of concentrating sufficiently to offer good targets for both air attack and potential use of tactical nuclear weapons. In that case in conventional-weapons combat it is possible—as it was possible in World War II—for that side to overcome strong anti-tank defenses, even though the defenses have been strengthened by the addition of ATGMs.

Of course by spending enough on the various anti-armor measures, including physical barriers, mines, defensive weapon systems, and weapon systems and forces suitable for counterattacks, the defending side can prevail. Unfortunately, the picture here is much the same as it was in the case of the air forces: The costs of Army weapon systems are increasing faster than the Army's budget. The most effective anti-armor systems, including the ATGM-launching Improved TOW Vehicle (ITV) built around the M-113 armored personnel carrier and the new Bradley lightly armored fighting vehicles, cost a significant fraction of what the tanks themselves cost—a quarter to over half as much. The latest attack helicopter, the AH-64 Apache, is now nearly as expensive as fixed-wing combat airplanes. Even with allowance for savings in the design and production of systems, these trends are unlikely to be reversed; therefore, proliferation of anti-tank precision-guided munitions in balanced forces incorporating the combined arms demanded by modern combat is no easier than proliferation of armored forces in the first place. If, for example, we felt we could not afford to match the USSR in armor, it is unlikely that we would be able to build up very effective anti-armor forces to much greater size than we could have built the armored forces. Recognizing, then, that the new weapons are much more effective than the old even while becoming more expensive, we see that the key problem is to acquire enough systems in such a mix that overall force effectiveness in combined arms combat would increase faster than the available numbers of systems decreases. As the discussion thus far should have demonstrated, this is no easy matter.

Given these complexities, however, we must further conclude, in answer to the question posed at the beginning of this chapter, that although guided anti-tank missiles have changed the nature of warfare using tanks and have made it more difficult and expensive, they have not yet made the tank obsolete. The two systems—ATGMs and tanks—exist in comparable numbers, and each has the ability to defeat the other in appropriate circumstances and with appropriate support. Both are evolving still. Tanks will have more powerful engines, making for more agility in negotiating terrain; they will have bigger guns and tougher armor, and they will be able to fire guided projectiles to achieve high accuracy at long range. Against today's ATGMs, they will be more effective and harder to stop.

However, ATGM technology may be said to be in its infancy. ATGMs currently deployed are at best of the second generation. The first wire-guided ATGMs of the French SS-10/SS-11 type, which had to be guided to their targets by manual control, were first generation; the addition of semi-automatic guidance, still using the connecting wire, led to the second generation of weapons that is in the ground forces today. Succeeding generations of these weapons, appearing at about seven- to ten-year intervals, can be expected to be faster and therefore to reach their targets in less time. They can be expected to be more flexible by freeing the gunner from the missile after launch. They are likely to have more powerful warheads to defeat the new tanks' improved armor, and those fired from helicopters will also have longer range. New types of anti-tank mines having sophisticated sensors and signal processing to "know" when they are within lethal range of a tracked vehicle or a tank and then to blow up may also be anticipated. These advances will help alleviate many of the disadvantages described for the current generation of weapons, although the offensive and defensive systems will probably continue to be similar in cost and therefore in numbers. Thus, the contest for dominance between the two technologies will continue. The only clearly predictable outcome at this point is their increasingly greater combat power and the higher and more rapid attrition they will induce as a consequence.

5

Ships and the Evolution of War at Sea

At the end of World War II the United States enjoyed overwhelming and unquestioned naval supremacy. Today we have begun to realize that differently constituted and growing Soviet sea power is challenging the United States' assumptions about its Navy's control of the seas. This is not the first time the U.S. Navy has been in serious conceptual trouble, as the quotation from E. E. Morison in Chapter 1 showed. But in that earlier time, there was no major threat to the country and its use of the seas, as we perceive from the USSR today. Our need to maintain links to other parts of the world was much less critical. The Navy was needed more for protection of commerce than for the security and perhaps the very life of the nation. So the troubles of the Navy today may be considered more acute (although today's troubles always appear to be more acute than those that were eliminated years ago), and the need to correct them has some urgency.

Background: The Purpose, the Threat, and Pressures for Change

The purposes of the Navy have always been, and still are, to protect the nation and to project its power beyond its borders. Today this includes protection of the vital linkages with our NATO and Japanese allies. In addition, the U.S. Navy is the main source of sea power protecting both our own and these key allies' connections with essential overseas resources. These purposes are fulfilled in wartime whether the Navy attacks threatening bases and resources directly, undertakes amphibious operations to put troops ashore, protects shipping, destroys enemy shipping, or destroys enemy warships intending to do any or all of the other things themselves. Capt. A. T. Mahan, whose 1890 analyses of the earlier uses of sea power have formed the theoretical basis for U.S. naval power for nearly a century, considered this to be the ultimate "object": to use the sea to enforce the nation's will on land in a confrontation with another nation.[1] To do this, it would be necessary to achieve the intermediate "objective" of destroying or neutralizing the other side's fleet to permit one's own side to get on with the other tasks.

There have been some changes since Mahan's day that affect, in implementation if not in fundamental philosophy and strategy, how the object and the objective can be achieved. One is the long distance the Navy can reach inshore, making the inland infrastructure as well as seaports accessible to its power. The ultimate expression of this change is the nuclear-powered fleet ballistic missile submarines (SSBN). In the the general purpose forces, land-based and sea-based aircraft and guided missiles have come to carry the main strike and defense burdens. Individual nuclear weapons can now destroy large ships or parts of the entire task force.

Mahan pointed out how difficult it was, in the days of sail and the first half-century of steam, to find a fleet at sea. He therefore stressed the strategic value of holding a position off enemy ports until the opposing fleets could be engaged. Now, with modern reconnaissance technology, finding surface fleets has become relatively easy. Most attack strategies are coming to depend on guided weapons having ranges of a few to a few hundred miles. The sub-surface naval force is the element of the fleet that has become hard to find, and the reconnaissance systems together with modern communications can be used to direct that force to positions from which it can attack the surface fleet.

Today's U.S. naval forces can be evaluated fully only in relation to those of the USSR, the only other major naval power in the world. Since the Soviet navy has been described in detail in many places, we are interested mainly in contrasting it with the U.S. Navy. Although the United States has pioneered the use of nuclear-powered attack and strategic-missile submarines, our general purpose naval forces are built mainly around seaborne air power. The large aircraft carrier is the main capital ship. There is a large variety of aircraft for tasks ranging from reconnaissance and early warning to air defense, attack of land targets and ships, and anti-submarine warfare. Other major combat ships are designed mainly to protect the carrier from submarine and air attack.

The Soviet Navy is described in Table 5-1.[2] The Soviet Union, like Germany in World War II, is an essentially land-locked power facing naval powers; and just as Germany did at that time, the USSR has stressed sub-marines and land-based aviation for maritime operations. Its surface fleet has grown slowly from the large number of small combat craft shown, with modern cruisers, destroyers, and frigates being added at a modest pace. The addition in 1976 of the *Kiev*, an intermediate-sized carrier with vertical-takeoff aircraft and anti-submarine helicopters, signaled an expanded interest in extending surface-based sea power. Additional striking power of a very different kind is added by the slowly growing force of modern Backfire super-sonic bombers being added to the old Badger and Blinder bombers of Soviet Naval Aviation. The "glue" that holds these naval forces together and

Table 5-1: SOVIET NAVY ORDER OF BATTLE

Submarines—nuclear powered

SSBN[a]	Ballistic missile submarines (Yankee, Delta classes)	62
SSBN	Ballistic missile submarines (Hotel class)	7
SSGN[a]	Cruise missile submarines	50
SSN[a]	Torpedo-attack submarines	60

Submarines—diesel-electric powered

SSB	Ballistic missile submarines	18
SSG	Cruise missile submarines	20
SS[a]	Torpedo-attack submarines	160

Aircraft carriers and aviation cruisers

CVHG[a]	VSTOL carriers (Kiev class)	2
CHG	Aviation cruisers (Moskva class)	2

Cruisers

CGN[a]	Guided missile cruiser (nuclear) (Kirov class)	1
CG[a]	Guided missile cruisers (SAM/SSM)	26
CL	Light cruisers (Sverdlov class)	9

Destroyers

DDG[a]	Guided missile destroyers (SAM/SSM)	38
DD	Destroyers	30

Frigates (escorts)

FFG[a]	Guided missile frigates (Krivak class)	28
FF/FFL[a]	Frigates/small frigates	140

Small combatants

Missile craft[a]	145
Patrol/ASW/torpedo craft[a]	395
Minesweepers[a]	395

Amphibious ships

LPD[a]	Amphibious assault transport Dock (Ivan Rogov class)	1
LST	Amphibious vehicle landing Ships (Alligator, Ropucha classes)	25
LSM	Medium landing ships (Potnocny/MP-4 classes)	60

Auxiliary ships

Mobile logistics ships[a]	150
Other auxiliaries[a]	605

Source: *Soviet Military Power* (Washington, D.C.: U.S. Government Printing Office, 1981), p. 40.

[a] Additional units under construction.

integrates their operations is a system of long-range reconnaissance and surveillance aircraft and satellite surveillance systems. There are also advanced communications for the tactical coordination of strike forces, rapid exchange of targeting information among air, surface, the submarine forces, and coordination of simultaneous strikes against surface naval targets in more than one ocean. These various capabilities have been demonstrated in worldwide maneuvers and exercises.

Thus, we have reached the situation where, although both the U.S. and Soviet navies have all of the elements of sea power in some degree, the United States seems to have stressed the large, concentrated, easy-to-find surface fleet, while the Soviet Union for many years concentrated mainly on building a hard-to-find submarine fleet supported by land-based air power as a means of defeating U.S. sea power.[3] Now, we find the Soviet Union building and using a surface fleet to carry out foreign policy objectives similar to those our Navy has supported.[4] The size and composition of this Soviet surface navy can challenge U.S. fleet task forces locally in such areas as the Mediterranean Sea and the Arabian Sea. Although these Soviet fleets are not yet as powerful as ours, they could easily become so over the next decade. Here, in a greatly oversimplified statement, is the reason the U.S. Navy has been the subject of broad controversy over the past ten years.

During the 1970s competing concepts of the shape of the Navy emerged rapidly,[5] partly as a result of extensive study initiated in the latter days of the Ford administration and demanded anew by the Senate at the beginning of the Carter administration.[6] The Reagan administration embarked on a major naval buildup, intended to modernize the surface fleet and enlarge it to an ultimate level of fifteen carrier battle groups.[7] This included provision for starting construction of two new *Nimitz* class nuclear-powered carriers at $3.5 billion each. The naval ship construction budget has therefore begun to grow rapidly and remains controversial. Thus what is written specifically at any point may well be obsolete by the time it emerges in print. But decisions taken and the trends they start in naval force structure take a long time to implement and are subject to change as policies are reconsidered and new trends in enemy planning became apparent. In the remainder of this chapter I will attempt to show, in more detail than has been brought to other discussions of the subject, how we arrived where we are, the nature of the current problems of naval force structure, and some directions that may make sense in trying to solve those problems. The reader should remember that because of the time and cost of building major ships (on the order of seven to ten years and $0.3 to $3.5 billion) and their long service life (now on the order of thirty to fifty years), any transformation of the Navy being talked about between 1982 and 1984 will not fully have taken shape before the end of this century. Trends initiated in the early 1980s might very well be changed again along the way.

The major technological developments that have affected the Navy since World War II are essentially the same as those that have affected the ground and air forces: nuclear weapons, jet aircraft, weapon guidance, and other applications of advanced electronics. In addition, since its vessels are large enough to use nuclear power plants effectively and since Navy missions can be enhanced thereby, it has also been influenced, both beneficially and adversely, by nuclear propulsion.

The Navy's main missions and the underlying concepts of naval warfare have not changed very much since the end of World War II, but, as with tactical air, the overall capability and the tools have changed quite a bit. It will be easier to review the missions after understanding how the Navy has come to its current form and state. Consideration of the missions is the key to deciding how the Navy ought to be structured.

Evolution of the Navy Since World War II

The public is most aware of the change from the battleship Navy that began World War II to the carrier Navy that completed that war. The main feature of this change was the use of the carrier as a floating air base from which tactical air power, otherwise too "short-legged," could carry the war to the enemy's territory. But since the advent of the SSBN force in the early 1960s, the general purpose Navy has not had the strategic mission of making a devastating attack on the enemy—for which read, Soviet or Chinese—homeland. Rather, it is intended to destroy the enemy means (land-based air, sea-based air, surface and subsurface fleets) of interfering with the main business of U.S. sea power: protecting the sea lanes for our and our allies' use, transferring materials of war, and landing ground forces where they might be needed. Twice, also, since World War II —in Korea and Vietnam— the Navy has provided a large fraction of the force used to attempt to prevent a lesser enemy, accessible from the sea, from reinforcing and resupplying his troops on the battlefield.

Not as commonly recognized, in addition, were the emergence from World War II of techniques and force structure permitting battle fleets to stay at sea and sustain operations for months instead of days. Also, the fleet's firepower came to be used primarily to support landing forces rather than to fight other ships. Long-range, land-based aircraft evolved into a key means of fighting submarines. World War II also saw the use of carrier-based aircraft to fight submarines, together with the land-based air, the more familiar destroyers and destroyer escorts, and the increasingly broad use of sonar (originated in World War I) as the underwater analog of radar.[8]

Thus there was, among other developments, a proliferation of means for contact and conflict between the surface and overhead forces, on the one hand, and those under sea, on the other. This was doubtless a tribute to the power of the submarine, imperfect as it was at that time. Since then, nuclear propulsion has eliminated one of the submarine's key vulnerabilities: having to come to the surface for air and to replenish its fuel and batteries. Simultaneously, this advance solved the related problem of having to move more slowly underwater for lack of power; and together with advances in materials, it permitted operations at much greater depths than had been possible earlier. Another vulnerability—noise—became more severe as a result. But with its underwater speed comparable to that achievable by surface warships and with continuing progress in reducing the noise from its machinery and from the flow of water over its hulls, the nuclear-powered submarine fleet has become a true undersea fighting force: powerful, elusive, and possible decisive in sea warfare.

Figures 5–1 and 5–2 and tables 5–2 through 5–5 illustrate the transformations in the U.S. fleet since World War II.[9] The basic comparisons we will make derive from the two naval forces shown in Figure 5–1. The force on the left is the renowned Task Force 58 that, under Mitscher's tactical command, won the battle of the Philippine Sea in 1944. The force on the right is a hypothetical one, assembled to permit the carrier's attack airplanes to deliver about the same weight of air-to-surface ordnance as the attack-airplane force of Task Force 58. (Calling the modern force a task force is, strictly speaking, artificial. If it were a true task force operating independently, it would have at least two carriers for mutual support, whereas a force with one carrier as shown would ordinarily be a task group, part of a larger fleet or task force. Either one would be assembled *ad hoc* for a particular task, and historically no two have been exactly alike. The comparison of forces based on equivalent weight of air-to-surface firepower is in keeping with the long-standing and current view of the Navy's most important functions. This firepower can be used in warfare against land targets, surface ships, or submarines. The results of the basic comparisons among naval forces that will be made throughout will not be affected by this simplification. Therefore, having alerted the reader, I will retain the artificiality as a matter of convenience.)

What do we learn from perusal of these tables and figures? Revival of a few Iowa-class battleships notwithstanding, naval gunfire has essentially disappeared as a primary means to deliver offensive fire. Defensive fire depends mainly on guided missiles (SAMs, similar to those used in land warfare), with close-in fire by a few radar-directed 5-inch automatic guns and 20-mm Phalanx Gatling guns. Carrier-based aircraft have assumed the antiship and the shore bombardment and attack missions, including attack of shore-side sources of danger to the fleet, preparation of landing zones, and carrying the war inland to the enemy (excepting, again, for the strategic

FIGURE 5-1: Comparison of Naval Formations—World War II and Now

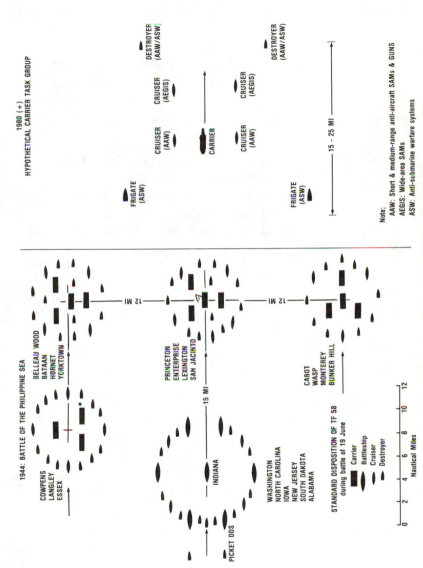

Source: S. E. Morison, *The Two-Ocean War* (Boston: Atlantic Monthly-Little, Brown, 1963), pp. 333, 336.

1:19-83-7

FIGURE 5–2: Progression of Some Classes of Major Surface Combat Ships
(Standard Displacement and Major Armaments Shown)

ATTACK CARRIERS

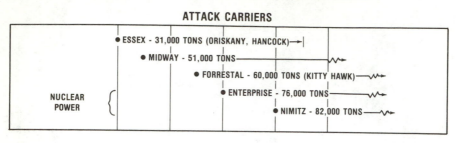

CRUISERS

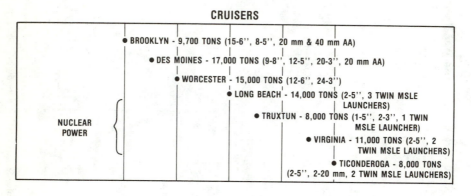

ESCORTS

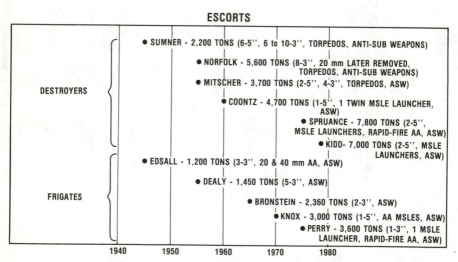

Source: Jane's Fighting Ships, (New York: Franklin Watts, for years shown. Listed under United States.)

12-29-82-4

**Table 5-2: COMPARISON OF AIRCRAFT COMPLEMENTS
OF CARRIER TASK FORCES**

1944 Task Force 58 (Battle of Philippine Sea)		1978 Hypothetical Attack/ Anti-Submarine Task Force	
Fighters 475		Fighters (F-4 and F-14).......... 24	
Dive bombers..................232 ⎫	a	⎧ Light attack (A-7).............. 24	
Torpedo bombers...............184 ⎭		⎩ Medium attack (A-6)............ 12	
Scout float planes.............. 65		Specialized aircraft[b].............. 14	
Total 956		Anti-submarine patrol............ 10	
		Anti-submarine helicopters........ ⎫	
		Utility helicopters............... ⎭ 6	
		Total 90	

Source: S. E. Morison, *The Two-Ocean War* (Boston: Atlantic Monthly–Little, Brown, 1963), pp. 333; and *Jane's Fighting Ships* (New York: Franklin Watts, 1978)

[a]Total weapon delivery tonnage by these aircraft in the two periods is roughly the same.

[b]See Table 5-4 for types.

nuclear-missile submarines). All this is not surprising. We have not perceived a surface fleet to threaten the U.S. Navy for nearly forty years; naval guns were designed to fight ships, while that and the other naval tasks could be taken over by airplanes and missiles having much longer reach and growing power over the years. The weight of airborne offensive firepower has remained about the same in today's far smaller task group as it was in a major World War II task force. It is delivered with much more concentration by far fewer aircraft. Roughly 10 percent as many ships and 10 percent as many attack airplanes can deliver about the same weapon tonnage; and as we saw in Chapter 3 this tonnage can be much more effective than it was in World War II. In parallel, the defense of the task force has been taken over by a relatively few very capable fighter aircraft, a few missile systems and some guns designed to be used against aircraft, a few ships with sonar, and anti-submarine helicopters and patrol aircraft. Except for cruisers, all ships have become heavier (and the cruisers appear to counter the trend only because some very heavy destroyers were redesignated as cruisers). The weight and complexity of carrier aircraft have increased, and the number of ships has

Table 5–3: EVOLUTION OF FLEET FIREPOWER: 1944-1980

1944 Task Force 58 (Battle of Philippine Sea)[a]	1980 Typical Carrier (CV/CVN) Task Force[b]
112 ships; 416 attack aircraft (dive bombers and torpedo bombers)	9 ships; 36-48 attack aircraft (A-6 and A-7)
Guns (estimated)	Guns (estimated)
100 3"	14 5"
350 5"	
56 6"	Missiles (estimated)
72 8"	2 Aegis long-range SAM systems
57 14–16"	2 Twin Terrier medium-range SAM systems
Several hundred 20-mm and 40-mm antiaircraft guns	(launchers double for Asroc anti-submarine rockets)
	2 Tartar short-range SAM systems
	2–4 Harpoon medium-range surface-to-surface missile launchers
	Possible
	6–8 Sea-sparrow SAM launchers
	6–8 Phalanx rapid-fire antiaircraft gun systems
Attack aircraft payload if all aircraft sortie: approx. 400 tons	Attack aircraft payload if all aircraft sortie: 250–400 tons

[a]Source for ships and aircraft: S. E. Morison
Source for armament per ship: *Jane's Fighting Ships*,
Fighter aircraft excluded; aircraft carrier armament excluded.

[b]Source for ships and aircraft, hypothetical
formation; see Figure 5-1.
Source for armament per ship: *Jane's Fighting Ships*, 1978.
Fighter and specialized aircraft excluded; attack aircraft payload
depends on force composition and specialized loading;
aircraft carrier armament excluded.

Table 5-4: AIRCRAFT COMPLEMENT OF ATTACK CARRIERS[a]

Mission	1944 Essex	1950–1953 Midway	1955–1957 Midway-All Jet	1963–1967[b] Forrestal	1963–1967[b] Essex	1970 CVAN	1978 CVN
General							
Fighter	41 (F6F)	28–36 (F9F Jets) or 48 (F4U, Prop)	60 (F3H,F4D,F8U, FJ-4,F9F,A4D)	24 (F-4B)	24 (F-8E)	24 (F-4 and F-8)	24 (F-4 and F-14)
Light attack	32 (SB2C)	14 (AD, Prop.)		28 (A-4E)	28 (A-4E)	24 (A-7 and A-4)	24–36 (A-7)
Medium Attack	18 (TBM/TBF)		12 (A3D)	9 (A-6A)	12 (A1H) (Prop.)	12 (A-6)	12 (A-6)
Specialized							
Reconnaissance			3 (F8U-1P)	6 (RA5C)	3 (RF8G)	3–6 (RA5C)	1–3 (RA5C)
Electronic warfare			3 (AD5Q, Prop.)				4 (EA6B)
Early warning			4 (AD5W, Prop.)	4 (E2A)	4 (E1B)	4 (E2A)	4 (E2C)
In-flight refueling			2–3 (AJ)			4 (KA3B)	4 (KA6)
Cargo			1 (TF)	1 (TF)	1 (TF)	1 (C1A)	1 (C1A)
ASW helicopters							8 (SH3)
ASW Patrol							0–10 (S3)
Totals	91	62	~85	72	72	72–75	82–106

Sources: Jane's, All the World's Aircraft, and *Jane's Fighting Ships* (for 1970–78);
Polmar, N., *Aircraft Carrier,* Doubleday & Co., Inc., Garden City, N.Y., 1969 (1944–mid-1960s).

[a] Aircraft types shown only as general indicators for those familiar with the nomenclature.

[b] Aircraft nomenclature was changed at beginning of this period.

Table 5–5: **ADDITIONAL ASPECTS OF FLEET EVOLUTION**

Category	1944	1976
Submarines	About 250—all Diesel	116—65 Nuclear attack (SSN) 41 SSBN 10 Diesel (SS)
Amphibious landing capability	1,354 amphibious assault ships	65 amphibious assault ships
	1,879 major landing craft[a] Simultaneous assault lift (water) for about 8 divisions, worldwide	105 major landing craft[a] Simultaneous assault lift (water and helo) for about 1 division, world-wide

Source: Janes's Fighting Ships (New York: Franklin Watts, years shown).

[a] Over 100 tons.

declined markedly—from about 30 carriers in the mid-1950s to 13 much larger ones today. Amphibious landing capacity has been transformed with helicopters that can overfly the shore defenses to interior landing zones prepared and covered by air support. Landing capacity is much reduced, but, again, after the Korean War and until the rise of concern about the Persian Gulf region in 1979–80 we did not feel we needed much (the deployment to Vietnam could be handled by conventional sea- and airlift). The transformation of the submarine force has been apparent to all. Note, finally, that the total number of escort ships for the one World War II task force shown in Figure 5-1, in one battle, was nearly half the number available to the entire U.S. Navy today.[10]

All this describes today's U.S. Navy. During the 1980s some surface ships will be equipped with the Harpoon and Tomahawk cruise missiles, capable of attacking targets at fifty to several hundred miles range. However, unless there are some drastic changes in naval force structure such as those to be discussed later, these missiles won't change the basic nature of our fleet design.

Modern Combat Operations at Sea

Although it appears sometimes that the Soviet naval threat appeared suddenly, there has in fact been constant awareness of its evolution. The fault, if one is to be identified, derives from the nature of our response and more particularly from the fact that the response is not always believed capable of meeting the threat as it has developed. It is worth reviewing the current form of the multitiered defense systems that the Navy has evolved through the years, to illustrate that, although the numbers of ships have shrunk, their tasks are more complex, if anything, than the comparable tasks of ship defenses in World War II.

The threat to a U.S. naval task force from the air is not posed by the kinds of direct, manned-aircraft attacks on ships that we would use. Rather, it comes as clouds of air-, surface-, and submarine-launched guided missiles, arriving from various directions and ranges, from various altitudes, and at various speeds[11]—in essence, the modern-day realization of the kamikaze attack. To meet the long-range, land-based aircraft that the Soviets would use to launch such missiles, a task force sends radar-bearing search and early-warning aircraft to patrol hundreds of miles from its perimeter. These aircraft are accompanied by a few long-range fighter/interceptors on combat air patrol (CAP). When an incoming raid is detected, the CAP is joined by additional deck-launched interceptors in the first part of a two-stage air defense far from the fleet. The fighters themselves launch long-range air-to-air missiles in an attempt to down the bombers before they can launch their weapons. Bombers getting through this screen, or air-to-surface cruise missiles the bombers are able to launch, must pass a long-range, area-type SAM defense based on a few ships covering a task force; and then they must pass through short-range missile and gun defenses defending each ship locally. Surface- and subsurface-launched cruise missiles also must pass by the local SAM and gun defenses and, depending on the launch range, by the long-range SAMs as well. Enemy surface ships participating in the attack are vulnerable to counterattack by submarines, carrier-based aircraft, or our own ship-launched missiles. As with most of the other aspects of fast-paced warfare using precision-guided, high-speed systems that we have examined, the timing, communication, and control problems for both the attack and the defense are severe. This complex attack and defense system is not unlike that for air warfare over land, but of course the target structure for the attacker is much simpler: it comprises the few ships of the surface fleet and any shipping they may be trying to protect. The interaction is illustrated in Figure 5–3.

The wholesale use of missiles in place of naval gunfire and aircraft to attack the surface fleet was pioneered by the Soviets because they had the greater need in building up their sea power. They faced a very large and powerful U.S. surface navy after World War II, and they did not have an existing investment that had to be transformed. (This is aside from all consideration of bureaucratic inertia that may have influenced the pace of evolution in a highly successful and dominant U.S. Navy.) The United States is now also, somewhat belatedly, adopting this mode as the growing size and power of the emerging Soviet surface navy become apparent. The Harpoon and

FIGURE 5-3: Schematic Drawing of the Air Defense of a Carrier Task Force

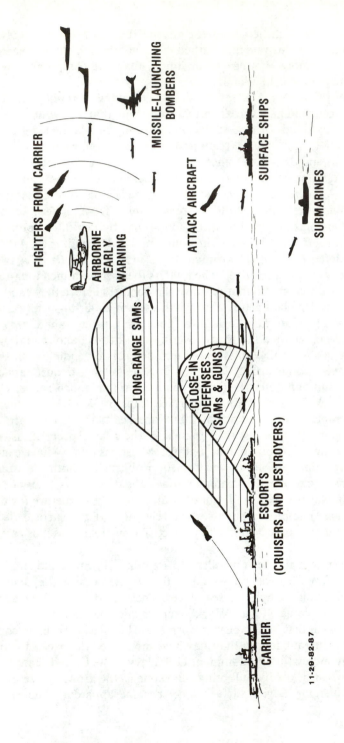

FIGHTERS FROM CARRIER

MISSILE-LAUNCHING BOMBERS

AIRBORNE EARLY WARNING

ATTACK AIRCRAFT

SURFACE SHIPS

SUBMARINES

LONG-RANGE SAMs

CLOSE-IN DEFENSES (SAMs & GUNS)

ESCORTS (CRUISERS AND DESTROYERS)

CARRIER

11-29-82-87

Tomahawk cruise missiles are entering fleet service [12] when a significant Soviet surface fleet begins to appear that can be shot at with missiles. Unlike that over land where target structures are complex, of widely varying magnitudes and importance, and buried in complex background noise, the seaborne environment is especially congenial for surface warfare that relies almost exclusively on expensive guided missiles. There are relatively few, high-value targets; the missiles are not so constrained in size since they can be launched from large, mobile platforms; and both target acquisition means and terminal-seeker guidance are aided by high-contrast target signatures against an essentially uncluttered background.

With the ability of unmanned weapons to attack over the horizon, of course, goes the problem of learning where the target is with enough accuracy to send a guided weapon against it. It is usually necessary also to provide external assistance in mid-course guidance for the longer-range weapons until the weapons' terminal-guidance systems can acquire their targets. Again, the Soviet Union pioneered the extensive use and dependence on long-range patrol aircraft, similar to those used mainly for anti-submarine warfare (ASW) by the United States for these purposes; and now they, as well as we, are able to make use of aircraft and satellite technology for such support. The use of inertial guidance (such as commercial aircraft use to navigate across the oceans) or other means, such as navigation satellites for mid-course flight to the point of target acquisition, is also available to the side that has the technology.

The submarines attacking the fleet can launch torpedoes, as well as cruise missiles, and the torpedoes are not all the classical, initially aimed, and free-swimming "fish" of World Wars I and II: many are guided, perhaps by sound emissions or other signals from their targets. The versatility and mobility of the submarine within a relatively opaque medium give it special advantages for attack and make it especially difficult and expensive to defend against. The main problem in such defense is to learn where submarines are with enough accuracy for weapons to be brought against them. The opacity of water has led to extensive use of underwater sound as the most viable means of "seeing" underwater submarines, although limited use of other sensors, such as magnetic detection, is also possible. Even with the use of sound, however, the medium remains relatively intractable, as the Swedish Navy demonstrated when it failed to find a mysterious submarine in Sweden's coastal defense areas during October 1982.[13] Variations in temperature gradient from the surface to deeper water lead to refraction of the sound waves in unexpected directions. This creates apparent boundaries across which sound waves will not travel and consequent shadow zones from which sounds cannot reach listening sources; it can also create unexpectedly long-range detection in some sound channels. The presence of the surface or the sea bottom leads to signal-masking reverberations; and fish, crustaceans, pelagic mammals, and surface ships emit confusing noise.

Some of these phenomena occur predictably, and some do not. Since the location of threatening submarines relative to surface ships is a somewhat random occurrence, depending on where the predators and prey happen to be when an encounter occurs, it is safe to say that in general submarine detection and tracking ranges are also random within broad limits. They are unlikely most of the time to be more than a few or a few tens of kilometers in extent.

Additional complications arise from the need to deploy hydrophone arrays of large dimension in order to measure accurately the direction from which emitted or reflected sounds arrive at the searching vessel. They also arise from the continuing trade between active and passive sonar. In active sonar the searcher emits a sound and listens for its reflection. He then has better data and decides when he will obtain the data, and he is likely to be able to detect at longer ranges. However, he also acts as a beacon announcing his position, in a geometric relationship in which the passive listener is thereby given a large advantage that he can use for evasion or attack. Passive sonar, which simply accepts sounds coming in, does not have this disadvantage, but it is more difficult to use. It is susceptible to self-jamming by the noise of the searcher's ship or fleet through the water, and it heightens the contest to quiet one's own submarines (which thus far the United States has been winning).

The physics of sound has not changed since the invention of sonar in World War I. But as in so many other areas, the understanding of the phenomena and the ability to treat them with modern electronics have led to continuing improvement in ability to detect and locate submarines within the fundamental limits of sound transmission through the media that were sketched above. Thus, the major advances in sonar since World War II have been in the area of automatic signal processing that permits extraction of fainter and more ambiguous signals from the incoming noise. These advances have extended detection range and increased the certainty that what is *suspected* to be a submarine *is* a submarine.

This area of warfare also has seen the appearance of multicomponent techniques for seeking, locating, and attacking submarines. Large hydrophone arrays can detect the appearance of submarines in a region. Long-range, land-based aircraft, in addition to their general search of areas where submarines might operate, can seed the region of initial detection with additional, more closely spaced hydrophones in sonobuoys that convey what they hear to the aircraft by radio. Within the limits imposed on accuracy by the number of sonobuoys an airplane can deploy and its onboard processing equipment, a submarine can be localized in a smaller area of ocean. Finally, fleet helicopter–launched arrays of sonobuoys (which, in this case, may be dipped or recoverable) and hull-mounted sonars or towed arrays on fleet escorts such as frigates or destroyers, all covering the area previously designated by the long-range patrol aircraft, can gauge the location of a submarine with sufficient accuracy for weapon delivery. Weapons, in the form of homing torpedoes, depth charges, or the Subroc and Asroc projected antisubmarine weapons, can be launched by any of the long-range aircraft, helicopters, surface escorts, or friendly submarines.

An important advantage of the aircraft, of course, is that they can press localization and attack rapidly before an initially detected submarine can move very far; also, they are not vulnerable to self-noise as the disturbances of their passsage do not cross the water boundary. The escorts, however, can carry much more elaborate detection and signal processing gear and many more weapons. It must be understood, also, that detection, localization, prosecution, and kill are not by any means certain. Countermeasures of various kinds can reduce the various probabilities still further from the levels associated with the physics of detection and accidents of position. Some submarines will escape, somewhere in the sequence, and some may turn on and damage or sink their attackers. If properly equipped with surface-to-air weapons, as they could be if long-range patrol aircraft were to become dangerous enough to them, they could shoot air attackers down. All these outcomes occurred in various circumstances during World War II,[14] and today's weapons make them equally, if not more, likely. The ASW analog of the multistage air defense is illustrated in Figure 5–4.

We have described here the basic sequences of operation in ASW, but many variations are possible. For example, mines in relatively restricted waters can be arranged so that they will destroy submarines passing through. Attack submarines can be used in barrier operations in such areas. The role of the land-based patrol aircraft is also fulfilled by smaller (but still relatively large) carrier-launched aircraft that can patrol far from the center of a task force. The land-based patrol aircraft can substitute in some significant measure for an escorting fleet in protecting convoys from submarine attack. Finally, attack submarines can operate on the far outskirts of a convoy or a task force, to attempt to clean the seas of opposing submarines where the friendly forces want to go. The nuclear-powered attack submarine in particular, because it can vary its depth to cross the sound transmission boundaries and can move at high underwater speed, is among the most effective ASW systems. But each type of system is more cost effective than any of the others in some circumstances and for some parts of the job, and in most circumstances several must be used together to give the fleet its requisite flexibility for ASW operations in various waters and under various tactical conditions.

104

FIGURE 5-4: Elements of the Multimode Defense of the Surface Fleet Against Submarines

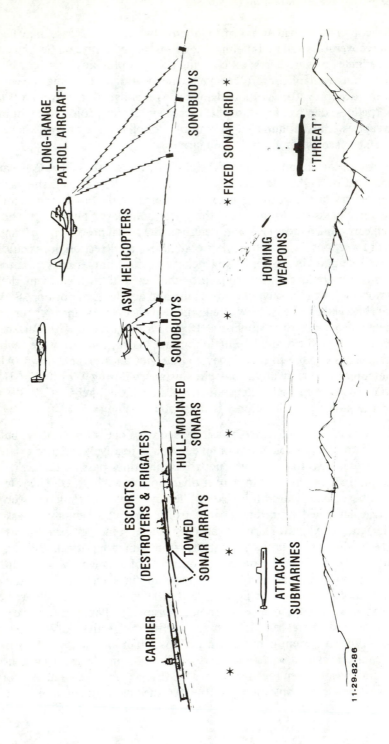

LONG-RANGE
PATROL AIRCRAFT

SONOBUOYS

ASW HELICOPTERS

SONOBUOYS

* FIXED SONAR GRID *

"THREAT"

HOMING
WEAPONS

ESCORTS
(DESTROYERS & FRIGATES)

HULL-MOUNTED
SONARS

TOWED
SONAR ARRAYS

CARRIER

ATTACK
SUBMARINES

11-29-82-86

Sources of Concern About the U.S. Navy

Whether comparisons between the U.S. and Soviet navies should properly be sources of concern depends primarily on whether the U.S. Navy, as it has evolved, is able to carry out its missions. This depends upon the potential enemy's missions and how well he can carry them out. Missions are obviously not independent of national strategy. Our own strategy vis-a-vis the USSR and in furtherance of our own interests in diverse areas of the world will be discussed in chapters 6 through 9; our naval strategy in particular will be considered in Chapter 9. The comparison with Soviet naval missions and strategy will be reviewed there. Suffice it to say at this point, based on our earlier review of Soviet naval trends, that we appear to be moving into a period where the assignments of the two navies are becoming more symmetrical. However, even if some parallelism does continue to grow, the Soviet and U.S. navies do and will continue to look quite different. Ours is both a source of strength and a source of worry and conflict for the nation.

Figure 5–2 and Table 5–4 showed, for major classes of surface ships, the growth in displacement of succeeding ship generations and the growing complexity of the weapons systems on these ships, as the Navy has given up guns and adopted guided missiles and aircraft for all purposes. The cost of ships is, of course, related to their size and the complexity of their weapons. In addition, the cost of the aircraft and the air weapon systems has been increasing rapidly. Finally, the congressionally imposed requirement that all major combatant ships be nuclear powered increased individual ship costs, while all the expected savings in reduced support did not materialize. Since aviation fuel and other supplies are needed at frequent intervals and represent a fair fraction of total underway support during a period of conflict, it has been found that whatever bookkeeping method is used (i.e., however the costs are reckoned), an all nuclear-powered navy would be more expensive than had been bargained for.[15] Also, gas turbine power for smaller ships such as destroyers and frigates has offered significant performance and design advantages. Therefore it has been agreed that nuclear ship propulsion will be reserved for carriers and submarines.

The picture of unit acquisition cost increase relative to budet growth for the U.S. Navy is very similar to these of the Army and the Air Force—costs of individual ships, aircraft, and weapons systems from one generation to the next have been growing, on average, faster than the Navy's budget over the past thirty-five years. The illustration in Figure 5–1 and Table 5–3 of the changes in naval combat formations over time is the logical outcome of such trends. However, if, as we have noted, the new combat force has much more effective air power per unit than the old one, there is as yet no basis to claim that the new, smaller task group is operationally inferior because of some perhaps arbitrary requirement for numerical ship strength. To achieve the greater air capability, of course, the individual naval aircaft and the ships' complements have grown in size and complexity. Where the 62 embarked aircraft on the *Midway* in 1950 were of three types, all fixed-wing, and weighed under a million pounds all together, the 90-some aircraft on the *Nimitz* comprise ten types, including helicopters, and weigh nearly 5 million pounds in the aggregate. These trends have caused growth in the carrier itself, because of the need for more aviation fuel, more hangar-deck space, greater strength and size of the landing deck to support the heavier aircraft with higher landing speeds, and so forth. As all parts of a design move together, the carrier, its power plant, its auxiliary services, and its crew have all grown. Growth in size and facilities means growth in cost. Whereas an attack carrier's cost (not including its aircraft) was about 1.5 percent of the annual Navy budget in 1950 (based on the average trend line), it is about 5 percent now.

Similar trends in shrinking numbers and growing capability can be shown for other naval missions. We could, for example, calculate the effective radii of operation of ships' detection systems and weapons and convert these to areas of effectiveness. During 1943–44 each of the approximately five 45-to-60-ship convoys spaced across the North Atlantic at any time had about 7 escort ships (such as destroyers or destroyer escorts).[16] There might also be two or three escort-carrier groups operating to cover the convoy routes. Together, these escort and ASW forces might be able to search for and attack submarines in 30,000 to 35,000 square miles of ocean at any time. Today, despite the variability in submarine-localization capability, the same number of escorts and one attack carrier (CV) task force in a screening position might nevertheless cover about 750,000 square miles in similar fashion. The carrier task force would not, however, be able to screen five convoys stretched across the Atlantic simultaneously, since the total distance along the shipping paths to be covered would be considerably longer than the radius of action of the task force. This problem could be solved by having fewer convoys, each with more ships if necessary or with larger ships if they were available, bunched under the wing of the carrier task force.

This arrangement would provide a much more lucrative target for submarines, and the latter will also have increased their operating areas enormously by using cruise missiles. In World War II, for example, there were on the order of 8 submarines operating against each convoy. These 8 submarines could shoot at ships in approximately 50 square miles of ocean. Today, given the size of the Soviet nuclear-attack and cruise-missile submarine fleet of about 110 boats (plus 180 diesel-powered submarines)[17] it might be possible for 20 submarines to attack the more highly concentrated convoy described above, and these submarines could shoot at ships within about 30,000 square miles of ocean. They would, of course, be hindered by the carrier screen and escorts, which would threaten any aircraft attempting to help with targeting in addition to threatening the submarines themselves.

It is apparent from the earlier discussion of the ASW problem that although the area and nature of this particular battle would be much changed and expanded, the probabilistic nature of the engagement would not have changed. Just as in World War II, neither side could achieve perfect kills but rather would exact a level of attrition on the other that would cause the battle to go on for some time. But the stakes of the engagement would be much higher, because the fleets are smaller and any lost warship, on either side, would represent the loss of a significant fraction of the fleet's total capability. In a sense, the protecting (U.S.) fleet will have lost heavily as soon as a carrier task force is assigned to screen or protect the shipping area, because the attack air capability of a CV may be unavailable for its attack missions while the CV is using its ASW assets to protect the sea lanes. This suggests that the CV task force may not be so assigned, significantly reducing the area of ocean covered by defending forces. Of course, some of the ASW protection that could be afforded by the carrier task force can be performed by land-based aircraft to a significant degree.

More serious than this virtual attrition of available sea power caused by reduction in numbers of ships is the increased potential for real attrition. This comes not only from the effectiveness of the weapons, which (nuclear weapons aside) has been growing as conventional high explosive warhead designs have become more powerful for a given weight. It derives also from the fact that there are many fewer targets for the weapons to shoot at. Let us illustrate the significance of the trend with another example from World War II, extrapolated to modern times, such being the only source of real data for this kind of combat.

The Special Problem of Vulnerability

During the Okinawa campaign from March through June 1945,[18] some 587 ships, of which about 320 were warships, participated in operations. Over this period, there were some 1,900 kamikaze attacks on the invasion fleet, with the attack strength varying from about 50 to 350 aircraft coming in waves of several tens of aircraft, recurring over one- to three-day periods. On the order of 150 aircraft per attack sequence was typical. These numbers may not be very different from the size of missile attacks that could be mounted by Soviet submarine and naval-aviation units against a carrier task force. Of the fleet off Okinawa, about 105, or 18 percent, of the ships were badly enough damaged to have been sunk or essentially eliminated from the war (36 of the 105 ships hit were made serviceable after more than thirty days). In the attacks, there were on the average about 15 to 30 kamikaze passes per ship hit; over the entire campaign 93 percent of the attackers missed their targets or were shot down, and on the average there were about 1.25 hits per ship damaged.

If we apply these statistics to a hypothetical Soviet attack on the modern carrier task group of Figure 5-1, with the attack taking place over a day or two, then the interesting results in Table 5-6 emerge. These results highlight the problem foreseen in increased vulnerability of the decreasing number of ships in the fleet, and they also point to some related factors not often brought out in the arguments about fleet force structure.

Assuming that the same high attrition can be extracted of incoming missiles as was extracted from the kamikazes, we conclude that an attack would have to be quite heavy to achieve more hits per target, on the average, than the kamikazes achieved. However, if the attacker's target acquisition system can select the carrier with reasonable success, even a fairly modest attack could score many hits on the carrier.

Although the damage potential of today's missile warheads is greater than that of the kamikazes, the phenomenon of ship damage is a complex one. Whether a hit sinks a ship or simply damages it, whether the damage knocks it out of action, and how many hits a ship can absorb, all depend on the kind of ship and on the location of the hit and size of the warhead. The accidental explosion of several bombs on the hangar deck of the nuclear carrier *Enterprise* off Vietnam did not sink the ship, although it broke off action and returned to port.[19] There were cases during World War II where several hits on carriers or other ships were required to knock them out of action.[20] Many of the carriers sunk went down after leaking and listing for many hours; a few were sunk by U.S. action because there was no easy way to salvage the ships. On the other hand, some ships (usually not carriers) were sunk by single, lucky hits that penetrated to magazines or boilers. Today's ships might easily be put out of action, even though the hulls and machinery might not be badly damaged, by a hit that cut many of the electrical cables that serve their radar and missile systems. This was demonstrated by the Argentine air attacks on the British fleet during the 1982 conflict in the South Atlantic.

The consequences of putting a ship out of action, but not sinking it, depend on the scenario and its magnitude. In a one-week war, the ship would be useless for the duration, after the event. In the previous example, the *Enterprise* was repaired and reentered the battle, off Vietnam. No major U.S. naval ships were lost because of military action in the two wars we have fought since World War II: the Navy was able to serve its purposes in those wars. (This judgment is independent of national political attitudes toward those purposes or those wars.) In a future war where the Navy *is* opposed, it may lose ships, as would the other side. The significance of the losses would depend

**Table 5-6: HYPOTHETICAL CRUISE MISSILE ATTACK
ON A MODERN CARRIER TASK GROUP**

Number of Missiles in Attack	Number Reaching Target	Average Hits Per Ship	Hits on Carrier if Half of Shots Aimed There[a]
1,000	70	7.8	35
500	35	3.9	17.5
300	21	2.3	10.5
150	10.5	1.2	5.3
50	3.5	0.4	1.8

[a] Assumes successful target discrimination and missile guidance.

on the relative loss *rate,* on what the ships were able to do before they were lost, and on what the remaining ships could do subsequently.

To achieve the higher weights of attack shown in Table 5-6, a substantial force would be required. For example, 50 bombers and a dozen submarines might have to operate over many days to deliver 500 to 1,000 missiles—a period offering sufficient opportunity for the task force to take lethal counteraction. It is apparent, on the other hand, that important ships (such as the carrier in a carrier task group) may not absorb hits "on the average." As shown by the last column in the table, they may in fact be the targets of concentrated attack and absorb a disproportionate share of the hits made. This distribution of fire will depend on the enemy's concern about the carrier relative to the other ships in the task force. For example, even with the carrier gone, the other ships can seriously threaten his aircraft and submarines when they try to attack other surface shipping, and he may not wish to ignore them. The distribution of fire will also depend on technical interactions of uncertain outcome: whether the target location means can distinguish among ships and locate them with sufficient accuracy, and whether midcourse guidance can bring the missiles to the point of acquiring the specific targets for terminal guidance with sufficient precision under conditions of active countermeasures and counterattack. (We might assume they could do so if wholly unopposed in a surprise attack—Pearl Harbor worked, too.)

Thus although today's much smaller task force can be said ab initio to be far more vulnerable than the much larger fleets of World War II, the specific elements of any attack would have to be considered in order to assess the potential validity of the inference.

All this tradeoff hinges, of course, on the assumption that certain historical attrition data would apply in the future. The World War II defenses included radar-directed guns that were used against large and slow targets—a combination calculated to favor the defense strongly. Guided missiles are smaller, faster, and show no combat degradation caused by stress on the pilot. On the other hand, their carriers and launchers are vulnerable to destruction. To minimize such vulnerability, it is desirable to launch them from long range, giving more time for detection and counterfire. These long-range launches enhance the chances of missing targets or acquiring the wrong targets as a result of system inaccuracies and countermeasures. The constraints of target-sensing and terminal-homing systems on board the missiles may make their trajectories more predictable for counterfire than those of piloted aircraft. Finally, what the missiles gain in reduced physical vulnerability owing to their small size and high speed may be compensated for by greater vulnerability to all forms of electronic warfare. These forms may include destruction of, or interference with, target acquisition means and countermeasures against guidance systems or sensors. There are, of course, also threats from torpedoes if enemy submarines can approach close enough to launch them. The defense, although formidable, may not work as well as planned, or it may be defeated by countermeasures. There are enough unknowns in this complex that the attrition of attacking craft—airplanes or submarines—or missiles cannot be predicted with any degree of certainty. Any attempt at an estimate would incorporate many technical assumptions that could be varied arbitrarily over a range of reasonable values, leading to a broad range of reasonable answers.

Thus far we have talked only about operation and survivability of the ship in a carrier task group. We must remind ourselves of the primary purpose of that task group, which is to launch aircraft to carry out attack missions against enemy forces, at sea or on and over the land. Especially in land attack, the carrier's airplanes may well encounter the kinds of defenses that were described in Chapter 3. The difficulties and uncertainties involved in overcoming such defenses would be just as severe for the naval air forces as for those based on land. Again, the outcome would depend very much on local conditions and circumstances.

Thus, it appears that the arguments and counterarguments as to whether the current and planned naval force structure is viable or should be changed can be said to depend on whether one wants to make a (usually unspoken) set of favorable or unfavorable technical and operational assumptions leading to prediction of less or more serious damage to the typical carrier force and its aircraft. To argue, however, that the risk to the task force or its air attack missions is low means that one has to make most of these assumptions in directions favorable for the defense, while assumptions about survival of attack aircraft must favor the offense. No prudent designer of naval forces on which the nation's safety depends could afford to make such biased assumptions knowingly today. On the other hand, it is always possible to assume a worst-case scenario in which the total and devastating Soviet first strike will always eliminate the Navy at the beginning of a war or in which all its aircraft will be shot down on their first attack mission. The problem is to reach a reasonably balanced view of what the Navy should do and should be.

Groping for Some Ways Out

The Reagan administration decided to meet the growing Soviet naval power by expanding the Navy in its currently conventional form: by buying more large carriers with their air groups and air-defense and ASW escort ships. This was described by the secretary of defense as "the most significant force expansion proposed by the Administration."[21] It made the Navy budget the largest of the four Services and entailed beginning construction of 39 major surface combatant ships over the five years from fiscal 1982 to fiscal 1987. With the ultimate objective of achieving fifteen carrier battle groups compared with the current thirteen and replacing or modernizing the oldest ships such as the *Coral Sea, Midway,* and *Forrestal,* there would have to be a similar high rate of combat ship construction until and beyond the end of the century to achieve the planned "600-ship Navy." This program places tremendous pressure on defense resources at a time when popular support for a vastly expanded defense program is shaky at best. More to the point, by expanding the Navy in the same form as that which currently exists the vulnerabilities and operational difficulties described above would not be solved; we would simply be providing more forces that have the same problems as the existing forces. And with more than the usual share of resources going into new ship and aircraft construction none would be left over to try new systems and directions that might help solve these problems. It is worth exploring what some of those new directions might be.

During the 1970s many schemes were advanced for reducing individual ship costs and thereby increasing the number of ships in the fleet. These include mini-carriers or sea-control ships,[22] midi-carriers,[23] strike cruisers[24] (which would really reinforce the trend toward concentration by incorporating vast—and expensive—multiple combat capabilities in a single ship), substitution of land-based air power for ships,[25] and reduction of the roles of the Navy.[26] Some of these proposals offer interesting possibilities for changing the way we exercise maritime power, but others could seriously weaken that power.

In these proposals the missions of the Navy were expressed as *projection* and *sea control*. "Projection" is taken to mean the use of seaborne tactical air power over land (perhaps in conjunction with amphibious landings), and "sea control" is taken to mean protection of shipping. The arguments tended to revolve implicitly around the possibility of a short war in Central Europe, where it can easily be shown that projection of power ashore by the Navy does not make sense and that sea control simply requires protection of reinforcement convoys for a month or two. For other areas, the reasoning in this direction maintained that there is no sophisticated threat requiring the maximum of combat capability. It was then argued that the Navy should emphasize the sea-control mission. Such emphasis would in the main require simpler and smaller ships, enabling the Navy to maintain or increase its size while keeping costs under control.[27]

Such arguments may well arise again when the resource pinch begins to be felt ever more strongly. I believe, however, that they tend to be short-sighted and simplistic. It is possible to restructure our maritime forces to achieve increased flexibility and reduced vulnerability by integrating the available technical components in different ways and without giving up the Navy's missions as we currently understand them. To support this argument it is necessary, first, to examine critically the projection versus sea-control dichotomy.

It would doubtless be difficult for the Navy to make a significant tactical air contribution to a land war in the central part of NATO Europe as such a war tends to be visualized today—i.e., brief and fought to exhaustion of materiel or until the Warsaw Pact overruns the NATO defenses. But there may be alternate scenarios involving more sustained conflict where sea power will figure more importantly (see Chapter 8).

Of additional concern are the potential influences of changes in the world scene over the thirty- or more year lifetime of a generation of ships. In that time it is, for example, possible for long-range bomber and submarine bases hostile to the United States and its allies to appear in Africa or in parts of Southwest Asia, dominating the critical oil-shipping routes across the Indian Ocean and the South Atlantic. This could happen if the USSR were invited by friendly governments to establish and use bases in an Ethiopia or an Iran hostile to the United States or in Aden (South Yemen) where they already have a strong presence. Without predicting contingencies, it is clear that such a vulnerability for the United States and its allies cannot be neglected, even though the events by which it might become real and part of some develop-ing conflict cannot now be foreseen. Although such bases would not be so powerful as those on Soviet territory, they could be well protected by SAMs and fighter aircraft. If the fleet is not to give up the option of protecting itself in wartime by attacking the bases that threaten it (a much more powerful option, in areas away from Europe where the base structure would be less formidable, than waiting for the attacks to arrive), it would need all the sophistication of its tactical air for the purpose. Thus, this sea-control mission, or others like it (e.g., off Japan and Korea), would seem to require essentially the same types of forces as are commonly thought of in connection with the projection mission—counterarguments can be made, but the possibility cannot be ruled out. If a combined bomber and submarine attack such as that illustrated in Figure 5–3 *were* mounted, the full capability of the fleet would be needed to counter it. Finally, some would argue that the Navy should at least maintain a degree of surveillance against the Soviet strategic submarine threat. Advanced Soviet SSBNs with missiles capable of 4,000-mile ranges greatly increase the area of ocean that would have to be covered in guarding against that strategic threat,[28] even if all Soviet SSBNs couldn't be kept under surveillance all the time in peacetime or prevented from firing their missiles in wartime. Such a mission might require a significant assignment of general purpose naval forces.

From these considerations, then, the projection and sea-control dichotomy seems a false one, especially when it is considered that many of the fleet's combat ships serve purposes associated with both missions; if fleet attack capability is reduced both missions would suffer, and naval power will have been diminished. Some other way to rationalize the structure of the Navy must be found.

None of the discussions of the Navy's missions in the literature cited above consider the projection and sea-control missions in terms of specific opponents and geographic locations. Projection of power where and against whom? Who is contesting sea control, where, and under what circumstances? Of course there can be many answers, and flexibility to meet many contingencies is the essential characteristic and requirement of naval forces. But failure to be specific in these respects constitutes the invitation to the pessimists to assume the worst-case scenario and to arrive consequently at conclusions we have seen. Although it is difficult to consider naval engagements independently of naval missions in specific strategic and tactical situations, we can outline the demands of those situations, which will be considered in more detail in the chapters of Part 2. Combinations of opponents and areas of operations might include:

1. Soviet forces in the North Atlantic on the approaches to Western Europe and in the northwestern Pacific on the approaches to Japan;
2. Soviet forces deployed to areas more distant from the Soviet heartland and main centers of military power, including the South Atlantic, Indian Ocean, and the western Pacific; and

3. Third-country forces in similar areas off Africa, Latin America, and the Asian rimlands; some of these forces may have Soviet equipment and training or, as we saw in the South Atlantic, they might be oriented toward the West in their equipment and tactics.

Each of these circumstances has its own demands for type and level of naval power. (The likelihood of war in the circumstances is a separate matter that will be discussed later; here, we assume the need to maintain armed forces that are ready for contingencies.)

Consider, first, the logic by which the size of the current naval force structure is assessed. In normal peacetime operations, for each carrier at sea there are 2 in port or in trials, in various stages of rest, training, refitting, overhaul, or modernization.[29] It is certainly possible to change this ratio in the surge of crisis or war, but the cost of changing it would be too high to sustain indefinitely, short of war. In any event, *all* the carriers are unlikely to remain at sea simultaneously as a matter of routine. Then, with 1 or 2 carriers in the Mediterranean (at least for political purposes*) or in the North Atlantic, and 2 active in the Pacific, the current 12 operational carriers are essentially accounted for. More or less, the numbers of escorts and auxiliaries will vary with the numbers of carriers. The Navy has thus felt that there is no flexibility, except for the surge possibility, in its structure. When a need for deployment into the Indian Ocean arose it was necessary to "borrow" the necessary ships from the sixth and seventh fleets in the Mediterranean and the Pacific. It was the combination of dissatisfaction with this situation and the strategic decision that substantial naval force deployments in the western Indian Ocean and the Arabian Sea would be needed indefinitely, together with a growing perception of weakness vis-a-vis Soviet naval power, that created the current drive to expand our own Navy. There are, however, other means to expand our maritime power to suit our military needs in the diverse situations described above, while reducing its vulnerability, increasing its flexibiity, and keeping the cost from growing to unsupportable levels.

First, it has become possible to engage in major offensive and defensive operations in and over "high threat" waters—i.e., those easily reached by massed Soviet air and submarine forces—without having large fleets of surface ships. Land-based aviation has now been developed to the point where it has intercontinental range, and it can attack any targets at sea (surface or subsurface—or airborne, for that matter) from bases on land. Indeed, this is the source of the Soviet air threat to our own surface forces.

---

*The issue of whether the sixth fleet is militarily viable is a separate and complex one whose treatment here is not essential to our main theme.

There is the obvious argument that land bases may be even more vulnerable to attack than sea bases because their locations are known and they are not mobile as are the aircraft carriers. However, with modern surveillance technology it is not as easy as it once was to hide ships in vast expanses of ocean. Moreover, if land bases are on the United States' or its key allies' home territory, while carriers at sea are more or less isolated from the land, the issues of deterrence of major attack become very different. In this context, in all except a major, all-out war, the land bases may indeed be safer than the bases at sea despite their greater accessibility. Moreover, active defenses in the form of interceptors and SAMs can be massed at a land base at much less cost than they can be massed at sea, and uniquely suited passive defense measures against nonnuclear attack, such as use of hardened aircraft shelters and proliferation of runways, are available to the land base at relatively low cost.

Long-range, land-based aviation can provide interceptor aircraft that could, for example, be adaptations of the F-111 attack aircraft or the B-1 bomber. These interceptors could carry many missiles like the long-range Phoenix currently carried by the F-14 fleet air defense interceptor, and they could operate in conjunction with radar search and control aircraft like the AWACS or with space-based sensors when they are available. Such interceptor and sensor combinations can be used to prevent Soviet long-range attack aviation from having the free run of the oceans. As we shall see later, the Soviet aircraft must sortie through relatively restricted passages like those between Greenland and the United Kingdom if they are not to pass over defended hostile territory, and this channeling of the attack helps to focus the defense.

For offensive operations aircraft like the B-52s or their successors the B-1s, carrying air-to-surface cruise missiles like the Harpoon or the longer-range Tomahawk, can be used to attack surface fleets at sea. We already use long-range, land-based aircraft for anti-submarine warfare, and these can be augmented. For example, these aircraft can already carry and launch the Harpoon against surface ships. It should also be possible to deploy appropriately designed and developed arrays of sensors to localize submarines with sufficient accuracy for attack and then to use the aircraft to launch long-range weapons against the submarines, just as is now done using the combination of land-based sensor aircraft and helicopters based on surface ships. The ASW capability of long-range aviation built up this way could be joined with the ASW strength of nuclear-powered attack submarines to increase greatly the anti-submarine strength of our maritime forces.

The combination of attack submarines and land-based aviation armed with cruise missiles, which we are building, could also keep the ocean basins that they cover clear of the ships of the growing Soviet surface fleet. Thus the most powerful weapons against Soviet naval aviation, surface fleets, and submarines in the high threat areas are likely to be land-based aviation together with attack submarines, assisted by sensors in space or carried aboard land-based airplanes analogous to current ASW patrol aircraft and the AWACS.

This would constitute the maritime power used to control waters like the North Atlantic and the North Pacific. Under the protective cover of this land-based and undersea force the surface fleet would also, as it now does, provide its own close-in protection against attackers leaking through the main, areawide defenses. The surface fleet would then be better able to engage in littoral campaigns in such areas as the southern Atlantic or the Indian and South Pacific oceans should the need for such campaigns materialize. The sea links to our main allies in Europe and the Far East would be protected without the need for large attack carriers. It must be remembered that such carrier forces weren't needed in the Atlantic for these purposes during World War II, either, so that the implied change of naval strategy is not as radical as it might seem at first.

It is worth making a few further observations in this connection. Up to World War II, surface fleets had the run of the seas and the oceans, limited in where they could go only by the very short reach of shore batteries or by opposing fleets. With the advent of effective air power in World War II it became clear that surface fleets couldn't operate where the opposing side had extensive land-based air power. Thus the Mediterranean was dominated first by the German and then by the Allied side as the balance in land-based air power shifted from one to the other. There were no extensive naval operations by either side in the North Sea. Some convoys were run across the Norwegian Sea to carry supplies to the Soviet Union, at very high cost as German land-based air power attacked them day by day on the long run to Murmansk; they succeeded at all only because the bulk of German long-range aviation was occupied elsewhere. In the South Pacific we weren't able to oppose Japanese air power effectively until Henderson Field on Guadalcanal was fully operational,[30] and the battle for control of the Coral Sea was simply the beginning of the contest for island airfields that would allow domination of the sea routes among Australia, Japan, and the Indonesian archipelago. Much of our naval war in the southern and central Pacific was fought for the purpose of destroying not only Japanese naval power but the air power based on the islands and on the Chinese mainland, to make the Japanese islands accessible for invasion.

Thus, in World War II there came to be areas as large as major seas in which naval power couldn't be effective because of the strength of opposing land-based aviation. Advancing technology has now brought us to the point where land-based air power, in combination with submarine-launched cruise missiles (which can be said to constitute another form of air power), can dominate entire ocean basins. The attempt to use mainly carrier forces to protect the sea lanes in such circumstances, or to operate them close to the USSR in areas such as the Norwegian Sea, would fly in the face of these long-term technological and strategic trends. Bucking the trends isn't necessary, as we have seen.

This doesn't mean that the day of the carrier is ended, however, or that carrier forces have become ineffective or useless as a general matter. In many parts of the world of vital concern to the United States and its allies, including vast parts of the Pacific Ocean, the Asian and African littoral, and the southern oceans, we have strategic interests that can be served and supported by surface naval forces. These areas fall within the second and third scenario descriptions on page 113. The argument that large carriers with all their combat aviation capability aren't needed in such areas doesn't hold, as even the brief 1982 engagement between British and Argentine forces in the South Atlantic demonstrated [31]—the small British carriers, without airborne early warning and long-range fighters, couldn't fully protect the invasion fleet against air attacks using Western-furnished aircraft and weapons. The situation would be much worse in areas such as the southwest Pacific or the Arabian Sea if Soviet forces of modest size could enter such an engagement.

Given current ship life of thirty to fifty years and the high cost of major ships, the current carrier force is likely, first, to be with us for a long time and, second not to grow very much if at all.[32] A decision to rely mainly on land-based aviation and submarines to provide maritime power in the North Atlantic and the North Pacific would mean that the size of our carrier forces wouldn't have to grow, although a low-rate construction program might be maintained to modernize and replace such ships as time passes and they become obsolescent or wear out. Would the carriers have to be as big and as complex as today's *Nimitz* class nuclear powered airbase afloat? Or should succeeding ships be smaller and cheaper? The large carrier has the advantage of consolidating many supporting functions for a great diversity of aircraft "under one roof," as it were. It therefore has the advantage of being able to bring more air power to a point or a region for lower cost than a multiplicity of smaller ships.[33]

Although through the accidents of continuity in history and long-lasting capital equipment the large carrier may remain the primary capital ship of the surface navy, where it can operate, long into the future, considerations of vulnerability may join with new technological opportunities to encourage the dispersal of various forms of aviation onto other naval ships. These opportunities include the advent of practical vertical or short takeoff and landing (V/STOL) aircraft. This class of aircraft includes helicopters for ASW and other purposes, fighters like the Marine Corps' AV-8A Harrier (soon to be replaced by a more advanced version, the AV-8B), and (potentially) utility aircraft that can perform the tasks of the current E-2C Hawkeye early warning aircraft and the S-3 Viking ASW aircraft. The use of V/STOL technology means that the functions associated with these aircraft can be carried out from smaller aviation-capable ships, which may look like the smaller British carriers that operated off the Falklands or like current U.S. Marine Corps amphibious assault ships. The advantage of dispersing such functions away from the large carrier is that more of the carrier's complement can be given over to the offensive aviation, which is (and has been) the carrier's main raison d'être. The dispersal of aviation functions among more ships also means that the total task group becomes less vulnerable to elimination of all its air capability by a few hits on the carrier. Moreover, the use of V/STOL designs would help maintain operations even on a large carrier if hits damaged the catapults or arresting gear or put holes in the flight deck.* The approach of using relatively small aviation-capable ships with V/STOL aircraft (helicopters and fighters) is already used by the Marine Corps for transferring air and land power across the water-land boundary, and these applications would extend the use of such ships and aircraft further.

It is also necessary to think about overcoming local air defenses to attack heavily defended targets on land as well as surface fleets. The tactical cruise missiles discussed in Chapter 3, used together with appropriately developed target acquisition systems and launched from aircraft, surface ships, or submarines, can serve this purpose. Although these weapons may be subject to countermeasures and counterfire, if enough of them are used they can saturate the defenses of seaborne forces including major ships (as we noted in considering the Soviet threat against our ships). Even if the missiles are expensive, it is not unreasonable to use a few million dollars' worth of missiles against a few hundred million, or a few billion, dollars' worth of ships.

---

*In pursuit of our main theme of the impact of technology, we might note that the fact that we think of V/STOL aircraft in all these roles at all, today, is an indication of technological progress from the specialized but marginal AV-8A Harrier currently being used to support the Marine Corps. V/STOL developments are becoming more practicable and perhaps more economic as a result of: the "supercritical wing" design that allows a thicker and therefore lighter wing structure for the same high Mach-number performance as conventional aircraft; composite materials permitting structural weight reduction; lighter-weight propulsion systems that benefit from advanced high-temperature materials and turbine blade–cooling technology; electronic advances that reduce the weight and engine-power requirements for cooling of onboard avionics; and computerized flight-control technology that permits smaller stabilizing and control surfaces. Although all these advances can help conventional aircraft as well, the benefit is greater for those that were marginal earlier. They make available a total technology, V/STOL, that was not earlier easily available for fixed-wing aircraft. In any case, the effects of other performance penalties, especially reduced payload, that must be accepted for V/STOL can be mitigated by using such aircraft in the conventional mode whenever circumstances permit.[34]

Indeed, as we have noted, this is the main Soviet attack scheme against our surface fleet. Sea-based tactical air operating against targets on land can adopt standoff tactics and weapon delivery techniques much the same as those that were described in Chapter 3. Massed cruise missiles for this purpose can be air- *or* surface-launched (from aircraft or from ships) to saturate and destroy enemy defenses where the latter are very effective. The necessary weights of fire to substitute for air attacks must be much larger in land war than in war at sea. For example, a carrier attack air force can deliver several hundred weapons in a few days, and if heavy cruise missile losses in standoff operations are accounted for the missiles may have to number in the thousands. Missiles for the anti-land missions must therefore cost much less than their counterparts for sea war. Even then, their cost will be high enough to require them to be reserved for use against "high-value" targets like air defenses, transportation choke points, and key fixed installations. Inventories of many thousands of these weapons would still be needed for any substantial engagements such as might be necessary in, say, the Persian Gulf area. Conventional warships could launch such missiles but they needn't—ships designed for the purpose might resemble, or use as their basic hulls, amphibious assault ships, various naval auxiliaries, or merchant ships. Missile bay designs could permit such ships to carry many tens, or even hundreds, of missiles each. When attacks by such systems succeed in reducing the land-based defenses, the much more efficient conventional carrier air operations against targets like moving land armies, using penetration tactics, can be undertaken.

The use of smaller ships than carriers for such diverse aviation-linked purposes as observation and surveillance, target acquisition, amphibious assault, some combat missions, and missile attacks against heavily defended targets on land and at sea means that overall task group vulnerability would be reduced because important targets (from the enemy's point of view) would be proliferated, causing the enemy to distribute his fire more widely than was shown in Table 5–6. In addition, such ships without the carriers would be available to distribute "peacetime presence" more widely, while smaller groupings of the ships could be detailed to carry out lesser naval tasks that now demand a large carrier because that is all that is available to provide a base for air power.

From all of the above it is clear that the combination of enhanced land-based air power for use in areas easily accessible to extensive Soviet military power, continued use of some large carriers having a changed aviation complement to emphasize offense more than defense, and the addition of some new classes of ships, aircraft, and weapons that can do things today's naval machinery can't do, can change the form of U.S. maritime power over the two or three decades it would take to implement these changes.[35] Since none of the scenarios considered is "pure" and conditions will vary, the new forms of naval power would add much greater flexibility than we now have. The land-based aviation could deploy to "rented" bases in low threat areas overseas, and the "low threat" ships could find significant uses in the "high threat" ocean areas. It would, of course, also be necessary to build and to protect the land bases on the rims of the North Atlantic and the North Pacific. Across all missions and scenarios, it appears that there would be value in strengthening the surface-based air defenses carried by smaller ships—cruisers, destroyers, and frigates—to deal with missiles that penetrate the outer defenses. Only detailed estimates could show whether more or fewer ships are needed. A change in their air defense structure to separate more distinctly the long-range and the close-in defenses would offer the opportunity to alleviate the complexity and, therefore, the cost of the attending command and control system.

There remains the question of budget. Relative budgets for the different kinds of naval forces discussed here are subject to decisions about numbers of ships, aircraft, missiles, and land bases, as well as kinds of each type that are to be acquired. It is known that smaller ships cost more per aircraft afloat than larger ones,[36] but it also appears that roughly equivalent firepower can be purchased in the form of land-based aviation for about two thirds the cost of sea-based aviation.[37] There is also potentially great budget flexibility in the rate at which large carriers would be phased out or modernized. A new generation of aircraft would be acquired. Some of them might be only somewhat different in cost from the new generation that would have to be acquired over that time period in any case. Close-in air defenses on all ships would be strengthened. We might want to build more attack submarines. Finally, it would be almost impossible to predict the change in operating costs over the years without designing the new naval forces in detail. This would depend in part on the added maintenance required for aging ships, such as large carriers, being retained to permit acquisition moneys to be spent for ships like the smaller aviation ships or the cruise missile ships and for land-based aircraft. Moreover, the distribution and amount of manpower for the new forces in comparison with today's forces could not be known without detailed analysis. The new Navy's size and cost might be adjusted more easily than those of today's Navy. Thus, it might eventually be found that the Navy could be redesigned, over twenty or thirty years or so, within a few percent of the overall budget trends of the past few years.

All these speculations about postulated fleet reorganizations and costs are so rough as to be worthy of consideration only as constructs for further investigation. They do, however, lend encouragement to the supposition that some of the problems facing the Navy are not completely intractable. They suggest that in a large number of important situations the naval forces and even the large carriers might not automatically be blasted out of the water, as some fear.[38] They suggest also that the undesirable trends toward concentration and increased vulnerability in the U.S. Navy, as the Soviet maritime forces grow, can be remedied by imaginative use of technological capabilities currently or imminently available, without the need to diminish U.S. sea power overall by giving up major missions or naval forces and capabilities. *The key to the changes is the recognition that modern technology offers the opportunity to dominate the oceans without necessarily building vast fleets of surface ships to sail in all of the oceans.*

Although the basic directions in U.S. naval posture as we enter the 1980s were established in World War II, advancing technology has made today's Navy into a force very different from the one that emerged from that war. The imaginative use of these same technological advances in different ways by the USSR is again requiring a change in the nature of U.S. naval force. A new naval force structure will not appear automatically or suddenly, given the rate at which ships and airplanes can be built and the lifetime over which we keep them. As always before, therefore, the change in the shape of the Navy is constrained to be evolutionary. But it is obvious that steps need to be taken, while they can be undertaken without major dislocation, to prevent the actual imbalance in naval-force design from becoming as severe as the perceived imbalance seems to be today. Just as we found to be the case with the Air Force, only a willingness to try the unconventional can get the Navy out of the financial and strategic straitjacket in which it finds itself.

Part 2
Using the General Purpose Forces

6
Military Power in the Twentieth Century's Last Decades

In the previous chapters we explored the significance of evolving technology for the form and functions of the general purpose military forces. We examined the impact of the technology on the capability of those forces, on their tactics, and on some aspects of strategy associated with their use. The problems of the individual military Services were considered in some depth, although an integrated view must yet be taken. In all this, the assumption was implicit that there would be national interest in the United States in fostering a rationally designed military capability. But that hasn't been an easy assumption to make in the post–World War II era. There have been several major changes in the United States' view of its armed forces and their role as an instrument of foreign policy.[1]

With the North Korean attack on South Korea in June 1950 the United States began to realize that warfare of less than worldwide scale might continue to be part of the post–World War II international scene. Many terms were coined to describe such conflict in its many manifestations: limited war; brushfire war; fringe war; counterinsurgency; stability operations; showing the flag. Many military and strategic theorists and historians wrote about such wars, their meaning for our future, and how to fight them. We were involved directly or indirectly in a number of military actions. The tide reached its high point in Vietnam. There, the United States' belief in the efficacy of military power as an instrument of foreign policy was shaken, and support for the use of military power for any but our closest and most vital security interests waned like the wash of a wave rushing back down the beach. Since Vietnam there has been little taste for the possibility of U.S. involvement in military action. This attitude was confirmed by events in Angola in 1975 and in Ethiopia and the Horn of Africa in 1978 and by the sensitivity displayed when we deployed a battalion of Marines to help restore peace in Lebanon after the Israeli invasion of 1982. On the other hand, we have made a commitment to defend the oil resources available to the Western world in the Persian Gulf area, and under the Carter and then the Reagan administration we embarked on a major effort to strengthen both our strategic and general purpose forces.

The nature of our varying national priorities as our economic strength has grown since World War II is illustrated in Figure 6-1. In this figure, we compare the long-term trend in national expenditures for defense and space, taken together, with the trends in expenditures for health and education. Many consider defense and space expenditures to be closely related and would prefer to see them decline. Health and education have been viewed (with other areas) as potentially worthy benefactors of the preference for other priorities. The rise in GNP, relating to the scale on the right, is shown for reference.

**FIGURE 6-1: National Expenditures in Selected Areas
(Years Ending June 30)**

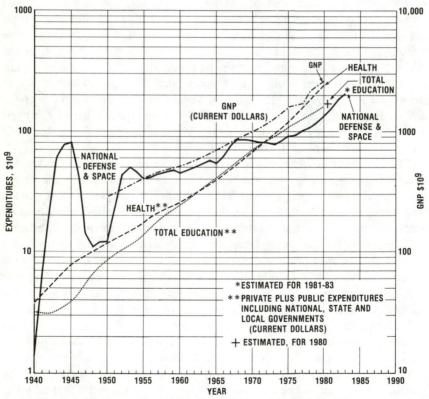

SOURCE: U.S. BUREAU OF THE CENSUS, STATISTICAL ABSTRACT OF THE UNITED STATES,
APPROPRIATE YEARS, WASHINGTON, D.C.

11-22-82-2

These curves are shown with a logarithmic ordinate, so that a straight-line increase in Figure 6–1 really represents an exponential increase—that is each year's expenditures are a given *multiple* of that of the prior year, not simply the prior year's expenditure plus a fixed amount.

After the large increase in defense expenditure during World War II, the level of expenditure in this area is seen, despite some large fluctuations, to have been rising relatively slowly in the long perspective of history. It declined after 1945, rose again after Korea, declined, and then increased with Vietnam and the peak of the Apollo moon program. (Before 1960 the budget for civilian aeronautical and space research was too small to appear on the scale of this graph.) Although defense and space expenditure again began to rise modestly with the inflation of the 1970s, and more sharply since 1980, the general trend over the past thirty-eight years has been to increase much less rapidly than the GNP. Total expenditures for health and education, however, have followed a strong and uninterrupted exponential increase, much more rapid than the rise of GNP, over the same period. Each area alone now accounts for more of the national wealth than the sum of defense and space; and although no exponential increase of resource use can continue forever, neither rise as yet shows much sign of abating (despite the struggles of the Reagan administration to control "social programs.") Although they have not been shown, in the interest of keeping this graph uncluttered, expenditures for other social purposes would follow a similar pattern (as the reader who wishes to browse in the *U.S. Statistical Abstract* can readily ascertain). It does not matter, of course, whether the dollars shown are of the current years or converted through the inflation factors to be equivalent to dollars for the same year, because the relationship among the expenditures would remain the same in either case.

This is the environment in which there has been increasing popular resistance even to letting the defense budget hold its own with inflation and in which the idea of using military power in the interest of international position has become anathema to much of our population. Although the events of the past few years in Iran, Afghanistan, and Poland have led to greater willingness to absorb more defense expenditure, perspective on the continuing nature of the trends noted above shouldn't be lost. Whereas in 1960 the United States was devoting 9 percent of its GNP to defense, this has declined to about 5 percent in 1980. Except for the short period immediately following President Reagan's election when there was general agreement on the need to strengthen our defenses, there has been bitter argument about an increase to just under 6 percent, and the defense program became a prime target in the fiscal year 1983 budget arguments.

This attitude is not unique to the United States, but it has been characteristic of the peoples in the Western world. It is of interest to compare it with the

trends in the nations associated with our chief military rival on the world
scene, the USSR. Figure 6-2 shows an indicator of relative expenditures on
social and military programs in the two major military alliances over the ten
years from 1967 through 1976. Social expenditures in NATO doubled relative
to military expenditures over this period, while they remained half as large
in the Warsaw Pact nations over the entire decade. Since both groups of
nations experienced economic growth, it is clear that NATO used the fruits
of its growth to improve its standard of living and the Warsaw Pact used
a much larger proportion of *its* growth for defense. The Pact countries and
especially the Soviet Union are, of course, much better able to enforce the
attending privations on their people, regardless of the relative economic
strengths of the two groups (although events in Poland suggest that there
are limits to this power in the Pact as well). The nations of NATO Europe
have barely met or are failing to meet the commitment made during the Carter

FIGURE 6-2: Ratio of Expenditures: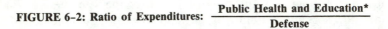

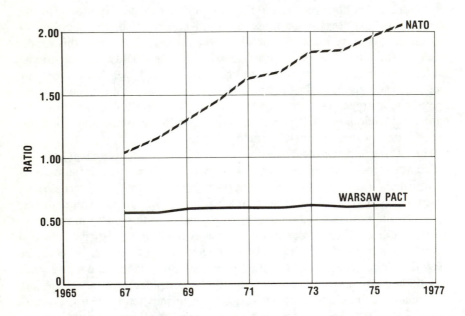

Source: Arms Control and Disarmament Agency, World Military Expenditures and Arms Transfers,
1967-1976 and 1965-1974.

*Public expenditures; does not include private expenditures.

1-20-83-1

administration to increase their defense expenditures by 3 percent per year in real terms—a much lesser commitment than the 5 percent to 7 percent increase being asked of the U.S. people by President Reagan. Such changes aren't resisted only on principle; the Western economies are no longer structured in such a way that such changes are easily made, especially in times of economic difficuilty.

These general trends occur at a time when, as we have seen, the military Services face severe problems in absorbing costly new technology and operational concepts. They raise a number of questions. *Can* we do anything with our military power on the international scene? Is it worth trying to solve the difficult new problems of structure in the general purpose forces? Where may it be possible to draw the line at some level of expenditure and effort and say, "This is enough"? What might be gained or lost by drawing that line at different levels?

Any proposal claiming to give definitive answers to such questions should be viewed with suspicion, because each observer will have his own views about what arguments may be persuasive or definitive. The necessity does become clear, however, of considering the general purpose forces in a broader context than that of their internal structure alone. After sketching briefly that broader context of international affairs and the politics of using military force, we will be in a better position to appreciate how the military Services function in an integrated way and to view some of the arguments that have arisen about the pace of technological change.

A Concise History of Warfare Since World War II

Most Americans are aware that there have been military actions in the world since World War II, but the extent of such activity may well be surprising. Table 6–1 lists a number of military actions or wars that have taken place since World War II, in the following three categories:

1. Conventional war—organized, regular forces were involved on both sides;
2. Unconventional war—organized, regular forces were on one side and guerrilla or paramilitary forces on the other; and
3. Deterred war—war in an area looked imminent; at least one major party moved forces into place to attack or intervene; but the war did not take place.

We can glean from the table that there has been much military activity; a considerably larger number of military actions has been unconventional than conventional; the United States, the USSR, and the People's Republic of

Table 6–1: SOME MILITARY ENGAGEMENTS SINCE WORLD WAR II

Conventional	Unconventional		Deterred
Arab-Isreal, 1948	Indonesian independence	Sudan	Iran, 1946
Kashmir 1	Greece	Indonesian coup	Taiwan, 1950—
Korea	Philippines I	Aden	Lebanon, 1958
Sinai campaign, 1956	Indochina	Israel-fedayeen	Kuwait, 1961
Suez intervention	Malaya	Jordan-fedayeen	Cuban quarantine, 1962
Quemoy-Matsu	Hungary	Palestinian terrorist campaign (worldwide) (?)[a]	Soviet-Chinese border, 1960s
Congo	Tibet	Lebanon (?)	Jordan-Syria, 1970
India-China border	Kenya	Rhodesia (Zimbabwe) (?)	Soviet intervention, Mideast, 1973
Yemen	Cuban Revolution	Portuguese Timor	Poland, 1980—
Morocco-Algeria	Algeria	Cyprus II (Turkish invasion) (?)	
Malaysia: "confrontation"	Cyprus I	Spanish Sahara	
Vietnam: air and "main-force" war	Cuba: Bay of Pigs	Philippines II	
Kashmir II	Laos	Cambodia-Vietnam	
Nigeria	Ethiopia (Eritrea)	Israel-S. Lebanon	
Arab-Israel, 1967	South Vietnam: internal war	Chad	
Czechoslovakia	Angola	Southwest Africa (Namibia, Angola, South Africa)	
Suez, 1970	Colombia	Morocco-Polisario (Spanish Sahara, cont'd)	
India-Pakistan (Bangladesh)	Yemem (continued)	Iran	
Arab-Israel, 1973	Cyprus—II	Afghanistan	
Mayaguez, 1975	Kurdish rebellion	Central American wars (Nicaragua, Honduras, El Salvador, Guatemala)	
Ethiopia-Somalia	Congof—II		
Thailand-Cambodia	Thailand		
Egypt-Lybia	Mozambique		
Iran-Iraq	Peru		
Israel-Iraq (reactor bombing)	Dominican rebellion		
Israel-Lebanon/Syria			
Argentina-Britain			

Source: Compiled from contemporary news reports by this author.

[a] (?) signifies circumstances are sufficiently uncertain to classify this as an incident where war *may* have been deterred.

China have not been directly involved in all of these actions; and where they were, the nature of their involvement has varied greatly.

These events all fall in the category, noted earlier, of limited wars or wars of similar definition. But we must observe that *limitation* refers to *our* view or to that of the other major powers. From the viewpoint of the countries whose people have been on the scene, in many cases the wars have been total. The local inhabitants' survival as a people, with their forms of government and culture, has been at stake. Thus, this list of limited wars or military actions really displays the evolution of the world's history and political structure since World War II. That is, we have seen nearly forty years of warfare following Clausewitz's dictum on the relationship between war and politics. In this sense, whether the United States is directly involved or not, the form of the world we live in is affected. These military actions have, as a consequence, influenced our place in a changing world and perhaps, over the long term, our own survival; this is true, also, for the other major powers. We can see this better if we examine the antecedents of these military actions— why they have occurred—and the trends in type of war.

Excluding Greece, which was part of the playing out of the de facto political settlement of World War II, virtually all the military events shown took place in the areas of the old colonial empires and in Latin America. In these areas there were generally three reasons for warfare:

1. Independence from colonial domination;
2. Mutual adjustment of borders, influence, and power among newly independent nations; and
3. Determination of the internal power structure and form of government of a country (i.e., internal war).

If we list all the wars from the Table 6–1 in roughly chronological order on a chart (Table 6–2) showing, for each, the derivation from each of the three sources and the kind of war, we can see some patterns.

With a few exceptions, the Western colonies' wars of independence were largely over by about 1960. The wars of mutual adjustment have almost all been conventional wars (as defined above). This is not surprising because by the nature of the definition, the armed forces of independent countries were confronting each other. (Korea is included here as a war between two independent countries, although obviously the internal form of government of South Korea was also involved.) The independence wars and the internal wars have been and are predominantly unconventional—and, again, they must be since in both cases an attempt is made to overturn an existing government from within the country. Except for civil war between two parts of a national army (as in Nigeria), the rebels must initially be irregulars. In the

Table 6-2: DERIVATIONS OF ENGAGEMENTS

ENGAGEMENT	ROUGH DATES	INDEPENDENCE	ADJUSTMENT	INTERNAL
INDONESIA	1945-47	X U		
GREECE	1946-49			X U
KASHMIR I	1947-49		X C	
ARAB-ISRAEL	1947-48		X C	
PHILIPPINES I	1948-52			X U
INDOCHINA	1945-54	X U		
MALAYA	1945-54			X U
KOREA	1950-53		X C	
TAIWAN	1950---		X D	
KENYA	---1953	X U		
SINAI	1956		X C	
SUEZ	1956		X C	
HUNGARY	1956	X U		
QUEMOY-MATSU	1954-58		X C	
LEBANON	1958		X D	
TIBET	1959	X U		
CYPRUS I	1955-59	X U		
ALGERIA	1956-62	X U		
CUBA	1958-59			X U
LAOS	1959-75			X U
KUWAIT	1961		X D	
YEMEN	1962			X C
CONGO I	1960-62			X C
CUBA, BAY OF PIGS	1961			X U
VIETNAM, INTERNAL	1959-75			X U
INDIA-CHINA	1959-62		X C	
ANGOLA	1960-75	X U		
COLOMBIA	1960-?			X U
CUBA	1962		X D	
YEMEN	1963-69			X U
MOROCCO-ALGERIA	1964		X C	
CYPRUS II	1964-65			X U
KURDISH REBELLION	1960-76	X U		
CONGO II	1964-65			X U
MALAYSIA-INDONESIA	1963-66		X C	
VIETNAM, U.S. ENTRY	1965-74			X C U
THAILAND	1964---			X U
MOZAMBIQUE	1964-75	X U		
PERU	1964---			X U
DOMINICAN REPUBLIC	1965			X U
KASHMIR II	1965		X C	
SUDAN	1965-69			X U
INDONESIA (COUP)	1965			X U
ERITREA-ETHIOPIA	1965---	X U		
ARAB-ISRAEL	1967		X C	
NIGERIA	1967-69			X C
PORTUGUESE GUINEA	1966-74	X U		
ISRAEL-FEDAYEEN	1968---		X U	

11-22-82-1

(Cont'd)

Table 6-2: DERIVATIONS OF ENGAGEMENTS *(Cont'd)*

ENGAGEMENT	ROUGH DATES	INDEPENDENCE		ADJUSTMENT		INTERNAL	
CZECHOSLOVAKIA	1968	X	C				
ADEN	1963-67	X	U				
NO. KOREA BORDER RAIDS	1967-70			X	U		
SUEZ (WAR OF ATTRITION)	1970			X	C		
JORDAN-FEDAYEEN	1969-71					X	U
PLO: WORLD TERRORISM	1968---			X	U		
JORDAN-SYRIA	1970			X	D		
USSR-CHINA BORDER	1960s			X	C		
CHAD	1969-81					X	U
SPANISH SAHARA	1970-76					X	U
INDIA-PAKISTAN (BANGLADESH)	1971	X	C				
BANGLADESH	1971---					X	U
ISRAEL-ARAB	1973			X	C		
SOVIET INTERVENTION (?)	1973			X	D		
(PORTUGUESE) TIMOR	1974-76					X	U
ANGOLA (UNITA)	1975---					X	U
ZIMBABWE/RHODESIA	1970(?)---					X	U
PHILIPPINES II	1972---					X	U
CYPRUS III (TURKISH INVASION)	1974					X	C
LEBANON	1975-77					X	U
SOUTHWEST AFRICA (SOUTH AFRICA vs NEIGHBORS)	1975---	X (NAMIBIA)	U	X (ALL OTHERS)	U		
MAYAGUEZ INCIDENT	1975			X	C		
CAMBODIA-THAILAND	1975---			X	C		
ETHIOPIA (OGADEN)	1976---			X	C U		
MOROCCO-POLISARIO	1976---	X	U				
LIBYA-EGYPT	1977			X	C		
ZAIRE-ANGOLA	1977			X	C(?)		
CAMBODIA-VIETNAM	1977---			X	U		
VIETNAM-CHINA	1978(?)-79			X	C		
ISRAEL-SOUTH LEBANON	1978---			X	U		
AFGHANISTAN	1979---	X	U				
IRAN	1979---					X	U
NICARAGUA	---1979					X	U
EL SALVADOR	1979(?)---					X	U
CENTRAL AMERICAN BORDER CLASHES	1979(?)---			X	C		
POLAND	1980---	X	D				
IRAN-IRAQ	1980---			X	C		
ISRAEL-IRAQ (AIR STRIKE)	1981			X	C		
ISRAEL-LEBANON/SYRIA	1982			X	C		
ARGENTINA-UK (SOUTH ATLANTIC)	1982			X	C		

KEY   X - PRIMARILY OF THIS DERIVATION   ▨ - UNITED STATES-COMMUNIST COMPETITION INVOLVED

KIND OF WAR   { U - UNCONVENTIONAL
C - CONVENTIONAL
D - DETERRED

11-22-82-1A

case of the Soviet moves to maintain Communist control of the Eastern European countries, the nature of the war was based on consideration of the actual or most likely potential sources of resistance—irregulars in Hungary in 1956, and the Czech armed forces if there had been resistance in 1968. The only wars that were limited rather than wars for survival, from the viewpoints of the participants on whose territory the wars took place, occurred in the mutual-adjustment category. Finally, it seems from the pattern of the chart that the military expression of conflict between the Western world and communism is declining. This is the result of a very complex set of interactions. Clashes of interest between the major parliamentary democracies and the Communist powers don't any longer tend to be mixed with the striving for independence from colonial rule, as the latter conflicts have been resolved. But except for a rather feeble reaction of protest when the USSR invaded Afghanistan, those democracies have not yet picked up the challenge of the new *Soviet* colonialism.

In three important geographical areas, the divisions are not clearcut. In the Near East the Arab-Israeli wars, the civil war in Lebanon, and the Israeli invasions of Lebanon have involved both conventional and unconventional warfare. Vietnam can be viewed as a similar mixture and also as a war of mutual adjustment in Indochina combined with internal war in South Vietnam. North Korea in the late 1960s adopted the tactics of unconventional warfare in an attempt to penetrate and undermine South Korea. The complex events of mutual adjustment and internal conflict in Africa, coming to the fore in the late 1970s, are seen from Table 6–2 to have had a much earlier genesis in the independence struggles of the previous decade.

The interests of the major Western powers including the United states have collided with the interests of the Soviet Union, and in a few cases with those of China, wherever there have been large questions of political orientation, economic ties, access to resources, and advanced bases from which tactical forces can exercise localized influence, strategic threat, and deterrence. Whether the United States elects to participate or not, there appears to be no reason to expect that the use of military force in the world will be discontinued. And we can also expect that, whether we participate or not, military events will continue to shape our future.

Strategic Developments and Constraints

Although it may appear from the preceding data that the world has changed little from the years or centuries preceding the world wars, this is not true. There have been many developments in both the context and the implications of warfare that are unique to our age.

One of the most apparent and disturbing changes is the increased loss of human life that attends the destructivenes of modern conventional weapons. Figure 6–3 shows, with selected examples, some of the history of conflict in the century and a quarter from the end of the Napoleonic Wars through the two world wars, as compiled by Lewis Richardson[2] in terms of magnitudes of deadly quarrels. The magnitude of a war is defined by Richardson as the logarithm (to the base 10) of the total number of deaths, military and civilian, estimated to have been caused directly by the war. If Korea and Vietnam were to be shown on this graph in the same terms, they would fall about in the range marked (1). Thus, four of the seven largest wars that would be shown on such a revised graph, and all but one in which over a million lives were lost, have occurred in the twentieth century. They have all been more destructive of human life then the notoriously bloody

FIGURE 6–3: Some "Statistics of Deadly Quarrels"

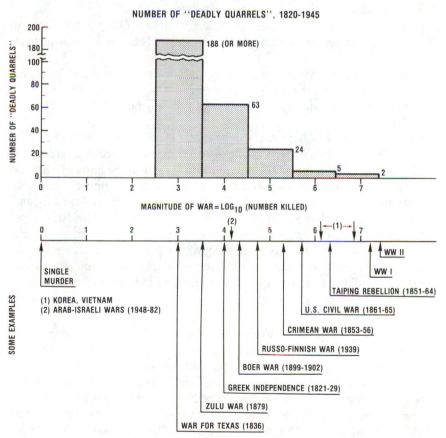

Source: Compiled and illustrated by this author from data given in L. F. Richardson, *Statistics of Deadly Quarrels* (Chicago: Quadrangle Books, 1960). Post-World War II wars, data estimated from contemporary news accounts.

1-19-83-6

American Civil War. This is not to say, however, that the importance or impact of a war to the surviving world population is related only to its magnitude on Richardson's scale. The position of the Arab-Israeli wars, shown by the mark at (2), indicates that wars of relatively small magnitude can sometimes have a profound effect on the course of world events.

What does make a war important? Obviously, it is all in the point of view. If one's country is about to be overrun and the government destroyed to one's detriment, improverishment, or death, the definition is different from what it would be if the same events were viewed by a stranger twelve thousand miles away. From the U.S. point of view, looking overseas, the importance of a war is defined by:

1. Its magnitude—if we are directly involved;
2. Our interests—if we or our major allies are identified with one side whose gain or loss becomes ours; and
3. Potential violations of important constraints—if they occur, they can lead to larger war or undesirable political and economic consequences.

A number of strategic conditions and developments in the post–World War II world have created the environment of constraints with which we must be concerned in considering the exercise of military power. These are listed in Table 6-3.

Most important has been the appearance of nuclear weapons and long-range delivery systems, which changed the implications of warfare to the extent that issues of immediate and literal survival of large parts of national populations are posed by the potential for their use. This immediately constraints the scope and purpose of military force used for political means. The avoidance of military clashes between the major powers obviously arises from the risks associated with escalation when both sides have nuclear weapons. This constraint has acted strongly in a number of cases we will examine later, under the heading of deterrence and escalation. At various times, it has allowed each superpower to defer to the other to avoid a confrontation, and it has given them a reason to bring a war between proxies to a close.

With nuclear weapons has come the growth of the so-called superstates: those with enough population and resources to be able to acquire large quantities of *both* the weapons *and* the delivery systems. At present, only the United States and the Soviet Union are in this category, and in the foreseeable future there are potentially only a few more: a unified Western Europe, Japan, and China. In addition, the OPEC states of the Near and Middle East wield enormous economic power. The presence of these major

**Table 6–3: STRATEGIC DEVELOPMENTS AND CONSTRAINTS
IN THE MODERN WORLD**

Important strategic developments since World War II

Nuclear weapons and delivery systems
Growth of the superstates
Global, asymmetric strategic patterns
War by proxy
Internal war as strategic war
Overseas bases of the superpowers
Export of sophisticated weapons
Two opposing ideological/political systems

Political constraints on military action by the superpowers
No military clash between superpowers
National borders are sacrosanct
Political/ideological affinity and conflict
Capability of the proxy
Popular support

power centers now demands that U.S. strategy be planned on a global rather than a regional scale.

All powers must be concerned about strategic attack on their lands by long-range weapons, but the United States and Japan must be more concerned with threats against supplies of resources and lines of communication, trade, and investment overseas than with threats of invasion. Japan has always recognized its dependence on imports—indeed, that recognition was one of the main reasons for Japan's entry into World War II. For the United States the phenomenon is a new one, since we had always deemed ourselves economically self-sufficient. Our imports have been growing apace, so that they have more than doubled relative to the size of our economy over the past twenty years. We now depend on imports for many critical materials such as titanium ore, bauxite for making aluminum, and some of the metals used in steel-making, such as chromium and cobalt, in addition to oil and natural gas;[3] the fuels have been only the most visible parts of this growing materials deficit. In addition, we are coming increasingly to depend on imports of machinery and other manufactured goods as other countries' ability to compete in these arenas grows. Again, although automobiles are the obvious example, our imports of other transportation equipment (such as subway cars) and machinery have increased over five times as fast as our GNP and over twice as fast as our exports in these areas. Although substitutions can mitigate our dependence in all these areas, these must be gradual, since they require heavy economic investment and can cause extensive economic stress. Moreover, we have found it in our interest to protect our allies' access to resources and trade, even in areas where we compete with them, in order to preserve the smooth functioning of an increasingly interdependent economic system that covers the globe.

Although the USSR may come soon to face similar resource problems,[4] thus far both that country and China have been concerned predominantly about a different set of problems. They are continental powers striving mightily to ensure the existence of friendly buffer states on their borders (except, of course, their mutual border). Western Europe, in many respects, shares both sets of problems. But the USSR, and China when her resources have permitted, have not been bashful about extending their efforts into other parts of the world when it appeared that to do so would help ensure their long-term influence and therefore safety. The collison of superpower interests in third countries has thus led to a unique twentieth-century emphasis on war by proxy. (By "proxy," used in this sense, we do not mean a puppet that slavishly carries out some master country's orders, but simply a nation engaging the interests, sympathies and support of a superpower in some way.) War by proxy operates on two levels, of course: the local level of the proxies, for whom the outcome is vital; and the level of the external supporters, whose interests in the outcome are much more limited, however important they might be. This being so, war by proxy must necessarily be limited insofar as the superpowers are concerned.

The combination of risk associated with war involving nuclear powers and the inability of democratic countries (or those aspiring to democratic forms of government) to keep a population totally suppressed by totalitarian methods has also encouraged the evolution of internal, unconventional war as a form of strategic conflict.[5] The reasons for considering it strategic are two, and they are interrelated: first, the initially inferior side can receive outside assistance from one of the major powers until it can win; and second, since that side will have been a proxy for that major power, the larger strategic balance will have changed.

The outside world has at least tacitly considered Soviet actions in Hungary and Czechoslovakia to have been taken within the recognized Soviet "empire." Other than these instances, Korea was the only case until the Soviet invasion of Afghanistan of an attempted total conquest of one country by another through direct invasion across a national border. From both the

Soviet and Chinese points of view, the price and risks in Korea were high. This was, one may postulate, one important reason for their falling back on support of internal wars or "wars of national liberation" as a means of extending their influence in the world. The ambiguity—Is there an insurgency or banditry? Is it conquest or civil war? Should we support the insurgents or the government? Is there Communist support for them or not? Does a mutual defense agreement apply or not?—precludes the kind of rapid response by the United States that the overt cross-border invasion of Korea elicited. Most of our alliance structure has been oriented toward the latter kind of situation.

After Korea, the world and one or both of the major nuclear powers have tended to try to stop any cross-border conventional conflict. Although Israeli attacks into other countries couldn't be stopped, they have been condemned by both East and West even when the larger interests of either might have been served by the outcome. The "occupied territories" are still identified separately in international negotiations and in the media. In the Iran-Iraq war neither West nor East has moved overtly to support either side. In Southeast Asia the United States chose to express support for a genocidal regime in Cambodia rather than appear to condone, even by silence, an invasion by communist Vietnam. Such history and the consolidation of Soviet and Western power in Europe, as well as Chinese power on the Asiatic mainland, have acted to make the pattern of borders emerging from World War II and the breakup of the Western empires, whatever its logic or illogic, virtually inviolable. Borders as they exist now are considered sacrosanct and not likely to be changed very much in the formal sense by *conventional conquest* for a long time to come. The breaking of this pattern by the Soviet invasion of Afghanistan was troubling precisely because it appeared to represent a loosening of this constraint by one of the powers tacitly pledged to uphold it. It has thus been condemned as an undesirable precedent. Even then, however, the USSR hasn't attempted to absorb Afghanistan as a Soviet Socialist Republic.

On the other hand, most borders in the free world are, in the late Gen. Charles Bonesteel's word, "porous." Although unconventional wars are much more difficult than conventional wars to fight, they are much more susceptible to outside support that does not carry severe political risks and penalties for closed societies capable of keeping the support clandestine.

Two additional developments have attended the superpowers' conflict, and they interact in a very complex way with those nations' struggle for security for themselves and for their allies. The first is the evolving overseas base structure, and the second is the worldwide diffusion of modern military capabilities.

The end of global war in 1945 found the United States and its British ally with a worldwide presence. Britain had expended all its strength and resources in the war and, when put to the test over the succeeding two decades, found that it could not and (perhaps in consequence) did not want to maintain that presence. The United States used the presence, however, as a means for building its worldwide military power structure to support the policy of containment of Communism in the USSR and China. The structure was indispensable to the prosecution of war in Korea and Southeast Asia and to the maintenance of our overseas deployment capability.

Gradually, partly in our own as well as Europe's reaction to the lengthy and unpopular conflict in Vietnam, and partly in response to the parallel growth of nationalistic self-assertion in the various host countries as a result of our failure in Indochina, the security of this U.S. base structure has been challenged. We have withdrawn from it in many ways, often despite the fact that our physical presence remains. Our base in Okinawa reverted to Japanese control, although we are still there, and Japan makes some of the rules about how we use it. Our bases in Japan proper have been subjects of periodic protests on various pretexts, such as visits by nuclear-powered or nuclear-armed ships. Germany protested the use of U.S. NATO-oriented airbases for resupply of Israel in 1973. Thailand saw no need for our continued military presence after 1975—it felt, in fact, that our presence would interfere with the business of making peace with its new Vietnamese neighbor. Both Spain and the Philippines have been driving hard bargains to accede to our continued presence. It thus becomes clear that no overseas base can be considered totally secure for purely U.S. purposes. Our presence at the bases must often be purchased, and our use of them depends on the host peoples' sympathy with our objectives in any particular action. This has been especially true of the contingent base structure we have tried to build in Kenya, Oman, and Saudi Arabia to improve our military access to the Persian Gulf region in case of a threat to our interests there.

Thus, even though long-range airlift and naval power can compensate in part for the loss of presence and staging capability in many places, our global presence has also been diminished. At the same time, the USSR is testing its ability to extend its presence, as we have seen in Angola, Ethiopia, South Yemen, the eastern Mediterranean, and (abortively) Portugal. Cam Ranh Bay in southern Vietnam is becoming a Soviet base for naval operations in the southwest Pacific. Some of these attempts have failed and some remain in doubt, but the general thrust of Soviet policy outside its borders has become apparent. However, events have shown that the Soviet base structure away from Europe is no more secure than ours. Shaky overseas bases for both superpowers have become a permanent feature of the political-military landscape for the 1980s and beyond.

Bases do not, of course, exist in isolation, but they emerge from association with allies among the great powers, with puppets, and with proxies in the Third World. Concomitant with these associations and of particular consequence in the Third World is the transfer of sophisticated military capability. The spread of Western (including Soviet) civilization was sparked by the total dominance of its military technology,[6] and the rise of imperial Japan in the 1930s and 1940s showed that this technology could be absorbed and turned effectively against the West. Table 6–4 lists some modern weapon types that the USSR has exported to its proxies; the United States and Western Europe export similar capabilities. The problems created for great-power exercise of military force by these exports have been noted in passing, in previous chapters. They created great difficulty for us in Vietnam. Terrorists have more than once been apprehended just before they attempted to launch SA-7 shoulder-fired missiles against airliners in Europe. As the Middle East wars have shown, this weaponry has brought the fast pace and great destructiveness of modern warfare within reach of many of the world's smaller political entities. The British faced mainly U.S. and French weaponry in their fight to retake the Falkland Islands from Argentina. Partly through the West's own efforts, its military technology no longer ensures its domination of the world.

Table 6–4: SOME IMPORTANT EXPORTED SOVIET CAPABILITIES

High-performance aircraft
Modern tanks
Anti-tank guided missiles
Battlefield and rear area air defense

    SA-2, 3, 6, 7, 8, 9—radar and infrared guided missiles

    ZSU-23–4 and other mobile, radar-directed guns

    Early warning, tracking, and fire-control radars

Anti-ship missiles

A strategic development to be noted finally, highly intangible but of great importance, has been the growth and maturation of two opposing political philosophies that, for reasons rational and irrational, have polarized the politics and economies of the world. These outlooks are interwoven with problems of military and economic strategy, giving ideological reasons for supporting one side or another in a third-country conflict and interacting with the constraints each side faces in the use of military force.

The behavior of the two superpowers is, of course, conditioned by their outlook on the world and by the view each has of what the other might do. Within the scope permitted by their internal freedoms and their relative control over the media, neither can, for very long, have a proxy of which its population and leadership disapprove, and the proxy must be a willing partner as well. Conversely, a superpower's attachment to a proxy for political and ideological reasons may transcend the logic of economics and political self-interest. For example, the United States supported Israel for many years virtually without question, for deep-seated reasons associated with our predominant religions, ideology, and culture. This attachment prevailed despite the obvious inroads by the USSR into the Middle East that this support encouraged. Only when our perception of the stakes was changed drastically, with the prospect that the other side might come to control an oil supply on which we were becoming more dependent, and the prospect of a serious breach with NATO Europe over the risks posed to their access to the same oil supply, did we change our policy to give more recognition to the Arab point of view.

Our freedom of action is inhibited by the nature of the support that our internal domestic politics will permit for a proxy. We saw in Vietnam and in the continuing difficulty we might have in supporting authoritarian regimes anywhere that the nature of our ally has a strong impact on the extent of support we can give. The Soviet Union, with a political system that gives it much more control over what its population learns about its government's actions in the outside world, is able to be at once much more flexible and more cynical in its military support of proxies. Short of getting its population directly and extensively involved in a war it must, perhaps, be more concerned about what the United States will do at the same time that it manipulates what its population thinks.

But ideological affinity must remain important to its leaders in their determination of the extent and kind of support they will allocate to other nations. Soviet behavior in many other areas suggests, for example, that if events were to shift Saudi orientation toward the USSR, the latter would not be completely happy unless it also attempted to change the monarchy to a Marxist regime— even at risk of losing its presence altogether. After clear signals that the United States would not interfere, the USSR used its Cuban puppet to establish a "fraternal" Marxist regime in Angola. It condemned French and Moroccan support for the Mobutu regime in Zaire. It freely abandoned the proxy and the base structure it had built in Moslem Somalia to play for bigger stakes in an Ethiopia newly turned Marxist,[7] again with reliance on the Cubans and support by the newly extended Soviet naval power. (Cuba is called a puppet rather than a proxy here because, despite the protestations of Fidel Castro to the contrary, we are increasingly seeing the Cubans in a role that violates the precepts of the Cuban revolution. These precepts call for support of "oppressed" peoples trying to liberate themselves.[8] Yet in Angola, Cubans were and are resisting the attempts of southern tribes and nationalist groups to avoid domination by the Soviet-supported governing faction.[9] In Ethiopia, at least for a time, they helped a radical military dictatorship resist an Eritrean independence movement of long standing, notwithstanding that Ethiopian rule was imposed on Eritrea as recently as 1950.[10])

If a major power commits some of its future world position to a proxy's success, it is helpful if the proxy is capable of fulfilling the role that may have been thrust upon it. The ability of the proxy to take care of itself obviously conditions what its sponsoring or supporting power can or needs to do. Both we (in Southeast Asia) and the Soviets (in the Middle East) have had the experience of supporting proxies that could not perform, and for each in its own way the result has been painful. However, although the Soviets may have lost treasure, prestige, and position, the United States has also expended the lives of its youth without a successful final result. Popular support in the United States for a war has proved impossible to sustain when there has been no clear ideological or cultural affinity with our ally and the threat to our interests has not been immediate. But a proxy whose capability has to be built step by step in the course of a war clearly makes for a long war; and after two such painful involvements in a generation, the prospect of a third acts to inhibit future military action by this country. This inhibition will be strongly reinforced by the War Powers Act of 1973, which raises any potentially unpopular involvement for public decision very early after it starts. The specter of the Act was raised even in connection with our noncombat-oriented deployment of Marines to help keep the peace in Lebanon in 1982. Any president must now assess his support before he acts to use military force in overseas actions if he does not want to risk repudiation at home and consequently much more severe losses on the world stage—a situation that makes for conservative action, to put it mildly.

The interacting U.S. ideological and political dynamics in localized wars, of which we may be a part but which are not central to our interest, have followed a pattern that is now easy to foresee. It happened in Korea and Vietnam, it arose very quickly in our support for El Salvador, and it appeared in the popular U.S. reaction to the Israeli seige of Beirut. In any such war the bulk of the population on the spot is probably not involved on either side, but it is affected by both. It is pressured, killed, displaced, impoverished. From the U.S. point of view, if we favor or assist one side, this becomes a matter of conscience associated with our cultural ethic. If U.S. troops are directly involved, we add our own suffering to that of the local populace. If the war is not settled quickly, we find that military means and human costs are escalating as the public, partly as a consequence, is revising its expectations downward. A war that ends quickly (as did the Israeli-Arab wars of 1956 and 1967 or our own move into the Dominican Republic) still raises all the questions and arguments and can have severe political repercussions. But the political conflicts take place after the *military* objectives have been achieved, and this inevitably gives them a limited and in many respects an ineffectual character. The situation is different if the war persists.

In that case, as the changing relationship between means and ends becomes increasingly apparent, segments of the public ask whether the price is worth the intended result. The latter changes its aspect as various groups answer in the negative. What would initially have been inconceivable comes increasingly to be accepted. France decided, for example, that it could survive without its Algerian "province" and gave up direct control over its other African colonies as well. Britain decided after Malaya, Suez, the Malaysian "confrontation," and fruitless war in Aden that it could survive without a military presence along its lines of communication to the Far East. The gradual British withdrawal into a defense of the home islands, associated with NATO, was thought to have encouraged Argentina to believe that Britain wouldn't resist a takeover of the Falkland or Malvinas islands. As the war in Vietnam wore on, large segments of public opinion in the United States concluded that we could live with a Communist-oriented Southeast Asia, as they had come to believe we could live with a Communist regime in China. But because *all* people have not accepted the implied changes in relationship between national interest and ideological interest, opinion becomes polarized around the issue of continuation or termination of the war.

As a result of this polarization, the country's view of its military also changes. The United States' military establishment would view it as simply cynical to fight wars without regard to winning or losing; our ethic and our training are competitive, patriotic, and oriented to success. If a war is long, if the original military objectives have not been achieved, if future political objectives have become fuzzy and subject to argument, and if the human and other costs of the war are increasing, then the civilians who question whether the war is worth the price come to view the military and their so-called conservative supporters as villains—the more so as pressure increases to escalate means to achieve the same or lesser ends. At the same time, the military come to view those who argue against continuing as not supporting them in a time of stress, when they have made sacrifices for the country, when they believe those sacrifices were necessary on behalf of the country's commitment, and when they need the country's support. The resulting severe political stresses have a profound effect on national politics and national defense in the long run. We are still, in 1982, feeling the effects of Vietnam in the public reaction to the need for increased expenditures to modernize our armed forces.

Shifting the burden of actual fighting to the countries directly concerned while we furnish military equipment and training, as proposed by the Nixon Doctrine, may make this conflict less acute; but it cannot be completely avoided. The commitment to support another country in a war commits our prestige and our future position to that country's success, in some measure. The consequences of failure in such a commitment, even where we are not directly involved, are best illustrated, perhaps, by the events in the world and in the United States following the 1949 Communist victory in mainland China, which was followed by two decades of recrimination over "who lost China." The same attitudes about ugly wars have been reflected in our reaction to the 1982 Israeli invasion of Lebanon. Since World War II, if a military conflict in which we have a stake hasn't been settled quickly the public taste for pursuing it has disappeared rapidly.

At some point, of course, if nearly all popular support for a war is lost it will be terminated. This process, too, can be arduous and painful, as the French learned after Algeria, as we learned in attempting to end both the Korean and the Vietnamese wars, and as both the Soviets in Afghanistan and the Israelis in Lebanon have been learning more recently. In the West each effort was and is being attended by profound political turmoil in the home country. The French suffered a near revolution. The end of our participation in Vietnam, after four years of attempted graceful disengagement, was particularly humiliating for the "helpless giant." Israel is suffering highly unpopular casualties to its occupation force and the humiliation of having been partly responsible for a massacre of Palestinian civilians in Beirut. The effects of continuing Soviet casualties in Afghanistan haven't been obvious, but if the numbers of killed and wounded continue to grow they would be difficult to hide altogether.

As a result of such reactions, it is clear, it would be foolhardy to project other U.S. use of military force for similar ends at an early date. But the world will not necessarily await our pleasure in posing the potential need, and indeed some nations may be moved to take advantage of our reluctance, as was the USSR in Angola and, perhaps, in Afghanistan. Moreover, as our current military buildup proceeds the visible signs of increasing military power could affect our attitude toward using it, at least in a political sense. All these possibilities will be considered later. Here, let us explore what the same history we have been considering shows us about deterrence and escalation in the context of less than strategic or all-out war.

On Deterrence and Escalation

The historical data on military actions since World War II that were presented earlier included some actions that did not involve shooting at all. These occurred at times and places, listed again in Table 6-5, when apparently the threat of military action by one side (or other adverse consequences, when the Soviet Union appeared to be preparing an invasion of Poland in 1981) was enough to discourage the other from making an attack, occupying territory, or intervening in an ongoing war, even though such moves may have been contemplated initially. (We must say "apparently," since obviously we cannot *know* what would have happened had the deterrent actions not taken place.)

With the frustration of Vietnam at a high pitch, we began to hear, again, in the early 1970s, about the military value of showing the flag,[11] the

Table 6-5: SITUATIONS OF APPARENTLY EFFECTIVE DETERRENCE

	Iran, 1946
	Taiwan, 1950—
	Lebanon, 1958
	Kuwait, 1961
	Cuban quarantine, 1962
(?)	Soviet-Chinese border, 1960
(?)	Jordan-Syria, 1970
(?)	Soviet intervention, Mideast, 1973
(?)	Poland, 1981

appearance of modest U.S. forces in an area where our interests are involved, as a reminder that we must be reckoned with. The revival of the concept has a wistful quality, a yearning for simpler days (say those between 1898 and 1959) when the world knew who we were and might easily how to our will. The tactic worked, at times when potential opposition was weak, disorganized, and easily subdued by battleships and Marine landing teams. It is still valuable as a visible symbol of our interest in a proxy state. But its value is suspect in most areas where we have serious concern about involvement in military conflict. Following are a few examples:

1. Neither the threat of our entry nor the presence of our forces nor the onset of bombing in the North deterred the North Vietnamese from pursuing their part of the war in South Vietnam.
2. Our presence in the eastern Mediterranean never deterred the Arabs from threatening or attacking Israel or the Soviets from resupplying them as the conflict progressed.
3. The same presence, and the NATO ties of both sides (and the presence of the Soviet flag nearby, one might add), did not deter the 1974 coup in Cyprus, inspired by the Greek dictatorship, or Turkey's subsequent invasion of the island.
4. The presence of our troops did not deter North Korea from its penetration campaign across the border to the South in the late 1960s; indeed, one of its objectives appears to have been to embarrass us by showing how vulnerable our troops were to such tactics.
5. The Indians did what they felt they had to do in Bangladesh and protested loudly at the entry of a few U.S. warships into the southern Indian Ocean.
6. Proximity to the sources of U.S. military power hasn't prevented apparent Cuban intervention in the conflicts in several Central American countries during the 1970s and early 1980s.

Thus, to use the presence of military force to stop a conflict, something more than simply showing the flag is needed, and what that is becomes apparent in reviewing more carefully the nature of the situations listed in Table 6–5.

Consider, first, all the cases except the possible Soviet invasion of Poland. It is of interest to observe that all these potential engagements would have involved conventional (rather than paramilitary or guerrilla) forces. We might note also that, although the forces on the spot that were ready to enter the conflict were small, they were backed up by buildups of forces that could enter the conflict early and more massively; and in some cases the opening moves included a strategic alert. This threat of much larger war, in which the parties who originally threatened military action saw it as obvious that the action might fail to attain its objectives and that a higher price would be paid than was warranted by the gains in prospect, clearly deterred the initiation of the engagement. We may note that, with some differences, deterrence here acts much as described in the theory of strategic war and that to achieve this effect the forces involved must be credible. That is, they must be available, ready, visible, and deployed with the apparent will to use them if necessary. For this kind of deterrence, as in the strategic case, the forces to fight the larger war must be prepared even though we hope not to use them.

The Poland case was different on the surface, of course. Given the stakes to the USSR, and the previous example of our inaction when it invaded Hungary and Czechoslovakia, it is unlikely that the Soviet Union anticipated that we would go to war over Poland in 1981. Nevertheless, there was the possibility of strong Polish resistance and the pattern of U.S. warnings combined with the example that (at least in the Soviet view) our reaction to Afghanistan was stronger than the USSR must have thought an action to secure its own borders warranted. All this, and our ability to marshal at least some degree of European support, must have persuaded the Soviets that unless the situation in Poland showed signs of getting out of control they had more to lose than to gain by direct occupation of the country to enforce their view of order. We can only guess at the lengths to which they went to avoid such a step, and at the Soviet/Polish government interactions that finally led to the imposition of martial law by Poland's own government. To the extent, however, that the Soviets went to some lengths to avoid an occupation of Poland, deterrence may be said to have worked in this case in much the same manner as it did in the more directly military confrontations listed in Table 6–5.

Unconventional war, as in Vietnam, Central America, southern Africa, or the many other conflicts of this kind listed in tables 6–1 and 6–2, presents a different picture. A characteristic of unconventional or revolutionary war is that a small force believes that by its techniques of organization, social and political action, and military doctrines it can defeat the much larger, established, conventional forces arrayed against it. There have been many historical instances when this in fact came to pass, or nearly did, and the required high force ratio against guerrillas testified to the potency of the strategy.[12] Since the insurgent side selects a strategy *designed* to meet its situation and believes it has selected the right time to start, deterrence cannot work because no credible threat can be posed against the initiators. This is independent of whether the insurgents ultimately win or lose—the point is, they start. So revolutionary warfare cannot be deterred, though it might ultimately be suppressed. (And this illustrates another reason why it has been so suitable as a chosen instrument of conflict by the USSR and the People's

Republic of China. It also illustrates why the Soviet Union has been having such a difficult time establishing firm control in Afghanistan.)

Escalation may be viewed as an attempt at deterrence during, rather than before, a conflict. Thus, deterrence and escalation go together as two sides of the same coin. And, just as deterrence of localized war may fail, so may escalation fail. Two examples of such failure are of interest: Korea and Vietnam.

Our entry into Korea and our buildup, through the march to the Yalu, were escalation on our part and were ultimately highly successful against the North Koreans. Chinese entry was a counterescalation that we chose not to try to top. In making this choice for the nation, Truman set the stage for the conflict between himself and MacArthur (i.e., between civilian and military views of the balance between means and ends that we discussed earlier). This was the first modern, major political conflict in the United States over the use of limited military force for ends only indirectly related to our national security and survival.

In Vietnam, our escalation was by any standards large, although it took place over some years. Ground forces went from about two hundred thousand South Vietnamese forces in 1963 to total "Free World Forces," including several hundred thousand U.S. troops, of a million or more in 1966. Air sorties in the theater, few in 1963, came to be numbered in the thousands annually over the same period. A large, varied, and powerful naval force was deployed against North Vietnam, off the South Vietnamese coast, and along the waterways of the Mekong Delta. To counter these actions the Communists, who had primarily guerrilla forces in 1963, increased their numbers to about two hundred fifty thousand, including Viet Cong "Main Force" battalions and North Vietnamese divisional forces. Because of the nature of the war they fought, this was enough to prevent our escalation from being decisive.

For the South Vietnamese and their allies, including the United States, to have overwhelmed the Communists by, say, increasing the ground force ratio to about the 10 : 1 rule of thumb for counterguerrilla warfare would have required nearly another two million men, a substantial fraction of them from the United States. This was a step we were not willing to take (as a nation), according to our collective view of the objectives and their worth. There would have been a much larger risk of China's entry into the war. (Even though China and Vietnam have long been enemies, as reflected in their subsequent border clash, the concern at the time was that China would enter the war on North Vietnam's side rather than see a massive U.S. force established on its southern border.) And such a large further escalation might not have been practicable in the time we felt we had available and under the constraints in matching means and ends that we felt, at the time, were reasonable. That is, fearful of losing a public support that was tenuous even at the best of times, President Johnson had decided to fight the war short of even partial national mobilization. (The nation may have resisted such mobilization. But this would simply have shown much earlier, and perhaps less painfully in the long run, where the American people drew the line in pursuing this particular military effort.)

These figures and events are cited to make the point that our escalation in Vietnam was not nearly so small as we sometimes seem to believe. Nor was the enemy's counterescalation so large. In both cases, the sides moved what they thought was enough, and until we disengaged it did not really do the job for either side.

These considerations (and the history of the other wars listed in Table 6–1) indicate that escalation works better for deterrence or toward a decisive outcome in a small war than in a large one. If the other side has the opportunity, the ability, the time, and the will to frustrate the initial move by counterescalation, escalation will not work. And if escalation does not use appropriate forces, it will not work. For example, the initial steps of escalation in Korea and Vietnam, which failed, used air power alone. As noted in Chapter 3, this could affect the ground action only in limited ways.

It appears, then, that the following rule about escalation emerges: If it cannot be shown in advance that escalation of a certain amount and kind will achieve the desired result, it is better not to escalate. It is better to lose small in one set of moves of a continuing conflict of worldwide proportions (i.e., the struggle for position among the superpowers) than to lose big. Conversely, if the stakes are high enough, the escalation should be big enough. Of course, the questions of how much is enough, of whether the force can be brought to bear in time, of whether the use of force will work, and of whether it is desirable are what the crucial arguments in the use of force to achieve political objectives in parts of the world remote from our shores are all about. It might be argued that we do not have the choice of deciding whether to escalate if matters of fundamental principle are involved, as in Korea and Vietnam. But similar principles operated in Hungary in 1956 and in Czechoslovakia in 1968. Both times we thought it prudent not to intervene. These examples illustrate that even if principles close to our national ethos are affected, the decision to escalate is not automatic.

Commitments and Prospects

Of the worldwide structure of U.S. military commitments that was built during the years of cold war and containment of Soviet and Chinese Communism,[13] only a few pieces have survived the bitterness and disillusion of Vietnam in any practical sense. These include alliances with NATO, Japan,

Israel, Korea, Australia, and New Zealand. Although the potential for conflict in the world that could affect us indirectly is much wider, we have firmly promised our protection by direct military involvement only to these countries. More recently, in President Carter's declarations of 1980, we have stated that the preservation of our and our allies' access to the resources of the Persian Gulf region is in our national interest, to the point of using military force to protect them if necessary. It is not obvious that the use of military force by the United States might be required in any of these areas, although the strength, commitment, and presence that would deter such conflict in these countries need continuously to be shown. The fears of the 1960s that our world support would be stripped away by "wars of national liberation"—viewed as a Communist-supplied euphemism for indirect Communist conquest—seem to many, in the aftermath of Vietnam, naive in the extreme. In fact, regardless of the arguments about whether it ever did exist, the perceived Communist monolith is no more. Even the postwar allies of Southeast Asia—Cambodia, Vietnam, and China—have been at each other's throats. The world is not the same as the one in which the structure of U.S. alliances and commitments was made.

With the general drift toward rapprochement between the United States and the People's Republic of China, uncertain as it must be until the mainland and Taiwan Chinese themselves make up their differences and hostility, the Soviet Union is left as the major rival state that we see threatening our interests and those of our allies. This is not to say that all would be peace and tranquility in the world if the Soviet Union were to cease trying to change the "correlation of forces" in its favor. Events in the eastern Mediterranian, the Persian Gulf region, southern Africa, the Caribbean basin, and even the South Atlantic attest to that. But we might feel that without Soviet pressure and mischief-making in these areas, and without the Soviet military buildup opposing Western Europe, the world would be a simpler place, militarily. For one thing, we and our allies could enforce a degree of world order with smaller military force. In addition, the intercontinental forces that help insure the safety of our own territory are neither as massive nor as complex as the general purpose forces we must maintain to insure the safety of our allies, our overseas interests, and our connections to them. Thus the USSR drives both the perception and the actuality of any threat to all these U.S. connections and vital interests.

It is a mistake, however, to view the Soviet "threat" as either simple or one-dimensional. It is highly complex and interacts strongly with our own and our allies' behavior in the military as well as the economic and political spheres. This doesn't necessarily mean that this behavior must include military action, although that possibility must always be a driving factor in the Soviets' view of their own security. It does, however, involve our own and our allies' military posture. That, in turn, must be said to be driven at present by two main concerns: the defense of Western Europe, and the defense of our own and our allies' interests elsewhere. The first involves the acquisition of massive land and air forces, with naval augmentation and protection of the sea lines of communication to Europe. There is also the possibility of broader naval action on the northern and southern flanks of Europe around Scandinavia and in the Mediterranean. The second concern appears to be pushing us toward what might be called an "augmented naval strategy"—a strategy of reliance on naval (including Marine) forces for military presence and power, with extensive land-based tactical air power and some ground forces deployable to potential areas of conflict. These aspects of our worldwide position, strategy, and commitments to use military power, for deterrrence and to protect our diverse interests by force if necessary, will be examined in the next three chapters.

The Soviet Union as "Threat"

We have seen in Chapter 6 that the post-Vietnam mood of the U.S. people and the absence of a clear polarization of issues directly threatening the United States make major involvement of our military forces in overseas combat operations, as in Korea or Vietnam, highly unlikely in the near future—over the 1980s, perhaps, in the absence of strong provocation. We have thus concentrated our attention on the military problems closest to our most vital interests, and these are not separable from our interactions in all spheres with the USSR.

These interactions, though worldwide, focused in Europe during the 1970s, and except for the Vietnam years they have been focused there since the 1950s. An agreement among the NATO nations to increase defense spending by 3 percent annually and the beginnings of a Long Term Defense Program to strengthen Europe's defenses were major initiatives of the Carter administration. There was also an attempt to reduce U.S. forces in the Far East, symbolized by the withdrawal of some units of the U.S. Second Division from South Korea. This move to turn Korean ground defense back to the Koreans was arrested early. Cubans in Africa, the Iranian revolution, Soviet use of the naval base abandoned by the United States at Cam Ranh Bay on the south central coast of Vietnam, and the Soviet invasion of Afghanistan all served to remind us that we couldn't concentrate our defense attention on Europe to the exclusion of events elsewhere in the world. The Carter administration enunciated a major new commitment—the "Carter Doctrine"—and began the planning for rapidly deployable forces to protect our interest in the Persian Gulf area. There was also a somewhat intensified discussion of the need for Japan to contribute more to its own defense. The Reagan administration, on taking office, reinforced these beginnings. In addition, much greater emphasis was given to building up the Navy. This accentuated further the military concern and orientation of our forces toward areas other than Europe. As at the same time the zig-zag course of rapprochement with the People's Republic of China continued, and China has not been viewed as threatening our interests since we withdrew from Vietman, all these actions to increase our military strength have mainly the USSR in view as the major opposing military power. This pattern in the general purpose force area is, of course, only part of a larger pattern involving the renewal and enhancement of the theater nuclear forces we have committed to Europe's defense and the strengthening of our strategic, intercontinental nuclear forces. Both of these actions also view the USSR as the only significant opponent.

Our military expansion as we enter the 1980s is based on the judgment that we have become militarily weaker vis-a-vis the USSR in all areas than is safe for our vital national interest and that of our allies. This positon was clearly stated by President Reagan in a speech to the nation on November 22, 1982. In the next two chapters we will examine the military aspects of this Soviet threat, with special attention to the impact of the new military technology on our relative strengths and capabilities. Here, however, we shall examine a different question: What is the nature of the "Soviet threat"? Do we really face the danger of a Soviet attempt to overrun Europe or sink our Navy, or is there some more complex and subtle underlying problem?

Looking East Toward the USSR

The North Atlantic Treaty states that an attack on one country of the alliance would represent an attack on all, and each country will respond accordingly.[1] The reason for the alliance was the perceived threat of Soviet expansion—a perception reinforced by Soviet consolidation of control over Eastern Europe after World War II, the Berlin blockade, and Korea. These events found the United States essentially disarmed (except for the very important fact of the possession of the atomic bomb) and Western Europe still prostrate from the war. Today, Europe is far from prostrate. The NATO countries of Europe taken together compose an economic unit about as populous and with almost as much gross national product as the United States. The view of the threat from the East has been modified, but it has not gone away.

The Soviet Union consolidated its hold over Eastern Europe after World War II in order to meet its need for a strong and deep buffer zone between the German and Soviet heartlands. It responded to the entry of the Federal Republic of Germany into NATO in 1955 by creating the Warsaw Pact. The Pact establishes in Soviet eyes the basis for a defense against potentially aggressive actions by NATO. It also gives the USSR a reason to station troops in countries where they may be needed to enforce internal security and prevent political and military developments potentially hostile to the Soviet Union.

In many ways through the years, the USSR has continued to give indications that it will hold what it has, that it will expand where it can, and that the West and NATO must still be on guard. It has applied pressure against Yugoslavia, reacted militarily to events in Hungary and Czechoslovakia, massed troops on Poland's borders, and prior to the 1971 Four-Power Agreement and the subsequent accord between East and West Germany it persistently tested allied steadfastness in Berlin. It has stimulated and supported countries on the Arab side of the wars with Israel. It invaded and has tried to subdue the population of Afghanistan. It has established a foothold in the Horn of Africa (using Somalia or Ethiopia as it deems appropriate and finds possible at specific times) and replaced Britain as the colonial occupier of the southwest corner of the Arabian Peninsula. Probes into southern Africa persist. The USSR attempted to "capture" the revolution in Portugal. Its forces in Europe, the Far East, and at sea have grown and have been strengthened and broadened in capability.

NATO's perception of risk has changed, however, as divergences among the NATO countries' economic and political problems and outlooks have evolved through the years. The United States and NATO military authorities, as well as some NATO governments, still perceive a serious Soviet military threat to Western Europe. However, a number of developments have caused Western Europe to give questions of national policy and well-being precedence over concern about the possibility of a Soviet attack:

1. The creation and consolidation of the European Economic Community (EEC);
2. France's need to build up her sense of independence and nationhood after two disastrous post–World War II defeats, in Indochina and Algeria;
3. The growth of West Germany as a major economic power and subsequent economic rivalry between France and Germany for a commanding role in the Western European economy;
4. Britain's gradual decline as an economic and military power;
5. Italy's continual political morass, with the growth of Communist strength threatening periodically to increase political divisions in NATO;
6. The revival of ancient mutual rivalries in Greece and Turkey;
7. U.S. preoccupation throughout the 1960s and 1970s with the involvement in Vietnam;
8. The United States' need to come to terms with the Soviet Union over strategic arms;
9. The divergence between U.S. needs and policies in the Middle East and those of the EEC, as dependence of Europe and the United States on Arab oil has increased;
10. The immediate problems of recession and inflation in the 1970s and early 1980s.

Some additional recent developments have exacerbated the divisive effects of these events and trends. Among them have been the dissension in Europe over U.S. and NATO plans to deploy long-range theater nuclear systems in Europe; disagreements within the alliance over trade with the USSR, exemplified by the conflict over the construction of the Soviet natural gas pipeline and projected Soviet gas sales to Western Europe; and heightened economic competition between the United States and European countries in such high-technology areas as computers, armaments, and commercial transport aircraft.

The Reagan administration's conventional force buildup has, of necessity, had to accentuate the threatening nature of growing Soviet military strength. Conversely, the USSR has gone to great pains to portray the United States as an aggressive power threatening to itself as well as to others in the world.[2] But it has not included Western Europe as part of its portrayal of the threat to the peace. The Soviets have appeared to be attempting to minimize any cause for increasing European concerns about Soviet intentions. Although their policies on a worldwide basis have been expansionist, there are countervailing perceptions that lead Europeans to believe that the chance of an attack on Western Europe is remote (although they continue to express concern about the Soviet military buildup). For one thing, Soviet fears of German resurgence and belligerence must be allayed by the firm interlocking of Germany with NATO defensive plans. The West German army is not even organized as a coherent whole but has its major combat formations interspersed among those of the other NATO allies.[3] The United States retains control of nuclear warheads on German soil. Politically, the Soviet Union has given every indication that it views the 1971 Berlin Agreements and the 1975 Helsinki accord as ratifying the division of Europe, with Soviet and U.S. spheres of influence as they emerged from World War II.[4] Soviet actions in Hungary and Czechoslovakia have tended to be viewed in the West as defensive—intended to maintain the integrity of Russia's Eastern European buffer zone. Indeed, the United States had to persuade Western Europe to take a firm stance in 1981 vis-a-vis the possibility of a Soviet invasion of Poland, suggesting that this view of Soviet interests and actions in Eastern Europe has persisted in the West until the present.

Elsewhere, the USSR has in many ways been circumspect. She has not committed Soviet forces even where, as in the Middle East in 1973, such commitment might have helped save a major element of policy carefully built over a long period. She has used proxies rather than her own forces in areas where there has been a clear opening, such as in Angola. The attempt was made by the USSR to portray her actions in Afghanistan as resulting from a localized border problem, and European reactions suggested that perhaps this argument was being accepted. At the same time, until the strong U.S.

reaction to Afghanistan the Soviet Union attempted to encourage openings to the United States and Western Europe to improve trade, gain the advantages of Western civilian technology, and purchase agricultural products to meet recurring shortages at home. Whether these overtures are sincere or are part of the Leninist approach of *using* capitalism to help destroy it—and there must be some elements of both involved—the fact that Soviet self-interest requires a lowering of hostility toward Western Europe is noticed there and is encouraged by those who seek economic and political gain from the process. The furor over the gas pipeline and purchases showed that despite the increasing hostility between the United States and the USSR the Soviet policy of detente toward Europe has persisted. This is not surprising, as it gives the USSR yet another lever to try to pry the NATO alliance apart.

In addition, we must remind ourselves that viewed objectively the military forces arrayed in defense of Western Europe are not inconsiderable, as we shall see in the next chapter. Although their strength has been eroded in many areas in recent years, they have gained strength in other areas, especially in the technical capability of major weapon systems. Moreover, there remains the backup of nuclear deterrents, both in the theater and in the U.S. strategic forces. Although, as we shall see, the Warsaw Pact's conventional forces in Europe are and remain much stronger than NATO's, if the alliance pays modest attention to maintaining its strength its defense would not look like a pushover from the other side. If it wanted to attack Western Europe, the Soviet Union would have to consider the military array against it, and its own vulnerabilites in Eastern Europe, very carefully.[5]

Thus, for many reasons, the NATO European population has had ample cause to doubt the immediacy of the threat of an attack by the Soviet Union and the Warsaw Pact. In summary, these reasons include Soviet revealed behavior, the absence of stimuli to Soviet belligerence in Western European policies, centrifugal political and economic developments in the Western alliance, economic developments in the USSR, and the alignment of potentially formidable military power in NATO's defense. As the popular view of such a threat has receded, the nations of the alliance have become increasingly immersed in immediate and internal problems that must be resolved because they are present and pressing, not future and potential.

Nevertheless, Soviet military strength has been growing steadily. The past several years have seen a major modernization of Soviet ground forces, the transformation of their tactical air forces from a purely defensive to a largely offensive posture, and the growth of impressive "deep-water" Soviet maritime power. The USSR continues to reaffirm its belief in the inevitability of Communist victory. Whenever openings appear, they are probed aggressively. All this suggests that the prospect that Soviet policies are expansionist and its forces are aggressively oriented cannot be ignored and that the possibility of a Soviet attack against NATO Europe cannot be dismissed. NATO as a corporate body continues to affirm this view, as in the communique from the June 1976 NATO defense ministers' meeting;

> Ministers were . . . given a briefing on recent increases in the military strength of the Warsaw Pact and voiced their concern that this continues to grow beyond levels justified for defensive purposes. They devoted particular attention to the implications of the increased emphasis on offensive capabilities in the Pact forces, especially air forces. . . . [They] took note with concern of the substantial advances in size and effectiveness achieved during recent years in every sector of Soviet military capabilities, confirming a clear potential to use military force, directly or indirectly, or the threat of such force, world wide.

President Carter repeated these concerns about the apparently offensive orientation of Soviet forces in Europe, in 1978 talks at Wake Forest University and the U.S. Naval Academy. General Bernard Rogers, NATO military commander, remarked in a Summer 1982 article in *Foreign Affairs* that Soviet "expansionism has been inspired partly by ideology but also by increasing Soviet confidence in the ascendancy of their arms and their ability to use military power for political gain". The drift of Soviet military power and the continuing view of its menace by Western leaders, as distinct from the European population, are clear.

The argument can be and repeatedly has been made, although it cannot be proved because history does not reveal its alternatives, that continuing peace and the subsidence or quiescence of the threat to Western Europe that existed during the successive Berlin crises from 1949 to 1961 are related to the presence of strong defense forces in Europe and in the United States. Now, trends in both technology and numbers suggest a change in the relationships and balance that have existed between Warsaw Pact and NATO forces, heightening the uneasiness expressed above. In addition, Soviet military and quasi-military activity in other parts of the world has become bolder and more open, contributing to this concern.

By a combination of apparent strategic planning and serendipity resulting from Soviet opportunism in diverse geographic areas, the USSR has come to exercise a significant measure of control in an arc of countries far to the south and east of Europe: Angola, Ethiopia, South Yemen, and Afghanistan (see Figure 7-1). The presence in Angola, exercised for the USSR mainly by Cuba, offers both a centrally located warm-water base for operations into the Atlantic and a land base for support of destabilizing insurgency in southern Africa. Southern Africa contains important parts of the West's mineral, gold, and diamond supplies, and it lies athwart the trade routes from the Indian Ocean to the West. The bases in Ethiopia and South Yemen at

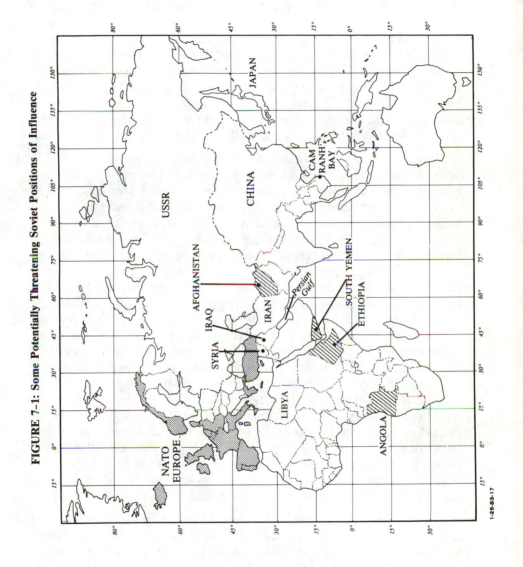

FIGURE 7-1: Some Potentially Threatening Soviet Positions of Influence

1-25-83-17

once help the Soviet Union secure its own passage from the Red Sea to the Indian Ocean, place it in a position to deny such passage to others, and provide a springboard for activities to destabilize both southern Africa and the Arabian Peninsula. The invasion of Afghanistan could have started as a move to secure the Soviet border in an area where there was some risk that the peoples of western China and the south central USSR might have found some affinity from the distant historical past. Clearly, if Soviet troops succeed in truly "pacifying" Afghanistan they would be in an excellent position to influence policies in both Iran and Pakistan by the persuasive force of their physical presence. They would also be well situated to foment rebellion in Baluchistan and attempt to dominate the strip of land from Kashmir to the Indian Ocean, even without marching their own troops through the areas.

Even though the Soviet Union may not use this presence for overt hostile purposes now, the presence is clearly threatening to much of the Western European and Japanese fuel supply in a time of crisis. This is potentially the kind of "soft underbelly" strategy Churchill used to talk about in the context of the European continent alone, but expanded to hemispheric proportions. In addition, even though revolutionary events in Iran and the Iran-Iraq war have caused the USSR to draw back into a period of watchful waiting, prior Soviet policy was clearly to exert a strong political influence in both those countries. Historically the countries have nourished a healthy suspicion of the USSR, and they have in general been standoffish even while buying Soviet arms and equipment. However, they are susceptible to pressure as they exhaust themselves in mutual conflict and the Soviet presence encroaches from both Afghanistan and Syria as well as from the USSR itself. The Soviet presence in Libya and extensive arms sales to that country have afforded the USSR a weak ally but also the opportunity for a future base area astride one of the most important U.S. and European access routes to the Middle East, the short route through the Mediterranean. Similarly, an increasing Soviet naval presence at Cam Ranh Bay would permit the USSR to operate more easily against the important U.S. bases in the Philippines as well as against another part of the critical oil routes to Japan. From this position it could also threaten the southern route from the United States to Japan and Korea in case of war and the denial of the North Pacific route.

It is also necessary to note the value of Cuba as a source of political destabilization in the Caribbean basin and possibly elsewhere in Latin America and as a potential Soviet fleet and submarine base area at a time of increased tension. Although we might believe that such a presence close to the source of our own military power would be easy to destroy if necessary, this would require extensive military forces at a time when those forces would probably be needed elsewhere.

It isn't necessary to posit a deliberate and totally-successful strategy of malevolent Soviet expansion to see that the distribution of Soviet military presence places the USSR in a position to do serious damage both to the connections among the U.S. and our allies and to the allies' fuel lifelines in a conflict short of all-out war. It isn't necessary to posit a Soviet plan for deliberate aggression to believe that the buiding of this set of interrelated strategic positions has been part of Soviet world strategy. By a judicious combination of choosing target countries and seizing opportunities, the Soviet Union has advanced and strengthened its position on the world chessboard at the expense of our own. We will examine the value of these gains for it after examining its possible motivations somewhat more closely.

Why Would the USSR Go to War?

War comes not from the mere existence of military forces but from political and economic dynamics that can ultimately lead to military action by accident or by design. To consider whether the necessary Western defense investments, which are driven in large measure by concern over potential Soviet aggression, can be fully justified we must examine why the Soviet Union might go to war.

One obvious reason for the USSR to go to war, at least in Europe, would be that she felt threatened. Soviet international policies have always been concerned, among other matters, with the defense of the USSR. The main threats are seen from Russia to lie primarily in the United States and the West and secondarily in China. The memory of the Great Patriotic War, as the Soviets call World War II, remains strong, and the one certainty in Churchill's "riddle wrapped in a mystery inside an enigma" is that the Soviets are determined to avoid such a war in the future or, if it comes, to win it quickly and not on Soviet soil.[6]

Part of this Soviet defensive policy has been to divide NATO, and it can be argued that this policy is succeeding, if not always through Soviet efforts alone. The recent absence of Soviet actions directly threatening NATO has made it easy for even the closely interacting nations of the Central and Northern Regions to pursue their individual political and economic policies without the inhibitions or forces for unity that would be engendered by an external menace. The drive for French independence from what in France's view was the U.S. tendency to dominate Europe began the dissolution of the kind of military and political coherence that would be necessary for NATO to undertake a war of aggression if it wanted to. The divisions between Europe and the United States over Middle Eastern policy and trade among themselves and with the USSR have also militated against such coherence. Additionally, of course, Soviet Middle Eastern policies with regard to both the Arab nations and Cyprus have, by design or by fallout, helped to foster the divisions. The

1982 test of wills between the United States and Western Europe over the Soviet gas pipeline exacerbated the growing differences among the NATO allies.

Although the Soviet probe into Portugal failed, the gradually increasing strength of French and Italian Communism has from time to time heightened the level of political anxiety within NATO. Although the potential role of Eurocommunism has been a subject for debate, the sensitivity about the question was illustrated by the blunt statements regarding the possible consequences of Communist participation in an Italian government made in 1976 by Secretary of State Henry Kissinger and West German Prime Minister Helmut Schmidt and reaffirmed by the Carter administration in early 1978.[7] Although in 1983 a Communist accession to power in Italy seems much less likely than it did then, the earlier strong reaction showed how near to the surface the anxiety is. Similar concerns were expressed, although not as openly, when the winning Mitterand coalition in the last French election included the French Communist party for a time. Greece has been drifting out of the alliance in the manner of France, embittered over the successful partition of Cyprus by Turkey and its unrequited claims to the Aegean islands near the Turkish coast. U.S. pressures on Turkey over Cyprus affected Turkey's role in NATO, which was in any case not being helped by the rivalry with Greece. Taken together with NATO's relative military weakness vis-a-vis the Warsaw Pact in conventional forces, these political developments do not make for a NATO structure that would currently appear threatening to the USSR.

Could this picture change? The greatest Soviet fear, from the Soviet's own expressions, has been of potential German "revanchism"—fear that West Germany will attempt reunification with East Germany by force.[8] Willy Brandt's *Ostpolitik*, continued in quieter fashion by Helmut Schmidt and not denied by the successor Kohl government, and the Helsinki accords were designed at least in part to alleviate such fears. It is obvious to the West Germans that they do not have the strength, military and economic, to undertake such action in defiance of Soviet opposition. Moreover, it is obvious from the outside that, although the hope of peaceful reunification must remain alive, the East German state has been going its own way and would be unlikely, without a major social and political upheaval, to welcome reunification on terms that would be acceptable to the West. Thus, from the point of view of both NATO and the Warsaw Pact it should be apparent that there is little prospect of a war over Germany that would threaten Soviet security.

What about an accidental war? This could occur if the USSR feels threatened even though it isn't. Periodically, in the Eastern European countries, there have been political developments calling, in local eyes, for military action to maintain stability—sometimes by the Soviets (Hungary, Czechoslovakia), sometimes by indigenous forces (in East Germany and twice in Poland). The enunciation of the Brezhnev Doctrine that once a nation (presumably one bordering on the USSR) is Communist it must stay Communist is really an admission that the Soviet Union couldn't feel secure any other way. This was made clear during the 1980–81 troubles in Poland, when the potential for a Soviet invasion of Poland hung on whether the Solidarity trade union would be allowed to become a recognized political force or whether there would be a strike on the railways connecting Russia with East Germany through Poland.

It is possible to imagine that events like those in Poland could occur in East Germany in a way that came to involve West Germany. Possibly the stakes and the issues could isolate West Germany politically; action by Germany alone might then be deterred, but NATO would be split. The realization of the potential damage to the West might then involve the United States, other NATO Central Region countries, and, gradually or suddenly, most or all of NATO. Although we cannot be specific about the nature of such events, history is replete with the unexpected, and we cannot rule these events out.

We cannot, also, rule out the possibility that Western policies could develop in a manner that would appear to threaten the security of the USSR. For example, as we noted in Chapter 2, the West decided to deploy a modernized force of intermediate-range ground-launched cruise missiles (GLCM) and Pershing II ballistic missiles in Western Europe as a counterweight to the growing force of Soviet SS-20s aimed at Western Europe. To the West this deployment seemed defensive. But the USSR, in the "negotiations" being conducted through the media, immediately stated that this would create a new strategic situation because now there would be weapons on *European* soil that could deliver nuclear warheads against Soviet territory. Before the GLCM and Pershing II decisions, Western nuclear systems on the ground in Europe could reach Soviet forces and bases in Eastern Europe only. Soviet statements subsequently suggested that with the short flight times of Pershing II (less than ten minutes) they would have to adopt a launch-on-warning strategy. They also were said to have offered to give up all SS-20 (and earlier SS-4/5) positions facing Europe except the number needed to counterbalance the British and French fleet ballistic missile submarine forces and the French land-based IRBMs if the United States would forego its proposed intermediate-range nuclear force (INF) deployment. This would appear to be a bargaining ploy, since the Soviet Union also has such submarines that can threaten Western Europe. Britain, France, and the United States rejected the idea, on the basis that the European-owned national deterrent forces are not at issue in these U.S. negotiations with the USSR.

Underlying this rejection is the Western notion that the SS-20s give the Soviet Union an advantage in the nuclear forces facing Europe and that it is important to have a U.S. force *in Europe* to counterbalance them, for reasons we will explore in the next chapter. It is possible, however, that by Soviet logic there is, indeed, no political separation among the U.S., British, and French nuclear forces facing them—that they fear a NATO that in their view is more unified in purpose and potential aggressiveness than we know it to be. In that case their response to the deployment of a NATO INF may indeed be destabilizing and could heighten the chance of an accidental war. (This reasoning doesn't argue against deploying the INF; it simply recognizes a possibility that must be faced in deciding to do so.)

From all this it is clearly possible that, although the West is in its own view neither strong enough nor united enough be aggressive, the Soviet Union could nevertheless feel the need to go to war to protect itself in certain circumstances. The volatility of the situation and the seriousness of the events that would lead the USSR to such a decision would have to be much greater if NATO'S military forces, including both the conventional and the nuclear deterrents, were strong than if they were weak. We shall examine the political and deterrent nature of NATO's military forces in more detail in the next chapter.

This brings us to the other major possibility that could lead to East-West war in Europe: The USSR might be tempted, after it has built great military strength for purely defensive reasons, to use that strength aggressively.

Although the West is concerned that the current military buildup and modernization by the Soviet Union appear to be more than are needed for a purely defensive strategy, we really have no idea of how much is enough in Soviet eyes. The Soviet Union could view the Western technological lead, the continual appearance of advanced Western weapon systems, the West's tactical and theater nuclear systems, and the West's enormous productive capacity, with a potential for turning out far more armaments than appear to be emerging from production now, as much more threatening than the West views all these conditions. U.S. attempts to encourage a buildup of Japanese defense forces and hints about selling arms to the People's Republic of China would exacerbate these views. The point at which the USSR feels it has enough strength may then be much higher than the point at which we would think so. The Soviet Union may well believe, as does Israel, that security lies not in military parity with its opponents but in outright and obvious military superiority over them. That this may be so was suggested by the late Marshal A.A. Grechko, former Soviet defense minister:

> [T]he aggressive nature of imperialism has not changed and as long as it exists, the threat of a new world war also persists. And there is no other guarantee

. . . against its outbreak than strengthening the economic and defense might of the USSR and . . . raising the combat power of the Soviet Armed Forces and of other fraternal armies.[9]

Secretary General Leonid Brezhnev stated at the Twenty-fifth Congress of the Soviet Communist Party, in the spring of 1976,

> There is no Soviet threat either to the West or to the East . . . . The Soviet Union does not have the slightest intention of attacking anyone. The Soviet Union does not need war.[10]

At Brezhnev's funeral, the new Party Chairman Yuri Andropov said,

> In the complicated international situation when the forces of imperialism are trying to push the peoples onto the road of hostility and military confrontation, the party and the state will firmly uphold the vital interests of our homeland, and maintain great vigilance and readiness to give a crushing rebuff to any attempt at aggression.[11]

This continues the defensive tone of the previous statements. On the face of it there seems no reason to interpret the Soviet *political* signals in this area as being excessively warlike.

It is also possible to speculate that the economic and political controls over the armed forces that act in the West are considerably weaker in the USSR. Although there have been continual rumblings among the Kremlinologists about guns-versus-butter arguments in the Soviet Union,[12] it is possible to hypothesize that in their bureaucratic society once a direction is set it may continue indefinitely within allocation constraints established many years or decades previously. In this case, the direction would be that of building strong, modern, and growing armed forces; and it may have been set in the early and mid-1960s, when the Soviet Union had to accept a rebuff over missiles in Cuba and when NATO's total defense budget appeared to be inceasing at a high rate because of the U.S. buildup in the Vietnam situation. Finally, the USSR clearly views China as a threat, especially in view of Chinese claims to vast territories that they say were taken from them during the periods of weakness of the Manchu dynasty. Recent attempts at Soviet-Chinese reconciliation haven't appeared to have high prospects of success. The USSR clearly must retain large forces in its Far Eastern areas.

Thus the Soviet's military strength could continue to grow, perhaps well past the point where even in their own view they have enough for their defense, even on two fronts. To this prospect might be added the repeated assurances of the Soviet leadership that the struggle against capitalism and imperialism must go on. Brezhnev also stated at the Twenty-fifth Communist

Party Congress that, despite the Soviet drive to improve East-West trade and other relations,

> as before, the Soviet Union will side with the forces fighting for the elimination of the vestiges of colonialism and the seats of racism, and for the removal of discriminatory barriers and manifestations of inequality in international economic relations . . . . We will work for these objectives with redoubled energy . . . . Certain people dislike the Soviet Union's principled stand of solidarity with the struggle of other peoples for freedom and progress, for the eradication of the remnants of colonialism, since this is in contrast to the old line followed by the advocates of exploiting and subordinating small and weak countries. These zealots try to picture Soviet solidarity with the cause of national liberation as "incompatible with relaxation of tensions." . . . This is either outright naivete or, more likely, a deliberate attempt to confuse people. It is obvious, after all, that relaxation and peaceful coexistence have to do with relations between states. This means primarily that disputes and conflicts between countries should not be settled by war, by the use or threat of force. *Relaxation of tensions does not to the slightest extent abolish or alter the laws of the class struggle.* No one should expect that because tensions have been reduced, Communists will reconcile themselves to the capitalist system or monopolists will become followers of the Revolution. [Emphasis added.][13]

There has since been no pronouncement modifying this policy. The growth of the Soviet Navy to the point where coordinated worldwide operations have been demonstrated,[14] the early Soviet demonstrations of the utilization of naval power, and the assurance quoted above that the USSR will continue to support struggles for national liberation all support the view that the Soviets believe the struggle between communism and capitalism continues and may continue until a final showdown.

Despite the current U.S. defense buildup, NATO as a whole is not increasing its miltiary strength markedly. The U.S. defense budget remains under fire (in early 1983) as poor economic conditions continue. Consider the prospect that defense efforts of NATO and the United States may remain essentially level or decline while Soviet military strength increases indefinitely, as it has been doing. Imagine further that the United States declines to compete in the strategic-force arena and thereby permits the Soviet renewal of strategic forces to reach the point where the value of our strategic deterrent is in doubt. A decision by Congress not to deploy the MX missile, and failure to provide some credible alternative, could be interpreted that way, whether that were the actuality or not. In such a case it is possible to conceive that in a subsequent situation of tension, the Soviet Union might seek a final solution in military action because it believes the United States would be deterred from a strategic response and that the Warsaw Pact could win easily in Europe.

In a military attack on Western Europe out of fear, the Soviet Union could be expected to use the maximum destructive power of its forces or at least to be less than concerned about the consequence for Western Europe if it does that. But suppose such an attack is motivated by the decision to use force to incorporate European industrial and agricultural capacity in the Communist sphere. In such circumstances, there would be a premium on preserving the population and infrastructure as nearly intact as possible or in reasonable enough condition to permit rebuilding to Communist advantage. The new Soviet strategy stressing the use of Operational Maneuver Groups[15] could help them achieve this if it could be implemented successfully. Western defenses that were weak enough to permit Germany and the Low Countries to be overrun in a few days by conventional means (with consequent political impact on the other European NATO countries if they were not attacked) would play right into such a Soviet scheme. A strong NATO conventional deterrent, placing the Soviet strategy in doubt and including the obvious will to build and sustain such a deterrent, would make it impractical—more important, it would make such action *appear* impractical.

Military deterrence is, however, only part of the problem, and its other political aspects could be taken to mitigate the need for stronger military forces. Germany presents special problems in this area. We could speculate that in some circumstances the Soviet Union might be tempted to attack the West to incorporate the fruits of capitalism into its own sphere, but it can as easily be argued (given the experience of China) that the USSR would not under any circumstances want to see Germany unified, even as a Communist state under its own influence.[16] The prospective drain on Soviet military resources to keep *all* of Germany safely suppressed or the risk of its resurgence as a militant rival on the USSR's western marches might well act as a *political* deterrent that needs no further military buildup by the West for credibility. It can be argued that Soviet policy is, and has always been, to keep Germany divided.

But what of possible Soviet actions to capitalize on political divisions within NATO, to weaken the European countries and make them more subservient to, or responsive to, Soviet policy? The possibility of such "Finlandization" can be considered in any case as a long-term objective in the Soviet drive to establish its superiority over the archenemy, the United States, and incidentally (but not unimportantly) to establish as well its safety and its power in world affairs.

History suggests that the USSR would move very cautiously. It would seek a succession of advantages, as in a chess game, but be prepared to backtrack if resisted. It would undertake political moves that had the backing of superior miltary force without actually using it, and it would attempt to present the kind of divisive ambiguity that saps its opponents' will to fight. The importance of each of the Germanies to the safety and political integrity of both the USSR and the United States suggests that military action by either side, of even a limited character, if it threatens the territorial integrity and, consequently, the political stability of either Germany, would lead to such a high risk of war with the prospect of uncontrollable escalation that neither side would attempt it. But suppose other situations were to arise that were not so central.

As Tito was nearing the end of his years, ancient rivalries among Yugoslavia's constituent groups began boiling up. They became quiescent after Tito's death, but given the turbulent history of the Balkans Yugoslavia could at any time explode into internal conflict. This would present a made-to-order opportunity for the revival of earlier Soviet drives. Here was the spark that ignited one world war and the focus of intense political and military activity by Western Europe—the Allies *and* the Axis—during another. Would the West initiate what could become a major war in response to a Soviet attempt to intervene in civil strife in Yugoslavia, even if it meant that, given free rein, the USSR could become firmly established on the Adriatic shore? Or would the West risk major war over Soviet political or naval intervention between Greece and Turkey? Would NATO find a reason for major war with the Warsaw Pact in an internal quarrel over an expanding role of Communists in Western countries, even if there were obvious Soviet political (but not military) intervention? Would the issues of where the Soviet-Norwegian boundary extends over the continental shelf in the North Sea, or Norwegian sovereignty over Spitsbergen, warrant major miltiary conflict for either side, even if oil is the ostensible point of difference (while military problems may be in the background)?

Let us also postulate for the sake of argument that the Soviet attempts to build strong positions and a base structure outside Europe, which we reviewed earlier, are defensive. They support Soviet attempts to neutralize, anywhere, economic power we could bring against them in case of conflict in Europe or the Far East. Moreover, they place Soviet forces in a better position to neutralize the strategic capabilities of the U.S Navy, anywhere, in case the world war they apparently fear should begin. Would the United States, much less the NATO nations of Europe, undertake armed conflict with the USSR to prevent it from establishing these positions, short of the highly improbable Soviet initiation of armed conflict? Despite all our expressed unhappiness, we didn't, in the cases of Afghanistan, Soviet use of Cam Ranh Bay, the Soviet/Cuban presence in Africa, and the Soviet presence in Cuba. A slice of salami isn't worth fighting over.

The Real Nature of the Threat

All the questions posed above are imponderables over which it would do little good to speculate. It does seem clear, on reflection, that behind all the possible political moves and countermoves must lie an awareness by both sides of their relative military capability. Having learned the lesson of the 1930s, the nations in NATO would presumably react to obvious provocations by standing fast—Berlin and Portugal attest to this probability. But whether or not it is questioned if NATO or the NATO nations individually (including the United States) or a rearmed Japan would have the will to fight as some situations such as those outlined grew severely threatening, it is clear that without the *capability* they would not really have the choice. If the capability exists, the possibility that they would react strongly would always have to be taken into account, and presumably this would counsel greater caution in any Soviet maneuvers on the international scene.

In the NATO arena the balance in the Central Region is pivotal. The geography of the Southern Region (the Mediterranean) and the farther reaches of the Northern Region (Scandinavia), with their waters and rugged terrains, favors defense. The forces there currently, including NATO naval forces in the North Atlantic and the U.S. Mediterranean fleet but excepting weakness on the ground in the far north, are nominally much more nearly in balance.[17] The area of potentially great relative weakness for NATO and of greatest reliance on the intangibles of the nuclear deterrents is in the Central Region. Both NATO and the Warsaw Pact must be cautious that conflicts and clashes in the far north and in the Mediterranean, which may involve posturing and even limited actions by military forces, do not escalate into major conflict in the vital center. The USSR would have to be cautious everywhere, in Europe or in the world, if faced with credible military oppositon in the Central Region. If that critical link in NATO's defenses did not exist or were obviously weak, the West's options, and even those of China or Japan, to oppose Soviet belligerence or expansion would be much reduced. Herein, then, lies the key to concern about growing Soviet military strength and the uses to which the USSR may at some future time be tempted to put that strength.

Similar considerations apply in the area of naval-force structure. Postulate, again, that the Soviet naval buildup is purely defensive. But suppose that the USSR continues to build its naval strength in the directions we have been observing, while that of the United States continues to deteriorate in the senses we examined: increasing vulnerability resulting from greater concentration of important capabilities in fewer vessels, without compensating changes such as greater reliance on land-based aviation and cruise missile ships to maintain our maritime power. Suppose, then, that Soviet and U.S. interests clash, in geographic areas where naval action by the United States could be important or could offer the only military means for response. The clash could have to do with NATO, political turmoil in the Middle East, or war or the threat of war in the Far East. Just as in Europe, if it became apparent in the crunch that fundamental U.S. maritime power had been allowed to deteriorate visibly and markedly vis-a-vis that of the USSR, our freedom of action will have been seriously curtailed. Conversely, if such a change in power relationships were not obvious, the USSR would have to be much more circumspect in how, where, and why it attempts to exert political or economic pressure against U.S. interests.

Thus, we see that the problem in deciding to maintain or build up our military forces, including ground and air combat capabilities important in a worldwide context, is not simply a matter of where we predict those forces will have to fight or of *expecting* war with the USSR or an attack *by* the USSR. It is as much a matter of creating a balance of capability, perceptions, and circumspection. The point is not whether there *is* a Soviet threat. It is rather that by maintaining our military strength and that of NATO we will be in a much better position to keep such a threat from developing, in the practical sense of constraining threatening actions the USSR might otherwise be tempted to take. The correct level of military strength unfortunately cannot be rigorously specified. No practically supportable force level can offer a certain prospect of victory in any of the possible military confrontations we will examine in the next two chapters. It is a matter of balancing risks, whose dimensions are brought out by the processes of political conflict and debate within each country.

There is some prudent force level where the prospect of military success, if we must use military force, although not absolutely certain might yet be credible. The likelihood of failure would increase visibly and markedly as the forces are allowed to become smaller and weaker from that level. The choice would thus seem to be to argue out what this prudent level of military capability might be and then achieve it or else to accept increasingly greater levels of risk. The risk would be counterbalanced by intangibles— whether the USSR would itself take certain risks in certain situations; what its perception of risk would become if the United States and NATO were to drift into increasingly apparent military weakness; or to what extent it might feel threatened as the U.S. builds military strength but NATO Europe lags behind. Since there is no certainty about Soviet response in either the building of our military strength or our letting it remain substantially weaker than that of the USSR, our problem for decision in the political arena would seem to be to determine which kinds of uncertainties we are most comfortable with.

At the present time it appears that the Soviet Union has achieved its national security objective: With its combination of conventional and nuclear forces, no nation or group of nations would attack it. But the USSR apparently doesn't see it that way, and it continues to modernize and build up its forces. Governments in the West have viewed this buildup as threatening—the USSR as a have-not and apparently insecure nation seems bent on geographic and political expansion. To some extent, though modestly, Europe has followed the U.S. lead, under both the Carter and Reagan administrations, in building stronger defenses. These buildups don't mean the two sides will necessarily go to war. There will be continued maneuvers for position and local conflicts that may involve the West or the USSR in various ways. Each side will behave in accordance with the dedication to interests and strength it perceives on the other side, balanced against its understanding of its own interests and strength. Although the West has much greater economic strength, some of the data presented in the previous chapter suggest that the two sides will use their strengths differently. The Soviet Union can much more easily than the West coerce its population into making the sacrifices necessary for a test of wills in building military forces. The relative outcomes and positions thus are not related in proportion to the relative economic strengths of the two sides, and over the long term the USSR could gain greatly in the contest for resources and political position in the world.

This is the real nature of the Soviet threat, and it is likely to persist to the end of this decade if not of this century. Let us now look more closely at the military and strategic issues that affect the perceptions of balance on both sides in viewing this threat.

8
The Defense of Western Europe

The strongest U.S. commitment that may involve the use of U.S. military forces overseas, and the only one that commands, at least in theory, the support of most Americans, is the commitment to NATO. Europe was the source of about 80 percent of our population, whose predecessors came in successive waves from the fifteenth into the twentieth century. We view it, accordingly, as the primary source of our history and culture. Although Europe has diverse and even rival nation-states, the partnership across the Atlantic runs deep, representing a unity of civilization that makes the United States and Western Europe one nation in the broadest sense. We would add the countries of Eastern Europe to this community if we could.

Thus, NATO, the deterrence of war in Europe, and the possibility of conflict with the USSR there or elsewhere came again, after the Vietnam debacle in 1975, to occupy most of our attention in the planning and construction of all those parts of our military forces not devoted directly to defense of our own soil. Since there had been no apparent threat to Japan, only since about 1980 have we begun again to look seriously at defense interests beyond Europe. Even then, the greatest attention is being given to protection of an oil supply, in Southwest Asia, that supports mainly Europe (about 10 percent of U.S. oil comes from the Middle East and North Africa, compared with about 60 percent of Western Europe's). To say all this is not to regret or to deplore it. We have proof from two major wars and a number of minor military actions since 1945 that a majority of the U.S. people do not consider the direct exercise of U.S. military force in peripheral conflicts in remote parts of the world, beyond a degree of "presence" or fast actions such as the *Mayaguez* affair, as essential for the defense of our own country. It is entirely appropriate and in any case unavoidable that we should devote our energies in the military sphere to the commitments and situations that do command our population's approval in some significant degree.

How well can this vital interest and alliance be defended? The answer is complex, but we shall seek some clues to it in this chapter.

A Comparison of Military Strength

Figure 8-1 shows a map of Europe with the various NATO and Warsaw Pact countries highlighted and indicates NATO's organization into major defense regions, Northern, Central, and Southern. The data for populations, gross national product (GNP), and men under arms for the individual

FIGURE 8–1: NATO and Warsaw Pact Boundaries in Europe

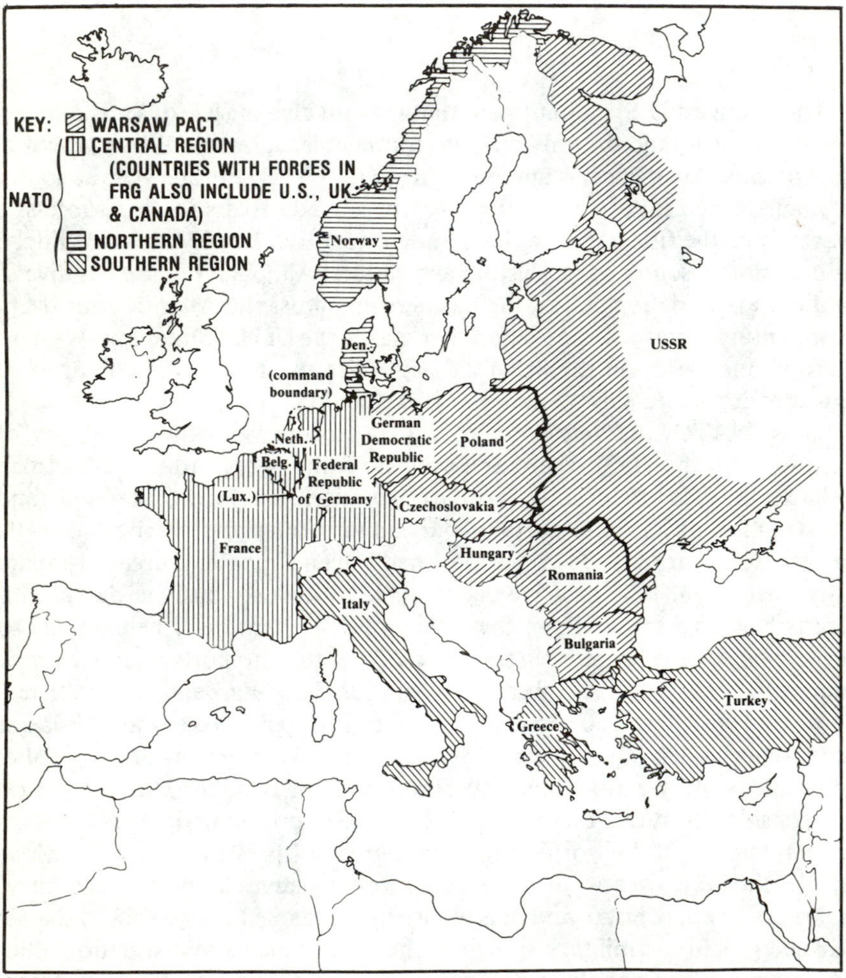

2-3-83-7

countries and the alliances taken as a whole show that by themselves, NATO Europe and the Warsaw Pact are roughly matched in economic strength (about 20 percent apart) as indicated by GNP, and they differ by some 14 percent in population—there is no substantial advantage for the Pact.* When the United States is included, NATO's population and GNP approximately double. Thus NATO, by the gross measures of both population and GNP, appears to be far stronger than the Pact overall. However, the Soviet Union, which represents most of the Pact's power, has been spending over three times as large a fraction of its GNP on defense as NATO Europe, and it has 35 percent more armed forces although it has 22 percent less population. U.S. defense expenditure per capita, although roughly the same as that of the USSR, is over twice as high as that of the remainder of NATO; our expenditure as a fraction of GNP is about 50 percent higher than Europe's on the average but yet less than half as large as that of the USSR. Some imbalances in commitment and effort are apparent, therefore, within Europe and between Europe and the United States. Some of the reasons for this disparity were noted in chapters 6 and 7.

Figures 8-2 and 8-3 show relative defense budget trends of the United States, the USSR, NATO, and the Warsaw Pact (Japan is small in relation to the others).[1] The difficulties of estimating the size of the Soviet defense budget, which represents most of the Warsaw Pact's budget, are legion, and they have been a matter of continuing controversy, with estimates varying from half to twice as much as the U.S. defense budget. Also, there is uncertainty about how much of the U.S. defense budget applies formally to the defense of NATO (presumably all of it does in the theoretical sense that a strong United States deters Soviet aggressiveness). The meaning of the relative defense expenditures of NATO and the Warsaw Pact, in terms of miltiary force, have also been controversial.[2] However, the data on relative military force strengths are consistent with the relative budget figures presented in figures 8-2 and 8-3.

---

*The various numbers extant for GNP, defense budget, and forces may contain many apparent inaccuracies, because all such figures vary from source to source and, for some, they depend on dollar-conversion factors. They are especially controversial for the USSR and the Warsaw Pact, since they are very difficult to estimate. To have a consistent set of figures for comparison and to avoid diversion into the arguments about how the figures were derived, we select a specific and respected source, *The Military Balance*, by the International Institute of Strategic Studies in London and the following remarks on population, GNP, and budgets are based on the IISS numbers for recent years unless otherwise noted.

**FIGURE 8-2: Comparison of U.S. Military Investment Outlays with
Estimated Dollar Cost of Soviet Military Investment Activities**

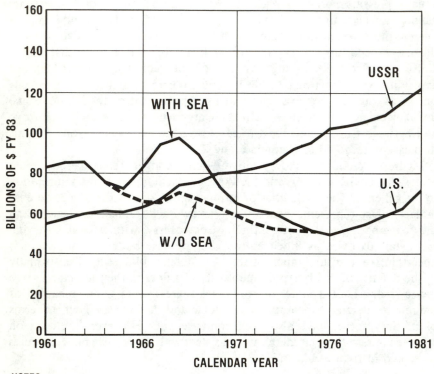

NOTES:

INVESTMENT INCLUDES RDT&E*, PROCUREMENT AND MILITARY CONSTRUCTION.

*Research, Development, Test, and Evaluation.

SEA: Southeast Asia

Source: Secretary of Defense posture statement, fiscal year 1983.

1-18-83-8

**FIGURE 8–3: Comparison of Estimated Atlantic Alliance + Japan
Military Investment Outlays with
Estimated Dollar Costs of Warsaw Pact Military Investment Activities**

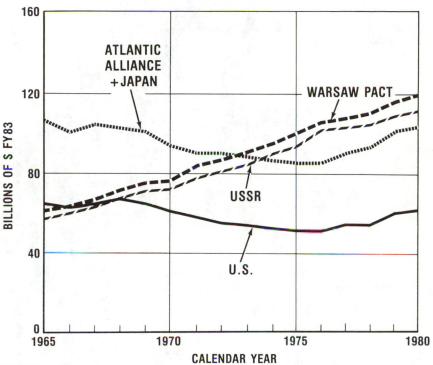

NOTES:

INVESTMENT INCLUDES RDT&E, PROCUREMENT AND MILITARY CONSTRUCTION.

U.S. TOTAL EXCLUDES VIETNAM INVESTMENT.

NON-U.S. ATLANTIC ALLIANCE DATA DERIVED FROM NONPERSONNEL DEFENSE OUTLAYS
CONVERTED TO DOLLARS USING CONSTANT EXCHANGE RATES.

Source: Secretary of Defense posture statement, fiscal year 1983.

1-18-83-7

Figures 8–4 and 8–5, and Table 8–1, compare various indicators of military
strength, and trends in two of the indicators.[3] The Warsaw Pact has nearly
three times as many tanks as NATO, overall. As we have seen, this is an
indicator of effective ground combat power. The Soviet tank force is being
modernized faster than that of NATO. Although both sides have about the
same number of tactical aircraft (eleven to twelve thousand, including all
types) NATO's tactical aircraft are decreasing in numbers while those of the

178

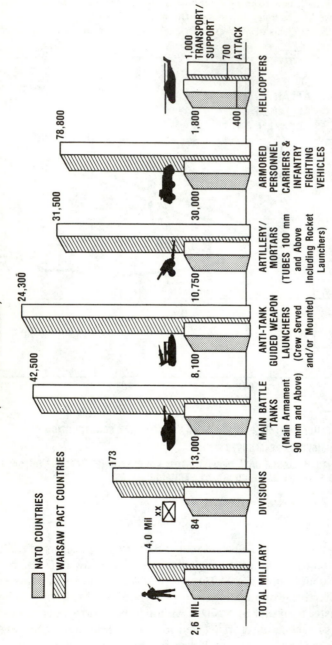

FIGURE 8-4: NATO-Warsaw Pact Force Comparison
(IN PLACE IN EUROPE)

NATO COUNTRIES
WARSAW PACT COUNTRIES

| | TOTAL MILITARY | DIVISIONS | MAIN BATTLE TANKS (Main Armament 90 mm and Above) | ANTI-TANK GUIDED WEAPON LAUNCHERS (Crew Served and/or Mounted) | ARTILLERY/ MORTARS (TUBES 100 mm and Above Including Rocket Launchers) | ARMORED PERSONNEL CARRIERS & INFANTRY FIGHTING VEHICLES | HELICOPTERS |

2,6 MIL — 4,0 Mil
84 — 173 XX
13,000 — 42,500
8,100 — 24,300
10,750 — 31,500
30,000 — 78,800
1,800 / 400 — 1,000 TRANSPORT/ SUPPORT / 700 ATTACK

NOTES: 1. WARSAW PACT DIVISIONS NORMALLY CONSIST OF FEWER PERSONNEL THAN MANY NATO DIVISIONS BUT CONTAIN MORE TANKS AND ARTILLERY, THEREBY OBTAINING SIMILAR COMBAT POWER.

2. FORCES IN PLACE IN NATO EUROPE, WARSAW PACT FORCES AS FAR EAST AS, BUT EXCLUDING, THE 3 "WESTERN MILITARY DISTRICTS" IN WESTERN RUSSIA (MOSCOW, VOLGA & URAL MILITARY DISTRICTS).

3. Source, this and subsequent NATO/WP Force Comparisons: Publication of the NATO Secretary-General.

1-18-83-5

FIGURE 8–5: Relative Trends in Main Battle Tanks and Artillery

IN PLACE IN EUROPE

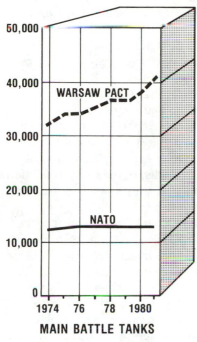

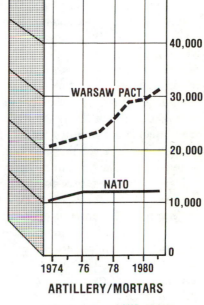

MAIN BATTLE TANKS

(MAIN ARMAMENT 90 mm AND ABOVE)

ARTILLERY/MORTARS

(TUBES 100 mm AND ABOVE INCLUDING ROCKET LAUNCHERS)

Source: Publication of the NATO Secretary-General

1-18-83-6

Table 8–1: NATO AND WARSAW PACT AIRCRAFT STRENGTHS
(Combat Aircraft in Place in Europe)

NATO/Warsaw Pact Combat Aircraft in Place in Europe

Group	Fighter-Bomber Ground-Attack[a]	Interceptor	Reconnaissance	Bombers
NATO	1,950	740	285	—
Warsaw Pact	1,920	4,370	600	350

[a]Many interceptors can be used in ground-attack roles.

Source: Publication of the NATO Secretary-General

Pact are increasing, and as we saw in Chapter 3 the Pact's tactical air forces have assumed an offensive capability comparable to that of NATO's. Of course, these figures show total budget and force numbers, including U.S. and Soviet strategic forces, and a significant part of the Soviet defense budget can be going into the parallel renewal of their strategic systems. The strategic forces represent about 15 percent of the U.S. defense budget.

It is of interest to extend our comparison of opposing strengths to the most critical part of the European theater, the Central Region. That is the area where previous wars that changed the political shape of Europe have been decided. It is the area where the Soviet Union and the other Warsaw Pact countries have concentrated their strength to achieve the most overwhelming advantage. What is learned in considering this region can be applied throughout. (Data on the Northern Region have been included, since they are presented in combined form in the source material; they are a small part of the total. The Northern Region presents problems unique to itself that were noted in passing, in the previous chapter.)

Figure 8–6 shows force comparisons for the Central Region similar to those that were shown for NATO and the Warsaw Pact as a whole. (Forces here are compared in terms of divisions in the source material. Soviet divisions have fewer people but more major weapon systems than NATO or U.S. divisions.) Since these are forces in place they do not include naval aircraft. It is assumed that those aircraft would have other, related missions and would not appear early over the European heartland. Also, they do not include the U.S. Marines or reserve forces that could be transported to Europe if there were time, and they do not include French forces of about fifteen division equivalents and about 800 tactical aircraft since France is not part of the NATO military command. In addition, since 1970–72, Soviet strength in the Far East, opposite China, has increased dramatically (from fewer than ten to forty-seven divisions), and this shift in orientation has been accounted for in the figures shown. The figures shown thus include only ready forces— those that could be assembled in Eastern Europe and the western USSR and moved to be in position to attack NATO after a short mobilization time, and the forces with which NATO could respond before reinforcement and before a French decision to participate. It is noted that the Soviets would know in advance that they planned to attack and would make every attempt to keep their preparations secret as long as possible.

The differences between the indicators of military strength are more severe in the Central Region than for NATO as a whole. In ground-force units the Pact is about twice as strong as NATO, and in the other key indicators of military strength its advantage is more than 2 to 1. It is over 3 to 1 for tanks, over 4 to 1 for artillery, and about 2 to 1 for tactical aircraft. Here, too, the Pact's tank and tactical aircraft advantage is increasing.

FIGURE 8-6: Defense of Northern and Central Regions

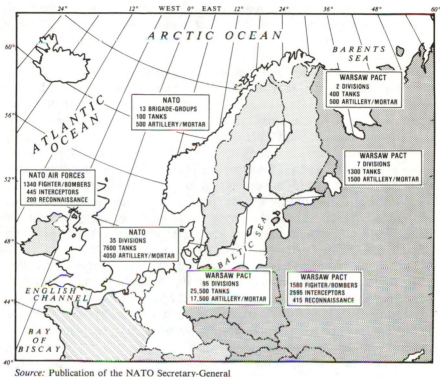

Source: Publication of the NATO Secretary-General
1-25-83-16

Now, several variables need to be considered further in order to appreciate the full meaning of these trends and the implications of the indicators. The great Warsaw Pact advantage shown in Figure 8-6 for the central front has led NATO to fear a Warsaw Pact surprise attack that would be undertaken without apparent mobilization, using the ready forces only. It has been feared that such an attack would catch NATO weak and without time to mobilize or to move its forces into the best defensive positions. The anticipation is, of course, that such an attack would overrun Germany in a few days.[4] Suppose, however, that there is adequate warning time—for example, a long period of increasing international tensions, during which both sides bring all their forces up to full strength and into position. The Central Region situation then would also include all the active forces on both sides, including those of France. (Although France was not included in the comparisons of budget and ready forces in the Central Region it remains a part of the alliance. The assumption seems reasonable that over a long period of political confrontation involving NATO as an alliance and the Warsaw Pact, France would find it in its interest to commit forces to the total NATO mobilization. The current posture would make it difficult for the French to become involved, even if they wanted to, if the Pact could achieve surprise and move as fast as the fears expressed above suggest.) The United States could add thirteen active divisions, including two Marine divisions,[5] and the equivalent of fifteen National Guard and reserve divisions and over 1,000 Air National Guard aircraft. European reserves, such as the German Territorial Forces, taken all together, would provide the equivalent of another seven divisions, and France could add approximately thirteen divisions to the two already in Germany.[6] The Warsaw Pact could add nearly forty divisions, mainly Soviet, without drawing from Soviet forces opposing southern Europe or those in Asia. These added forces would increase opposing manpower and, therefore, the ability to use supporting arms like artillery and anti-tank weapons, but the *relative* armor and artillery strengths would not change substantially. Tactical combat aircraft would be increased by about 1,000 on each side, not counting naval and Marine tactical aviation and helicopters organic to U.S. Army divisions.

Thus NATO ground forces would come up to about eighty five divisions while those of the Pact would total about one hundred forty, and the Pact would remain rather stronger in total tactical combat aircraft numbers. The net meaning of all the above comparative force numbers would remain that before or after a period of mobilization of active and reserve forces the Pact appears considerably stronger in conventional forces than NATO. It can be argued that the disparity in the key element of tank strength would not be critical; NATO would have the advantage of strong defensive positions, with many anti-tank guided missiles and enough armor for counterattack if it held the initial attack successfully. There were also, in the past (say, in the early 1970s), arguments about quality of weapons, in which NATO was considered to have more advanced technology and better performance in its major weapons systems, especially tactical aircraft. This was considered to have made up for the disparity in force strengths. However, we have seen that with the passage of time the Soviet Union has developed the advanced weapons systems, such as improved ATGMs and air-delivered, precision-guided munitions, which make up much of the higher quality attributed to NATO forces. The effect of a uniform command and control system on the Warsaw Pact side, compared with fragmentation into national forces with an imperfect command overlay on the NATO side, is imponderable but intuitively one feels it must favor the Pact. On the other side, however, the political cohesion within the Pact is unlikely in many circumstances to be as strong as that within NATO, and this could act to tie up Soviet forces in what amounts to guard duty to preserve the security of their rear. Finally, this kind of static comparison of conventional forces cannot portray the potential contribution of tactical nuclear weapons to the assessment of the balance of forces in Europe. NATO has been relying on them heavily for its defense, and the USSR has also acquired them in large numbers, with consequences we shall examine shortly.

Clearly, a simple comparative examination of gross force numbers such as we have undertaken thus far is inconclusive. Many uncertainties and arguments can be shifted about to lead to alternate results.[7] A more definitive means of comparative assessment is needed. Although it is impossible, short of the event, to predict with any degree of certainty the outcome of a large-scale military conflict, it *is* possible to consider many of the factors and their interactions in a dynamic way, leading to insights that the simple comparison of numbers and qualitative reasoning cannot quite achieve. Such consideration is made possible by computer simulation techniques that have been under continuous development by the operations research community for the past thirty years.[8]

These techniques in general portray the outcome of a hypothetical war based on relative casualty and resupply rates on both sides, on the analysts' partly subjective representations of weapon performance, and on rules established by the analysts for the computer to determine what the forces should do next when relative casualties reach certain levels. Nevertheless, in modern warfare in Europe casualty rates, especially losses of particular kinds of weapon systems on each side, can be expected to be high. The outcome thus must depend in some considerable measure on the initial strengths of both sides and on the imputed quality of their weapons—their relative ability to find target weapons and forces on the other side and to damage or destroy them. The models cannot describe the effects of politics, ideology, training, and morale. They also cannot capture the random impact of extreme events that have often occurred in warfare: loss of the will to fight by one side; poor use of overwhelming force by the other; collapse of a retrograde movement into a rout. However, they can describe what would happen in a war based on the interplay of resources alone. This is not beyond utility; although Lee, as a commander in the American Civil War, performed tactical miracles in winning battles against the superior Northern armies, he could not withstand the overwhelming resources brought to bear by Grant when they were used in a determined and consistent way, despite enormous attrition suffered by Union forces in successive battles.[9]

This type of analysis applied to the possibility of a conventional—nonnuclear—conflict in central Europe, and allowing the Pact the advantage of initiating the battle (in keeping with NATO's defensive orientation), would show that with today's forces the Pact would win. Their greater mass would tell, and there would be no doubt that NATO's conventional forces could be overrun. This would remain true whether the battle were fought with in-place forces or with forces augmented by the reserves on both sides that were described earlier.

However, the USSR and the Warsaw Pact are not the only ones improving their forces; NATO is doing so as well. In a few years these forces will be augmented by large numbers of ATGM systems, including types, mounted on armored fighting vehicles, that afford better protection against artillery and air attack. Other steps include acquiring the improved tanks now emerging from development (U.S. M-1, West German Leopard II, and UK Chieftain) and developing its tactical air further. The tactical air will come to incorporate, especially, the means to overcome ground-based air defenses from standoff ranges and improved fighter and attack aircraft now in production (F-15, F-16, Mirage F-1, A-10, Jaguar, Tornado). The new airplanes will afford higher ground-attack payloads and more effective air defense capability. These changes in NATO forces will increase their fighting power to the point where the Warsaw Pact would need much more than the in-place and ready forces facing the Central and Northern Regions to be certain of success against NATO's ready forces if the latter were alerted. The ultimate balance after incorporation of all the conventional force improvements planned and under way in NATO will be close enough, in fact, that it might be possible to conceive of a scenario in which NATO could hold the attack, even with its smaller forces and without nuclear weapons. It would be an interesting diversion to sketch such a scenario as a concrete illustration of the exercise of military power using the new military technology discussed in earlier chapters.

Defending Germany with the New Weaponry: An Illustrative Scenario

We hark back to other times when major changes in the way forces were constituted and weapons were used permitted relatively small forces to defeat larger, heavily armored, mobile armies—the English longbowmen at Crecy (1346) and the Swiss halberdiers in their own country (fourteenth and fifteenth centuries).[10] The English could negate the armor by firing at it effectively from long range (modern counterpart: long-range ATGMs and air-launched PGMs), whereas the Swiss negated it by closing with it (modern counterpart: short-range ATGMs and other anti-tank weapons). We might also note that in more recent times inferior forces (as, for example, in Vietnam) have been able to win wars while losing many battles by operating in great depth, attacking widely dispersed population and military centers, and using multiple ambush tactics, causing the superior side to disperse and be worn down piecemeal.[11]

Suppose we assume that the forward-defense strategy in Germany permits deployment of NATO's forces in sufficient depth and dispersion that an attacking or exploiting armored column must, wherever it goes, pass by a large succession of positions, each having a number of ATGM units. NATO's armored forces would be held in deep reserve for counterattack. We must also assume that NATO's tactical airfields and aircraft could continue to operate, despite the anticipated Pact attacks on them. Perhaps the aircraft could use reserve airfields in France and England, if the conventional war were not carried immediately to those countries, or the many civilian and secondary airfields in Germany and the Low Countries. Finally, we must assume that NATO's forces have time to reach their fighting positions before the attack and that its command, control, and communications systems continue to function effectively.

With NATO ground forces of current size and strength, in light of the force ratio requirements for breaking through a well-prepared defense, the Pact would be able to mass for breakthroughs at a few locations along the central front from Denmark to Austria. As we showed in discussing breakthrough tactics, Pact forces in the spaces between these main thrusts would be weaker, with only enough strength to pin down NATO's forces during the breakthrough attempts elsewhere. The dispersed defensive deployment in depth would be designed in part to encourage breakthrough attempts at locations desired by NATO and to inhibit the Pact's enveloping maneuvers.

In the first stage, the defense would use its long-range anti-armor defenses, including tactical aircraft, to deplete and to slow the attacking columns, like a pillow absorbing a punch. Infantry armed with the short-range weapons, in the areas between the columns, would then close with them from their flanks. The intent would be that even if the forward elements of the columns could reach the western part of Germany they could not consolidate positions there. The situation might be similar to that which faced MacArthur's columns on the way to the Yalu in December 1950—these columns were moving up the coastal regions and were attacked on their flanks by the Chinese from northern Korea's mountainous center.[12] The increasing urbanization of Germany would also serve to slow the movement of armor attempting to exploit along the roads. Every built-up crossroads, village, or town would harbor many anti-tank positions. At the same time that the Pact's breakthroughs were engaged, NATO's armored reserves and tactical air would attack eastward, between the penetrating columns and at their bases of support. The counterattack would be designed to deny the essential and continuing logistic support that armor needs to fight. With their support threatened or cut off, their momentum slowed, and their flanks under attack, the advancing Pact units would be likely to have to withdraw. If the Pact strategic reserves entered the battle at about this time, they would be engaged on Pact territory, in a complex war of maneuver different from that which they had initially planned. If NATO's intent were to prevent the Soviet and

Pact armies from occupying West German territory and reaching the Rhine and beyond, this outcome would be consistent with that objective.

The Soviet Union has been aware of the increases in NATO force strength that are pending. It has also had ample time to contemplate the potential impact of evolving NATO strategy that the new weaponry encourages, along the lines described above. The Soviet strategic response is to design an even more rapid and massive attack than their tactics described previously (chapters 2 and 4) imply. This includes plans for airborne and air-landed operations and rapid movement through openings in NATO's defenses using Operational Maneuver Groups (OMGs), which might range from battalions to divisions or even armies in size. These groups would be designed to seize key objectives such as airfields, nuclear-weapon sites, transportation and communication nodes, and supply dumps on which NATO's effective defense on the ground would depend. The whole would be accompanied by heavy air attacks and strong air defense to defeat NATO's air attacks. The purpose of these operations would be to confuse and disrupt any NATO defense, so that the main Soviet forces could break through before a NATO decision to "go nuclear" could be taken—perhaps a few days to a week.[13]

The problems these tactics would pose to NATO forces are severe. NATO is committed to a continuous-front defense, but the Soviet tactics would create a fragmented front. The tactics would require very fast command reaction, but the current NATO command structure requires multicountry agreement on major military steps—an inherently slow process. NATO's component national Corps have diverse tactical concepts without highly integrated and uniform military doctrines and practices. NATO's airfields are critically important to its ability to mass firepower rapidly against superior forces, and given the disparity in ground-force strengths there would be a paucity of deep reserves to meet both the OMG onslaughts and the main breakthrough and exploitation attempts.

To recognize these difficulties is not, however, to grant that the Soviet strategy must necessarily succeed. That strategy requires a high degree of surprise, timing, and ability to pierce the "fog of war" to obtain virtually perfect "real time" knowledge of friendly and enemy force locations and battlefield conditions. Such results have been achieved in this century only by Israeli operations against the Arabs, on about a tenth the scale the Soviets would have to contemplate in Europe. Any disruption of the flow of supplies and weapons to their forces, counterpenetration by aggressive NATO response, more effective NATO air defense than the Soviets would anticipate, or delays due to confusion and poor coordination between Soviet and other Warsaw Pact forces could face the Soviet attack with the same denouement the Allied forces under Montgomery experienced in their attempt to take Arnhem in 1944.[14]

Also, the Soviet ability to succeed in this strategy depends on whether the NATO allies have prepared for a confused early period of fighting followed by the ability to stabilize a zone of resistance and sustain a conflict of more than few days' duration without resort to nuclear weapons. If NATO has been prepared in this way, and has had adequate warning (which was believed and used) to meet the attack, the strategy of response by containing and destroying penetrations while counterattacking against supporting and follow-on forces might succeed.

Thus both the results of analysis, however constrained, and the subsequent flight of fancy that these results encouraged as an illustrative example suggest that NATO might withstand a Central Region attack if the circumstances, as reflected in all the assumptions necessary to set up the successful outcome, were favorable. The validity of those assumptions in the real world is very uncertain, even apart from their political ramifications, which we will examine shortly. It is clear that in most circumstances, with relative force sizes as we currently know them, the Warsaw Pact's initiative gives it a much better than even chance of negating those assumptions and defeating NATO on the central front in an all-out attack using conventional weapons and tactics only. This would be true in the examples we have considered even if the superior quality of NATO's weapons, which has always been supposed to outweigh the Pact's greater numbers, is maintained. About the best that could be said is that with appropriate attention to maintaining the strength and readiness of its forces and developing their defensive tactics to best advantage, NATO could mount a substantial and stalwart conventional defense against such an attack.

However, this is a key point because it has never been argued that conventional forces in Western Europe must, by themselves, be able to withstand an all-out attack by the USSR or the Warsaw Pact. The strategy of flexible response was proposed by the United States during the early 1960s and is now generally accepted by the major European countries, at least in principle.[15] The intent of this strategy has always been twofold. First, NATO should be able to withstand an attack by nonnuclear forces, with strength sufficient to discourage the Soviet Union from making militarily minor but politically devastating incursions along NATO's borders. Second, the strategy's intent has been to discourage the Soviet Union from thinking it could overrun Europe without becoming involved in a major conflict. It has always been expected that nuclear weapons would have to be used to meet a major attack. Tactical nuclear options have been accepted since the 1950s, and U.S. strategic forces have been considered the ultimate deterrent. It is obvious, then, that we cannot think about the defense of Western Europe only in the terms outlined thus far but that we must bring into consideration the use of nuclear weapons and the entire question of deterrence. Before going into this question, however, it is necessary to round out the previous discussion with several observations about the long-range implications of the results regarding conventional defense.

Preparing the Conventional Defense

All the analyses of the problem, at whatever level and by any technique, show that if such conditions as training, morale, and command capability are considered equal on both sides, NATO's main chance to withstand Warsaw Pact conventional forces of superior numbers derives from the greater capability of its weapons. As we have noted repeatedly, this capability is changing all the time, on both sides. If NATO were to rest on its current lead by reducing significantly its expenditures on military research and development while the USSR continued to bring the Warsaw Pact's weapons up to the current capability of NATO's, the potential outcome would shift unquestionably in favor of the Pact as long as the latter maintained its quantitative advantage. This it could certainly do if maintains its current level of defense expenditure as a fraction of GNP while its economic strength grows. Thus, for NATO's conventional forces to have any credible chance of defending Western Europe at all, the United States and the European nations must continue to devote effort and resources to maintaining their technological lead over the USSR.

It is also obvious from the analyses described that NATO's forces can best meet the threat if there is time to mobilize and to augment the ready forces in the theater by reserve forces if possible. At least, it is essential for NATO to be able to move existing forces out of their peacetime locations into position to fight at all. To the extent that NATO's potential defense looks increasingly formidable, the Pact's preparations for war must be increasingly massive. As this happens, the prior Soviet mobilization time must increase, its mobilization must become more obvious, and the chance of delaying NATO reactions by deceptive stratagems must be reduced. Moreover, if NATO's conventional forces are to act as only part of the overall deterrent, with nuclear forces forming the other part, NATO needs time for the consultations required by its various internal agreements to decide which of its forces to commit to NATO (rather than national command) and whether nuclear weapons should be brought into play. Prior consultation during a period of warning and, at least, a decision to hand control of conventional forces to NATO military commanders would be essential to meeting the newly developing Soviet OMG strategy. The nuclear decision would depend on how the conventional war proceeded. For the requisite time to be available for such decisions both advance warning and the ability to fight successfully and conventionally for more than a nominal period are needed. This raises the issue of how long a conventional war to plan for. The view that has consistently been held of the speed with which the Pact might overrun Germany suggests that any conventional war may be very short—a matter of a few days or a week. If the war becomes nuclear, with escalation, the level of destruction would certainly bring it to a close in a short time. The tendency in European thinking, therefore, has been that planning should be for a short war, and before the Reagan administration there were indications that the United States was coming to this way of thinking as well.[16] This was a natural consequence of the desire to hold defense budgets down while system costs have tended to drive them up.

The length of war that forms the military-planning basis affects not only the budget but the organization of the operational forces. It has been noted that there is an asymmetry, expressed in terms of "teeth-to-tail ratio," between the Pact and NATO.[17] The pact has appeared to be configured for an intense, short war, and, therefore, its forces have not appeared to include a very large logistics tail to provide resupply, field maintenance and repair, and other long-term support. Since NATO's forces, on the other hand, incorporate extensive logistic and combat-support capability, they could sustain longer-term combat by forces whose teeth could be extended (e.g., by activation of reserves) with the tail already in place to support them. If this picture is accurate—and in many respects it is— the Pact is in a better position to win the opening battle, and NATO would not have the chance to take advantage of the potential for greater endurance inherent in its force structure. From this, it was argued that NATO must reduce its tail and add teeth to its ready forces, in order to be able to fight the short war—essentially the opening battle—successfully.

There are several problems with the argument that is drawn from the observations about teeth-to-tail ratio. First, what exists may not be all that it seems. The Soviet—and, therefore, Pact—mode of operating is different from NATO's. NATO provides continuing logistic support to its combat forces and provides a continuing flow of replacement equipment and personnel from replacement pools and depots. The Pact has been configured to replace entire units with their basic loads of weapons and supplies and reconstitute depleted units in their rear to feed them into the battle subsequently.[18] This places a premium on their reserve forces; it allows echelonment of units in battle, thus always permitting fresh units to be brought forward; and it does indeed bring more combat power to bear early on. But modern armored forces, too, have a strong need for a continuing flow of fuel and ammunition and for frequent equipment repairs and replacements. In one Soviet work, for example, it is noted that

. . . under present conditions, the organization of rear support includes new, larger measures than in preceding wars. Thus, the rear of the Land Forces should carry out an increased amount of work in a shorter period of time and in the course of the offensive more often bring the storage areas closer to the troops, utilize all means of transport with maximum effect and comprehensively, increase the rate of road rebuilding, carry out measures related to protecting the rear against nuclear weapons, maneuver the rear units and subunits, support the troops operating on individual axes, and eliminate the consequences of nuclear weapons used by the enemy against the troop and rear objectives.[19]

Although Soviet ready units may have more major weapons per man than NATO, it is not necessarily true that they do not have or do not need the tail to sustain even a short war. Their forces are simply constituted differently.

This line of reasoning does not mean that NATO does not need to add fighting strength up front. The force additions talked about earlier would, in fact, provide this. But it does counsel caution in case there may be thought to neglecting NATO's capability for sustained combat. If NATO also configures itself for a short war, as it perceives the Pact has done, then it would be trading one vulnerability—the risk of losing the opening battle—for others that might hurt more in the long run.

First, even if NATO, could ultimately hold, it is likely to have to fall back under the initial onslaught. This has been the outcome in nearly every major armored attack since the beginning of World War II, and (although it would be politically infeasible ever to admit it) this might even be the battle plan under a scenario such as the one sketched earlier. If NATO's forces at that point faced a lack of reserves and supply, the war would have been conceded de facto. Second, battles and wars almost invariably tend to take longer than the paper plans call for. The five to six weeks allocated for the 1914 execution of the modified German Schlieffen plan were extended ten days when the forts around Liege refused to fall, giving the French the opportunity to build their later defense on the Marne.[20] Goering thought Britain would be subdued from the air in three days, and Hitler thought he would defeat Russia in three months.[21] The major exceptions in modern times have been the Israeli victories in 1956 and 1967, when their opposition was significantly weaker in the key but intangible areas of training, morale, and sophistication in using modern weapons and forces. The prospect, made apparent by NATO strength, that a quick victory might *not* occur would be a major factor in the deterrent value of the conventional forces, both in terms of warning (as we have noted) and to cause the USSR to doubt the possibility that its contemplated quick conventional victory would work at all.[22] Conversely, it is obvious that if NATO were to plan for a war that would last for a very short time and this were to become apparent to the other side, the latter would have only to plan for a significantly longer war—ten days instead of five, or a month instead of a week, for example—in order to win.

The freedom to choose between planning for a long or a short war is, of course, inhibited by the demands of modern war itself. As noted previously in several contexts, modern weaponry produces very high loss rates, and, thus, the time available for intense fighting must be limited, all other considerations aside. This means that both sides, if they went to war even with conventional weapons only, would soon be depleted. The implication is that the relative initial strengths and inventories will exert great influence on who can win, at least in the first round. *NATO must continually remind itself that it does no good to have laboratory versions and test quantities of advanced and highly effective weapons if there are insufficient numbers of those weapons to turn the tide against vast operational inventories of technologically inferior weapons.*

The further implication is that defense budgets must account for the acquisition of the new weapons in significant quantities, however unpalatable that prospect may be in stringent economic circumstances. Although World War II generally—and, in the main, correctly—has been viewed as a war in which relative production capabilities played a decisive role, the initial forces involved faced both sides with force-depletion problems not unlike those of today. The thin ranks of the RAF during the Battle of Britain have been much publicized.[23] Not so well known is the fact that the Luftwaffe, during the early days of the war, was also hard put to maintain its strength. For example:

> Though the remainder of the French campaign [after Dunkirk] presented the Luftwaffe with no great problems, it needed to rest and recoup when it was over. *Insufficient force was available for an immediate attack on England.* Above all, the necessary ground organisation had to be built up in northern France. The Royal Air Force utilised the interval to strengthen its defences. Both sides were getting ready for the coming conflict.[24] [Emphasis added.]

German production of fighter, bomber, and attack aircraft was only about 1,500 in 1939, increasing to 6,000–7,000 in 1940 and 1941; losses in those years, both over Britain and in the East, accounted for a significant fraction of German air-combat power. In fact, the small number of available fighters was in large measure responsible for Germany's failure to protect its bombers from the counterattacks of the RAF and, consequently, for the failure to defeat the RAF.

One of the lessons of this convergence of cautions and history appears to be that U.S. and European defense planners should not focus on the opening battle to the exclusion of downstream contingencies. It is possible to conceive, for example, that, if for some reason the denouement of an initial Pact attack were not a nuclear exchange, the war could take place in phases, of which the first would be the short war we have been talking about and the second would take place after both sides rebuilt their combat strength.

All these considerations revolve around NATO's need to continue to improve the capability of its conventional forces and to achieve, partly by doing so, sufficient warning to be able to prepare to meet an attack. This places what amounts to a floor under the size of conventional forces NATO should have available: These forces should certainly not be smaller than today's, and they must continue to be extensively refitted and modernized. If Soviet forces continue to grow in size, NATO's forces may have to grow as well, distasteful as that prospect may be.

The Nuclear Deterrent

It is convenient to begin discussion of the nuclear deterrent in the military area with some speculation about the impact such weapons could have on the conventional battle discussed above. It is readily apparent that if NATO's central-front forces were exceedingly weak, nuclear weapons would offer the only feasible opportunity for a substantial response to a major attack. In addition to all the unresolved uncertainties of the nuclear battlefield, there would be a paradox attending the use of such weapons in the European context if near total reliance were placed on them: it is desired to minimize the yields and numbers of the weapons used to reduce collateral damage to the civilian population; but in achieving this goal, the use of the weapons themselves would become less effective in stopping massive attacking forces. The need for effectiveness, in the absence of other alternatives, would work against control of yields and numbers. In this sense tactical nuclear weapons cannot be considered a substitute for strong conventional forces unless total nuclear destruction of friendly as well as enemy areas in which they are to be used is contemplated as a real possibility. This prospect would be even more certain if Soviet strategy in using Operational Maneuver Groups led them to "hug" the populated areas that contain their special targets during their initial onslaught. Alternatively, this tactic could preclude use of nuclear weapons at critical points in the battle, without the conventional forces to compensate.

If, however, the conventional forces are strong, the military requirement for tactical nuclear weapons changes. Suppose NATO's conventional defenses can hold in most areas except for a few where Pact forces are massed overwhelmingly for a breakthrough or where the latter have broken through and threaten NATO's rear. Then the number of points at which the Pact will be able to achieve such superiority will, from force ratio considerations, be fewer as the defenders become stronger. The chance would be much greater that a few nuclear weapons, possibly with small yields, used in those critical locations, might turn the balance. From the NATO point of view, then, the way to depart from the tactical-nuclear weapon paradox in Europe, as first stated, is to have stronger conventional forces. This would then permit thinking about minimizing the numbers and yields of tactical nuclear weapons.

Of course, this reckons without the Soviet view. It must be presumed that if the USSR and the Warsaw Pact decide to go to war in Europe, making a major attack on the West and accepting the risk that the U.S. strategic forces will be used, the issue over which they decide to do so would be vitally important to them, and they would intend to win. If they thought they could accomplish their military objectives quickly without resorting to nuclear weapons, they might well attempt to do so. They would be encouraged by the view of a NATO weak in conventional forces and deterred from using nuclear weapons by fear of escalation or by ambiguity of U.S. willingness to bring its strategic forces into play. Suppose, however, that NATO were strong enough conventionally that a small number of nuclear weapons might turn the balance in its favor, placing the outcome of a conventional attack by the Pact in doubt for the USSR. If the issue leading to war were vital enough and if the USSR felt, from its assessment of intelligence on NATO war plans, that NATO *would* resort to nuclear weapons, it is not unlikely that the Pact would initiate the conflict with a nuclear strike on key targets. Such targets would include command centers, supply depots, airfields, nuclear-weapon storage areas, and possibly some key transportation and shipping hubs.

This possibility is not beyond Soviet thought: Their military writings have been replete with references to the advantages that surprise use of nuclear weapons could bring,[25] especially those writings reflecting the period up to about 1972 when there was little doubt about NATO's ultimate reliance on a nuclear defense. The Soviets in those circumstances could view a massive nuclear initiation, rightly from the purely military point of view, as the means to prevent NATO Europe from putting up any sensible defense at all. They would, of course, have to be willing to accept punishment from the British and French strategic nuclear forces, which include sea-launched ballistic missile (SLBM) submarines. They would have to believe that the United States, either because it had signaled, somehow, a lack of will or because it had allowed the USSR to achieve a clear strategic superiority, would not call its strategic forces into play. Alternatively, they would have to be prepared to undertake a strategic nuclear exchange with the United States if their attack escalated to one.

The stakes would have to be very high to cause the Soviet Union to initiate such a war in Europe. The increasing scale of contingencies makes it apparent what would be happening as NATO's strength in the conventional area increased: the level of military force at which the Warsaw Pact would have to plan to go to war would increase, and as a consequence the issues involved in a decision to undertake major war would have to be increasingly important. NATO would have raised the price of entry for undertaking major military conflict to resolve a political or economic issue.

Now, all this is what deterrence is about. NATO has always said that its forces are for the purpose of deterring a Warsaw Pact attack. Further, the preceding discussion shows the interrelationship of the three elements of the triad of deterrence.[26] These are: conventional forces, theater nuclear forces, and U.S. strategic forces; and they are inextricably interwoven.

The need for a strong conventional part of this triad was not always recognized throughout the alliance.[27] The European view of NATO deterrence in its early years was that Europe's defense would rely on nuclear weapons—to some extent those in the theater but primarily those of the U.S. strategic forces. The conventional forces, and especially U.S. Forces in Europe, would be a "tripwire," and would, if attacked, initiate the chain of events leading to the strategic nuclear exchange. Facing this prospect, the USSR would be deterred from starting a war. This approach had a number of inconsistencies, which gradually came to be recognized. For one thing, it offered NATO little flexibility in responding to potential Soviet military initiatives that could be very dangerous for NATO, politically, but that were not in actuality large enough to warrant a nuclear response that could lead to all-out strategic war. This realization led to the 1962 McNamara proposal that NATO should strengthen its conventional forces.[28] NATO should have the nuclear deterrent in the background but at the same time be able to respond to lesser provocation with appropriate means.

At about the same time, de Gaulle pointed out that Europe and the United States were increasingly following their own interests. This was borne out at the time by growing U.S. involvement in Vietnam and would be dramatically illustrated in the 1973 Middle East war by divergence over U.S. support for Israel from the European base structure. Also, the USSR was changing the nuclear balance, building up its own weapons and thereby eliminating the overwhelming U.S. nuclear superiority. In consequence, de Gaulle claimed, Europe could not always count on the United States' putting its cities at risk to save Europe.[29] This was the beginning of French withdrawal from military involvement in NATO.

The arguments of the time merely accentuated the issue, but they reflect a deep ambivalence of concern and internal conflict in Europe that persists in various forms to this day. The advent of cruise missiles, for example, elicited the same duality of concerns in another guise. NATO Europe feared that the United States would bargain away, in the strategic arms limitation negotiations, a new weapon that could add to the tactical deterrent. But then there were countervailing fears that if the United States were to give Europe the technology to build its own cruise missile deterrent, this would weaken the commitment of the U.S. strategic force, part of the NATO deterrence traid.[30] Similar sensitivity was evinced in consideration of the value of enhanced-radiation weapons in the theater nuclear-deterrent leg of the triad. This expression anticipates that such weapons' reduced collateral damage qualities may increase the chance they will be used. This is seen as increasing the chance of escalation to major nuclear war, the fear of which is at the very heart of the European deterrence concept. Yet there is concern that the availability of these weapons will somehow weaken the deterrent. Most recently, Europeans have been torn between wishing to deny the new intermediate-range nuclear force (INF) of Pershing II and cruise missiles a base on European soil and wanting those weapons there both as an earnest of U.S. commitment to "strategic" war—a strike against the USSR eliciting a return strike against the United States—if Europe is attacked—and as a "bargaining chip" in the "Eurostrategic" standoff.[31]

Analysis of possible means for a successful conventional defense of Germany showed that one of the essentials would be deployment of defensive positions in great depth, leading to a war, like World War II in many respects, that would be fought on German and other Western European soil. Indeed, a conventional deterrent, to be credible, may have to be planned obviously in this mode (which is the opposite of the current forward-defense strategy) so as to face the USSR with the clear prospect of a long war, with all its stresses and dangers, rather than the chance of a rapid military coup de grace by simply piercing NATO's forward defenses and overrunning its rear. But the prospect leads the United States' NATO allies in Europe to to want to rely on the nuclear deterrent; conventional war is unthinkable. The use of nuclear weapons in the event of an attack, especially if they must be used against a number of major breakthroughs and if the other side responds in kind, would, however, devastate Western as well as Eastern Europe—much more than conventional war would. A nuclear war in Europe, which to the United States would be tactical, would to the Europeans be the equivalent of strategic nuclear war to the United States. For the same reasons, therefore, theater nuclear war is also unthinkable. Deterrence must act, and the ultimate deterrent is the prospect of a strategic nuclear exchange between the United States and the USSR.

Because European nations rely on this view of deterrence, it has not been obvious to them that stronger conventional forces would be to their advantage, and at least some of the nations have held back in building up their forces. The analyses described earlier show that even forces of about current size, if appropriately configured, might in favorable circumstances be strong enough to repel an attack, or at least to make the anticipation of cheap and easy victory untenable. This uncertainty adds to the conventional part of the deterrent triad. We have, further, argued here that strong conventional forces might well increase the prospect that any war in Europe, if it breaks out, would be nuclear. By raising the stakes, this would in turn make war less likely. That is, increasing the conventional strength in the triad enhances deterrence in *all* respects.

The prospects for enhancing NATO's conventional defenses enough to deter an attack, in the senses described here, led McGeorge Bundy, George Kennan, Robert McNamara, and Gerard Smith to make their 1982 proposal that NATO adopt a no-first-use policy with regard to nuclear weapons.[32] They argued that the growth in numbers of nuclear weapons on both sides renders the prospect of a successful nuclear response by NATO to a Warsaw Pact conventional attack both strategically unsound and untenable because of the risks posed to humanity. They argue, further, that the United States and NATO should renounce any intention to use nuclear weapons first and that NATO's conventional defenses should be strengthened instead. Such strength can be built at a reasonable cost, they say, and the first edition of this book was quoted in subsequent public discussions as showing that the stronger NATO conventional forces described earlier could be obtained for perhaps a 3 to 4 percent real increase in defense budgets.[33] Although much has changed in the costs of weapon systems and military forces since that edition, Gen. Bernard W. Rogers, current supreme allied commander in Europe, noted more recently that by his headquarters' estimates a 4 percent real increase in NATO defense spending for six years would achieve a credible conventional defense.[34] Thus the earlier estimate of the cost of a conventional deterrent seems to be holding up.

After careful consideration, however, I have had to conclude that these modest cost increases can apply only in a situation where ambiguity about possible use of nuclear weapons is preserved. First, the uncertainty itself is necessary to force the USSR to contemplate the use of nuclear weapons to assure victory. As I have argued above, this would raise the stakes for going to war so high that in the absence of a direct military threat there would appear to be no issue so powerful as to warrant the risk of massive nuclear exchanges.

Second, from the military point of view it appears that a 4 percent defense budget increase would purchase stronger conventional forces but not very much larger ones. But the quality of Soviet military hardware is also increasing, as we have noted. Given the disparity in force sizes described earlier in this chapter, the absence of a nuclear weapon threat would permit the USSR to concentrate much more powerfully for a breakthrough than they could currently allow themselves to do. This is the significance of the discussions about a nuclear battlefield and armored warfare tactics in chapters 2 and 4. The ability to hold a conventional attack in the face of such concentrations, even with the added strength conferred by a 4 percent increase in defense spending, would be much less certain. This budget increase is more consistent with a strategy in which the defensive nuclear threat is retained. In the absence of that threat, NATO forces might have to approach those of the Pact in size to constitute a credible deterrent.

Finally, both the United States and the USSR have large tactical nuclear arsenals, and enforceable agreements to dispose of them do not appear achievable in the foreseeable future. Thus the nuclear capability will remain, and neither side could be certain that the other would honor a no-first-use pledge if pushed to the limit. In times of extreme tension with national survival apparently at stake, the pressure to maintain the nuclear threat must increase greatly. Especially at such times, the Europeans could see a U.S. no-first-use policy as threatening the dissolution of the deterrent triad and therefore of the alliance, in the manner presaged by de Gaulle.

Thus we seem to be faced by the need to balance equally unpalatable risks. One is the risk, however remote, of possible nuclear war if the current deterrent triad and strategy for Europe are retained. The other is the risk that in the absence of a conventional arms buildup that NATO has shown great reluctance to undertake, departure from the nuclear deterrent policy would encourage the USSR to exercise more aggressive policies toward Europe. This could then belatedly stimulate a massive conventional arms race or increase the chance of war by miscalculation, in which nuclear weapons might come to be used anyway. It appears that military safety and security have elusive qualities in a world having powerful military forces.

Concluding Comments

There obviously remains considerable latitude for interpretation, within the theoretical dynamics of all the previous arguments about deterrence, of how much conventional force is appropriate for the three-tier deterrent. This is what any arguments in the United States and Europe about force size and defense expenditure in the NATO context boil down to. The nonnuclear forces must be big enough and appropriately designed to achieve their deterrent ends by showing the Soviet Union a credible conventional war-fighting capability but yet not big enough to be provocative. Also, unspoken but in the background, the European components of those forces must be big enough to satisfy the United States that Europe is doing its share toward its defense, but not so big that the United States sees no need to keep its forces involved there. That involvement is part of the unity of the deterrent.

The nuclear forces, while they exist, must be big enough to persuade both NATO Europe and the USSR that they constitute a viable deterrent force to balance the Soviet SS-20s and other forces. But they can't be so big or constituted in such a way that they frighten both our allies and our opponents into political actions inimical to the stability of Europe.

Finally, in this day of inflation, recession, and unemployment when the United States and Western Europe are attempting to keep their economies in order against such pressures as the OPEC price fluctuations, industrial stagnation, and impending collapse of Third World economies, the question also becomes involved in the domestic politics of defense budgets. Few Western nations have been thinking extensively about how defense spending can be increased, and although the United States has added significantly to its defense expenditures, most NATO nations are thinking mainly about how such expenditures can be decreased or at least kept level. As the fiscal year 1984 budget debate begins in the United States, the key political question is whether the defense budget can continue to climb while expenditures for social programs are curtailed. The military, the political, and the economic problems may all be separable in theoretical arguments, but they clearly are not separable in practice.

Rapid Deployment
and the Uses of the Navy

Development of Strategy

Brief and broad reviews of strategy and its development must of necessity oversimplify exceedingly complex events and international relationships. Such a review is nevertheless necessary for a full appreciation of the directions in which our military forces have developed and must develop in the future on a worldwide scale. The following paragraphs will try to make a few key points about our national strategy without doing too much injustice to the sweep and intricacy of the events and their attending relationships among nations.

Since the emergence of the fundamental rivalry between the Western and Communist economic and political systems after World War II, the basic outlines of U.S. national security strategy haven't changed. Regardless of the various phrases (like "massive retaliation," "containment," or "flexible response") used to describe it, this strategy has included a structure of alliances to contain or to meet Soviet military expansion, and Chinese expansion when that appeared to be a threat. It has stressed the maintenance of a "strategic" deterrent, or the ability to strike militarily at the Soviet and Chinese homelands if our interests are sufficiently threatened by attacks on us or our closest allies. And it has emphasized the maintenance of a worldwide military presence and "general purpose forces" able to reinforce that presence where our interests or those of our allies are threatened on less than a vital scale. However, there have been a number of fluctuations of geographical and military emphasis within this broad strategic orientation, in response to changes in world conditions and to events brought about in part by the very directions of emphasis in that strategy at particular times.

Although the defense of Western Europe has been consistently in the forefront of the parts of this strategy that look beyond our own homeland, we have fought two major wars in Asia in furtherance of the policy of keeping Communist dominion from spreading. This was a matter more of necessity than of choice; there was no military attack in Europe, but there were such attacks in Korea and Vietnam. It can be argued that deterrence worked in Europe but, for a variety of reasons (some of which were reviewed in Chapter 6), it didn't in Asia.

Although Korea and Vietnam were in the main wars with proxies on behalf of proxies, we tended to view them as necessary to prevent Chinese dominance of southern and eastern Asia and to protect our presence and relationship with Japan. Japan has come increasingly to be viewed as an integral part of the community of free, democratic, industrialized ("Western") nations that we lead. Further in the background, the prevention of Chinese expansion was viewed as related to the prevention of Soviet expansion, including expansion in Europe, which we still view as the ultimate threat to world peace and freedom.

It can be argued that although neither of our post–World War II Asian wars was particularly successful for us on the spot—we deliberately fought to a stalemate in Korea[1] and abandoned South Vietnam ignominiously[2]— they were nevertheless successful in the broader context of our long term policy and strategy. Although we have been taking a new view of that strategy, expressed in terms of limitations to power, our relationship with Japan remains strong and seems likely to survive even the stresses of economic competition. That relationship could have weakened significantly had we stood aside and let Japan come to terms on its own with overt military conquest in Korea and Southeast Asia. China, too, seems to have been rethinking the limits of the exercise of power beyond its borders. Ancient rivalries with the Vietnamese have bloomed anew, and there has been a slow movement toward rapprochement between the United States and the People's Republic of China. This has been fueled and prodded by distrust and fear of the USSR by both countries. At the same time, even though there is uncertainty about whether we would become militarily engaged in another area—as there was before both Korea and Vietnam—the facts that we did do so in those cases and that the results of those engagements were even more painful for those on the other side than they were for us must surely counsel caution against direct military aggression in areas where our interests are known to be involved. It is quite possible that our actions in those wars, which on the surface had many divisive effects on our alliances, have also helped to hold them together because we *did* demonstrate willingness to act militarily. Thus Korea and Vietnam helped to establish the boundaries among the Western and the Soviet and Chinese areas of dominance, probably closer to the Soviet and Chinese borders than they would have been otherwise. For all the talk about dominos falling or not, this appears to have been a practical outcome of our military policies and conflicts worldwide.

As we have noted, the immediate effect of our political defeat in Vietnam was, however, an intensified concentration on Europe. From the viewpoint of our armed forces, this concentration provided both the opportunity and the demand for modernization of our general purpose forces. Although there are currently (in 1983) extensive arguments about the level of defense expenditure and about which expensive military system is or is not needed, it is generally recognized that extensive procurement of "current" fighting forces and expendables during the Vietnam years led to a slowing of development of new major systems. In part, the current surge in defense spending derives from the attempt to rectify the effects of that lag on an accelerated scale. The acceleration is spurred by the gradual realization that the USSR has been steadily modernizing its forces so that, with their greater numbers, they face the West with the risk of being hopelessly outclassed militarily.

This growth of Soviet military capability and its assumption of a worldwide scope for action well beyond Soviet borders have led to the view of the Soviet threat that we reviewed in Chapter 7. That view, combined with the economically threatening events attending the Iranian revolution, has led to another of the periodic shifts of emphasis within our broad national strategy that we referred to earlier. Although Europe still has the highest defense priority beyond our own borders,[3] we have come increasingly to stress the importance of the Middle East and Southwest Asia to our national interest. We have suggested that Europe will have to fill the military gap as our forces are diverted to that area.[4] We are building military forces having capabilities tailored to that area. And the largest force expansion and modernization we have undertaken have involved the Navy, which offers the readiest and politically least challenging capability for military presence and rapid response to attack in many parts of the world not otherwise easily reached for political or simple geographical reasons.[5]

Thus, in the practical sense of forces and their orientation, our strategic emphasis is assuming a more evenly balanced worldwide outlook than it had in the 1971–81 period. To judge whether this makes sense, and its significance for military force structure, it is worth examining the potential for military conflicts in the parts of the world outside Western Europe. It is as well to note at the outset that such a survey will undoubtedly miss the possibility of some unexpected events in an unanticipated area. Just so did Great Britain fail to anticipate the need to retake a small archipelago in the South Atlantic from Argentina. But just as in that case, if the military forces are built to encompass the appropriate capabilities the exact geographic location where they may be used is of less military than political importance.

The Prospects for Conflict

Figure 9–1 shows in schematic form, using the terminology developed in Chapter 6, where the most important conflicts in which the United States

FIGURE 9-1: Present and Potential War Areas of Concern to the United States

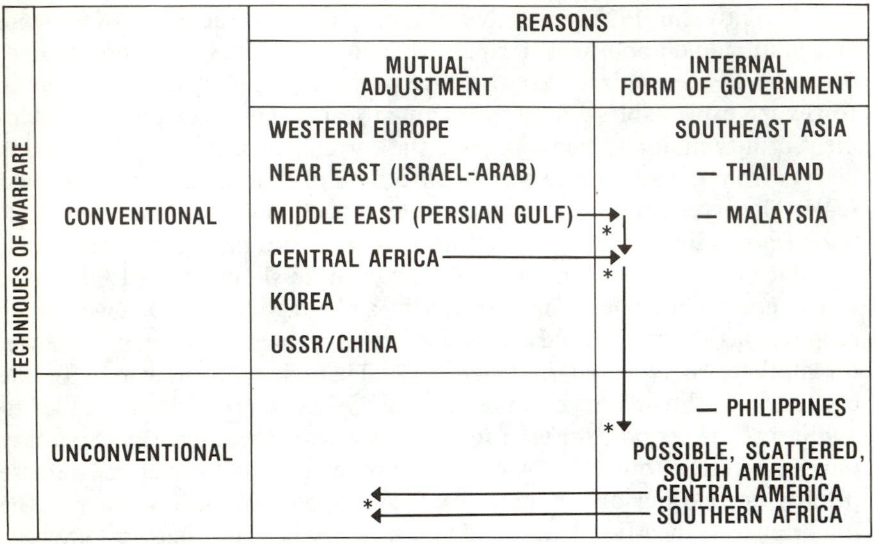

		REASONS	
		MUTUAL ADJUSTMENT	INTERNAL FORM OF GOVERNMENT
TECHNIQUES OF WARFARE	CONVENTIONAL	WESTERN EUROPE NEAR EAST (ISRAEL-ARAB) MIDDLE EAST (PERSIAN GULF) CENTRAL AFRICA KOREA USSR/CHINA	SOUTHEAST ASIA — THAILAND — MALAYSIA
	UNCONVENTIONAL		— PHILIPPINES POSSIBLE, SCATTERED, SOUTH AMERICA CENTRAL AMERICA SOUTHERN AFRICA

*Could be either kind.
3-9-83-1

could be involved may threaten during the next two decades. As we observed in the earlier chapter, the problem of independence wars has gradually gone away: few if any remain to be fought. One can postulate without fear of error that the remaining issues involving friendly nations in Southeast Asia are likely to be resolved (or even to drag on unresolved) before a new political generation in the United States would be willing to permit involvement there on any scale but that of political presence and bases to support operation elsewhere. As we shall note later, this could be troublesome if unexpected events in the Philippines threaten the base structure needed to defend Japan. Barring another Soviet surprise in the Caribbean basin invoving the nuclear deterrent, the trends in Latin America until very recently have appeared to be away from any but a minimal requirement for U.S. military action. The reaction to our 1965 "stability operation" in the Dominican Republic and the recognition of the vulnerability of the Panama Canal to guerrilla action during the debate about the Canal treaty appeared to signify that in general we had eschewed the idea of intervention with military force in that area unless there were to be some direct and obvious threat to our vital interests.

In the late 1970s and since, that outlok has changed in a very complex way. The attempt by the Carter administration to come to terms with the Marxist Sandinista regime in Nicaragua was not notably successful. Posi-

tions on both sides have hardened since, and Nicaragua has engaged in skir-
mishes with her neighbors to the north. Especially, she has been accused of
being a conduit for Cuban arms to guerrillas in El Salvador. The Reagan
administration took a strong position in support of the government in El
Salvador, as had the Carter administration before it. But there has come to
be greater stress on military aid, a military training program, and a few
military advisors (fewer than fifty). Even these actions, mild by any objective standards, raised a hue and cry in Congress and in the press about
parallels with Vietnam and our possible involvement in another "quagmire."
Clearly, then, the sensitivities remaining from Vietnam haven't gone away.
They lie dormant, ready to flame into irritation with but a slight provocation.

In recognition of this sensitivity the administration has called for a much
broader Caribbean basin initiative with stress on economic development rather
than military aid. But at this writing (in the spring of 1983) that proposal
hasn't caught on like wildfire. Even though the area is far closer to home,
the popular attitude about both the continuing conflicts in the area and the
continual building of Cuban military strength by the Soviet Union appears
to be more one of indifference than of deep concern, at least on the part
of most of our population. The popular hostility to nondemocratic regimes
that was highlighted in Chapter 6 is acting here as well.

It can be argued that a policy of "benign neglect" toward the *internal*
quarrels in Central America—many of them dating from the days of the con-
quistadores and the Maya tribes before them—and attention to our main
external interests would best suit this popular U.S. attitude. Such a policy
would leave the quarrels on the land to run their course while attending to
the physical security of the Panama Canal, guarding against overt Cuban
intervention, and guarding against the direct buildup of Soviet naval and
air power in the area. This would amount to a revival of the Monroe Doctrine
in its purest form. To pursue it as described, however, would probably require a tolerance we haven't displayed to the spread of Marxist governments
and a belief that covert Cuban and Soviet intervention doesn't really threaten
us. We would have to wink at potential Communist mischief that didn't
involve an overt attack, and we would have to feel comfortable that whenever
a future threat to the canal arises—even a guerrilla threat—we could contain
it.

Such equanimity in our government's view of the evolution of events in
the Caribbean and Central America is as unlikely as is direct intervention
in internal wars there. We thus appear to be in for a period of policy
dissonance in which our air and naval power tend to enforce the alternate
military policy just outlined—which they can do with relative ease so close
to home—while we use mainly political means to try to influence events on
the ground. If these events were to develop in a way that led us to put troops

on the ground, we would likely find that we could move them there quickly but that once there they would find ground operations as difficult and expensive in terms of equipment and sickness as such operations were in Southeast Asia.

With respect to Africa it is easy to extrapolate from the Rhodesian example to predict that, from a combination of domestic political outlook, the level of our interests, and the capability of the country, we would assiduously avoid taking sides *militarily* in any conflict that might develop in southern Africa. Although Soviet penetrations in central Africa, in Angola and the Horn, may pose long-term dangers in the form of a nascent Soviet base structure that can dominate vital resources and supply lines, this appears, in the late 1970s and early 1980s, remote and indirect. it certainly does not appear to warrant or command U.S. military involvement. The Carter administration was almost apologetic about providing some logistic support to the French-Belgian rescue mission to Shaba, Zaire, in 1978. However, this outlook could change if a Soviet presence should appear threatening to our Persian Gulf supply lines or access to other resources. We will return to this possibility in a somewhat different context shortly.

Let us now consider each of the possibilities for military involvement in the areas, outside Europe, of the upper left quadrant of Figure 9–1.

The "conventional wisdom" of the political observers says that a war between the People's Republic of China and the USSR would be dangerous for the United States.[6] In some respects, such as potential nuclear fallout, the danger is obvious. But I believe that with regard to the issues of whether we would be drawn into such a war, or whether, even if we weren't, there would be serious and negative political fallout for us, the "conventional wisdom" may be questioned. The consequences to us depend in part on how the scenario develops. Soviet forces might reach Peking in a few weeks, regardless of nuclear resistance or assistance. What happens next? We would certainly have to worry about the new political situation and the appearance of a more serious threat to Japan. The United States would not like, again, to face a nuclear-armed, closely coupled Soviet-Chinese alliance, and one could visualize direct or indirect materiel support to the Chinese to help them keep Soviet forces enmeshed in a very large country with a very hostile population. The history of the attempted Japanese conquest of China suggests that with or without such help, the events subsequent to a successful Soviet march to Peking would not play out or let the USSR disengage decisively or quickly. It is difficult to see that this would either be inimical to our long-term interests or necessitate our direct involvement. Deterrence of war in Europe might well be easier in the circumstances.

Korea remains a dangerous location for potential U.S. involvement, at least for as long as Kim Il Sung lives, provided repressive regimes in the South do not achieve for him what he cannot: the departure of the United States because of ideological reasons at home. The Carter administration attempted such a withdrawal. Not only the added threat to Korea but the significant possibility of weakening Japan's security made the attempt abortive. The North maintains a warlike stance, however. In consequence, this may be the most likely region outside Europe where the nuclear deterrent must act; and this very fact of nuclear potential makes less likely the retention of Japanese bases for essential support in case of war in Korea. We have a major interest in protecting Japan, but it is difficult at this point to see who would threaten Japan militarily. (Threats to Japanese lines of commerce and supply would be another story. But they would in many ways be threats to our own connections overseas as well.)

One can forecast with reasonable confidence based on past history that barring a Soviet miscalculation, the United States and the Soviet Union will continue to act to prevent a military confrontation between their own forces or an irrevocable decision in favor of one side or the other in the eastern Mediterranean. The half-consummated peace between Egypt and Israel, even in the aftermath of the Lebanon invasion and even if it could ultimately be successfully extended to the West Bank and Jordan, will simply serve to modify the alignments among the Soviet and U.S. proxies in the area without changing the nature of the superpower confrontation there. If anything, the Soviet commitment to a presence in Syria seems to have been strengthened by the defeat of Syrian air and land forces during the 1982 war in Lebanon.

The greatest change in the outlook for engagement of U.S. arms overseas occurred with the 1979 Iranian revolution. In the new situation an apparently secure U.S. position in the Persian Gulf area became precarious for the United States and its allies in the industrialized world. The traditional rivalry between Iran and Iraq flared into open warfare. The positions of the "traditional" states on the Arabian peninsula began to seem precarious and in danger of subversion by Iran's militant Moslem fundamentalism. Although the Soviet Union has been meticulously careful to avoid taking sides among the parties to the various conflicts, the United States felt that its interests in the area had come under serious pressure. President Carter deployed naval forces into the Arabian Sea. He declared that we would defend our interests in Southwest Asia by force if necessary and initiated the buildup of a Rapid Deployment Force (RDF) to respond to attacks on friendly nations or oil fields in the Gulf or Arabian region.[7] A series of tentative basing agreements was sought with the right to use the bases for movement into the area if necessary, with Egypt, Kenya, Somalia, and Oman. Some joint exercises of modest scale have been held with Egypt and Oman, to the tune of much regional political sensitivity in the latter case. Several AWACS airplanes were deployed to Saudi Arabia to help guard the Arabian oil fields when the Iran-Iraq war broke out.

Currently (in 1983) the planned size of the Rapid Deployment Force, which if it deploys is to be integrated into a new Central Command to cover the area generally from the Horn of Africa and the eastern shore of the Mediterranean through Pakistan, is on the order of 220,000 men.[8] It includes designated Army forces including three and one-third divisions (including the Eighty-second Airborne); carrier battle groups of variable size but including amphibious landing forces; a 45,000-man Marine Amphibious Force; and about 500 Air Force aircraft in seven tactical fighter wings.

These forces clearly are not usable to solve internal conflicts in the nations on the Arabian peninsula. They are aimed at deterring Soviet movement into the Gulf region—a possibility that appeared more real after Afghanistan and the Iranian revolution. However, the USSR can easily pose a threat of over twenty divisions, plus supporting airborne and tactical air forces, to move through Iran or Iraq to the Gulf.[9] The planned RDF, especially if its buildup is less rapid than desired—always a likelihood in "real life"—might have trouble fighting a force that large that had the military initiative while the RDF itself faced the problems of landing, establishing defensible positions, building up, and engaging the Soviet attacker seriously, all at once. The retreat to the Pusan perimeter in Korea comes to mind.[10]

However, Soviet movement from its borders through the rugged and undeveloped terrain to the Gulf region would not be as easy as running down a superhighway. Airborne landings can't be made too far forward if they may face serious opposition, and a linkup with ground forces may be delayed. Thus, if there is *"strategic warning" that is heeded,* a "preemptive presence" could be established by the landing and beginning of a buildup by significant parts of the RDF. The characteristic Soviet caution noted in Chapter 7 could then operate to forestall any overt Soviet military move to the South. Thus, just as in Europe, the key to the success of the RDF is not that it could with certainty beat Soviet forces on their own ground in an all-out army-to-army fight. Given the short Soviet interior lines of supply, and the U.S. need to operate at distances that characterized the British move on the Falklands, success for us in such a fight would be problematical. The role of RDF, like the role of conventional forces in Europe, is to create doubt in the Soviet mind about whether the USSR could win easily in a war it could contain. As in Europe, many political factors surrounding the presence and use of the force are at least as important as its military capability.

Rapidly Deployable Military Capability

Of course, such capability doesn't come without penalty. As we have noted, the buildup of the RDF diverts forces that would otherwise be available to reinforce Europe in the event of a crisis.[11] In addition, most of the major weapons and equipment of these forces will have been developed with Soviet opposition in mind (since that is the most capable opposition), and if they are tailored for any theater it will be for Europe. The experience of Korea and Vietnam was that forces developed primarily for operation in Europe are imperfectly matched to situations elsewhere. They have been and can be adapted, of course. But this takes time. We have also seen that the military world is different now from that of even the recent past. Given current circumstances, can modern military capabilities be as effective elsewhere as they are expected to be in Europe, or even more so if there is a lack of technically sophisticated opposition? The answer to this question has several parts: the nature of the opposition; the effects of the physical environment; and our ability to get the capability where it is needed in time for it to be decisive.

Weapons and systems designed to operate against Soviet opposition in Europe should do as well in Southwest Asia if the opposing weaponry were the only matter of concern. However, the environment is of great concern as well. The disaster of the Iranian rescue mission showed that we operate in ignorance of potential physical stresses in the environment (such as extreme heat or unexpected dust storms) at great peril to the missions involved.[12] Aside from climatic, weather, and terrain stresses, we would find in such areas that facilities are greatly lacking, while the distances involved for communication, logistics, and other support are enormous (Iran alone is roughly as large as the United States east of the Mississippi), and water is scarce. All these factors would affect our ability to operate, whereas the USSR, if it were the attacker, might have planned to meet the problems—although perhaps not perfectly.

In keeping with the lessons of all post–World War II history, though we may plan our forces with Soviet opposition in view we are more likely to fight non-Soviet forces if the RDF becomes engaged militarily. As we note at several points in earlier chapters, impressive military capabilities are being transmitted to various potential combatants in areas of the world that may at some future time be of miltiary interest to us. Although all the recipients of modern military equipment may not use it with maximum effectiveness, even relatively primitive armed forces so equipped can cause serious damage to the most modern armed forces. This does not necessarily mean that U.S. forces could not prevail ultimately if events should come to a conflict against "typical" opposition—or even Soviet opposition—in the Middle Eastern deserts or other undeveloped areas. It does mean that more time than we would wish to spend would be required for our forces to succeed in such military missions while minimizing casualties. As with a potential full military buildup in the Persian Gulf region, adapting to the conditions will take time when we wish instantaneously to create a new political situation based on credible and instantly effective military force.

Paradoxically, too much of our capability can be effective only against similarly equipped opposition. Many of the major advances in weaponry derive from improved electronic technology, reflected in target acquisition and improved weapon guidance and control. Some of the guided weapons, as we have seen, will by virtue of their precision in hitting targets lead to economy of force and to a reduction of war's vast incidental destruction to an extent that is not yet fully understood. But much of the advanced target-location capability is specialized for use against electronic (radio and radar) emitters or to recognize "signatures" convertible to electronic data. The guidance, especially for standoff air-delivered weapons, is closely associated with such acquisition capability in potential tactical applications. To the extent that a military opponent is *less* well equipped with modern weapons and is adept at hiding, the new capabilities can be degraded or will be difficult to bring into effective use. Indeed, this was the case in operations against Communist forces in *South* Vietnam, where multimillion-dollar airplanes often had to bomb colored smoke at the edge of a tree line thought to harbor enemy forces of unknown size. This is another difficulty that could translate into more time and greater force requirements than we might hope to use in any military action. Thus, from many points of view the diffusion of modern weaponry puts us in danger of making errors similar to those attending our entry into Vietnam. We must recognize that even apparently primitive opposition might require a greater military investment than we would wish, on careful political consideration, to make.

Our ability to bring forces rapidly to where they are needed has grown since the mid-1960s, as evidenced by the massive 1973 airlift into Israel. However, remember that now no base on foreign soil can be considered secure in all political circumstances. Bases providing access to the Middle East will be difficult to prepare in advance of need. Use of our bases in the Philippines or Japan will also depend on political circumstances surrounding the immediate events. Deployment capability can become limited even for long-range aircraft such as the C-5, which can be refueled in the air. Support of operations into, say, Korea or the Persian Gulf area would be very difficult in the absence of staging in Japan, southern Europe, or some points in the Middle East. But study of the globe shows that it can be done—again, at the expense of time, as a deployment hampered by lack of intermediate bases and overflight rights would have to reduce payloads and perhaps fly less than direct routes. To meet this problem for the RDF we are stationing a few (about a dozen) fast logistic ships at Diego Garcia. They will carry the heavy equipment for ground forces that can be deployed by airlift. This suits a strategy of "preemptive presence," but it can present insuperable vulnerabilities in a war where the oceans are not sanctuary.

Finally, we must note another factor, totally independent of military technology, that affects the time to act, namely, intelligence and warning. Although the intelligence community is often blamed when an event like the 1973 Middle East war or the major Soviet lift of Cuban forces into Angola takes us by surprise, the fact is that most failures of warning can be traced to the assumptions of the recipient. It is usually found that the data were there but not recognized or were ignored for various reasons.[13] To be safe we must conclude that the one who wants to initiate military action can probably achieve tactical surprise. Again, if the United States should want to act, its response would automatically be delayed unless we preempt by moving forces in anticipation of events. Such moves are difficult in a climate of political tension, because the "locals" who grant us our base rights are likely not to want to appear provocative by granting those rights just then. If at some time the political climate should be conducive to preemptive action, we would be doubly frustrated if we had failed to build the technical capability to undertake it.

Thus, all the factors affecting our own time to move with credible forces and for those forces to accomplish their missions, in areas outside Europe, appear to extend the potential duration of any military action we might undertake. The so-called surgical strike to achieve carefully delineated objectives in almost no time and with no incidental damage is but a dream born from misunderstanding of the limits of military power, even power using modern military technology. Practically, this means that situations in which political constraints of all kinds make even small wars difficult for us must tend to dominate our use of military power, despite the great advances of military technology. Concentration on NATO affairs and the Soviet threat in building our forces, as we have seen doing, can only reinforce these trends. Again, this does not suggest that the military capabilities being built for Europe would be ineffective outside Europe or that they would be built very differently for use in potential wars elsewhere. But there are some things that obviously should be done to ease the path for contingencies in which policies may change rapidly.

1. Long-range aircraft capacity should be built to a level that would accommodate the flight times attending a paucity of staging bases for deployments into such areas as the Persian Gulf or the Southwest Pacific; in any case, this can only help support deployment to Europe in time of crisis. This has been undertaken, in an atmosphere of great domestic political conflict over whether we should buy more C-5s (C-5B), used 747s, or a wholly new airplane, the C-17.

2. The amount of airlift and sealift is only one part of the problem of deploying rapidly to remote geographical areas. Forces configured to fight in Europe must of necessity be armor-heavy, with tanks, self-

propelled artillery, and other armored fighting vehicles. Such forces
are not easily airlifted. In part, this problem is being solved in Europe
by storing the materiel of reinforcement divisions there. It is being
solved for the RDF by storing heavy equipment on the rapid deployment ships to be stationed at Diego Garcia. There are also the
beginnings of experiments with lighter forces, such as a High
Technology Light Division experiment being undertaken by the Ninth
Infantry Division at Fort Lewis, Washington. Such forces might use
light tanks, for example, which have not been part of the U.S. Army's
regular equipage. They would be well equipped with ATGMs, SAMs,
lightweight artillery, and armed helicopters and designed for rapid
deployment and to take ground rapidly in areas where there are few
facilities and only moderate opposition. Such forces, and the Marines,
operating as the vanguard of a heavier force, might be able to secure
areas where Soviet opposition is expected, but they wouldn't have
the fighting power of divisions designed for Europe.

3. Naval and amphibious forces are more important in furnishing an
   available, rapid-response capability for areas outside Europe. This
   would require changes in naval-force structure of the kind discussed
   in Chapter 5, as well as attention to the size and capability of the
   Marine Corps. As we have seen (Table 5–5), our amphibious capability is none too large, and until recently it was shrinking. Many
   of the necessary changes in naval and amphibious force structure have
   been started, but many remain to be undertaken, and there may be
   distortions in the naval development, as we have noted. We will return
   to the problems of the naval buildup shortly.

4. We must also make certain that our new target acquisition, guidance,
   and control systems can be adapted to other geographic and military
   environments than those (in Europe) for which they are mainly being
   designed. The lead time for developing and adapting such technical
   capabilities requires this attention much before, not when, the
   capabilities are needed.

In the sense of militiary-system acquisition, none of this is a very great change
from what we are doing now. But all of it is important, and it will cost money
that, in the short run at least, reduces what can be spent on what we have
viewed until now as the primary missions.

It is worth noting in this connection that from the U.S. viewpoint alone
there are alternatives to military action in the Persian Gulf region, just as
there are alternative strategies in the Caribbean. For example, the synfuels
program undertaken by the Carter administration, and permitted by the
Reagan administration to decline before it was effectively begun, might have

lessened our Persian Gulf commitments. The program makes little economic sense in a time of declining oil prices, and it would always be vulnerable to destructive pricing policies by oil producers, now that the price obtainable for natural oil has climbed far above the basic cost of extraction and transportation in most cases. Taking a broader view, however, the cost of a six-division war in the Persian Gulf region and a subsequent occupation by U.S. forces for an indefinite period, judging from the Vietnam experience, could equal or exceed even the $100–150 billion originally designated for the synfuels program. Another factor in weighing our involvement in the Persian Gulf is that although we could position the United States to dispense with Middle Eastern oil, our European allies and Japan are far more heavily dependent on it.

Thus we find again, as we did in both Korea and Vietnam, that we are undertaking a military strategy that is in our national interest mainly in the sense that it helps to maintain the alliances among the industrial nations that we believe are fundamental to our long term national security. We may also find that, just as in the previous two Asian wars, these key alliances are in many ways weakened by the actions we take to hold them together. Perhaps this is one of the unavoidable penalties of exercising leadership among nations.

It is also true, however, that the forces being designed for this role would give us a flexibility to meet the unexpected that we don't now have. For example, a sudden turn of events in the Philippines analogous to the fall of the Shah in Iran, and the need to give up our bases in the Manila area, could be very threatening to the security of Japan. We are not currently well positioned to respond to such events. As noted in Chapter 6, the American public would probably object to U.S. military action to sustain a regime they view as oppressive. Military forces might not in any case help very much by direct intervention in such essentially political events. But the ability to move effective military forces rapidly can help influence those events, in conjunction with other political and economic policies. In particular, an augmented military presence at the right time could help avoid the later need to choose between participation in a shooting war or withdrawal.

The Navy in the Newly Developing Strategy

The Navy is being built to meet Soviet naval power. But it will be needed most in Third World areas if the idea of rapidly deploying land and air forces to those areas is to make sense. With naval forces able to carry military power to the African and Asian littoral of the South Atlantic, the Indian Ocean, and the southern and western Pacific, as well as to waters closer to home including the Caribbean, the Gulf of Mexico, and the Pacific shores of Latin America, the need for bases and an intrusive U.S. presence on land is much reduced. Naval forces can bring a U.S. military presence to an area without intruding on the sovereignty of nation. Using the Marine ground and air forces, the Navy can land combat forces if necessary to start a military buildup, and if events press the buildup that far these leading contingents can protect any further deployments of Army and Air Force units. Once such a presence is established the Navy can, together with the air forces that have landed, protect the line of communication and supply to the newly established military presence. None of these actions may involve the Soviet Navy in any way. As we have noted in Chapter 5, however, we can't ignore the possibility that they may intervene in any action we undertake if they view that action as sufficiently threatening to their interests.

It should be apparent from all that has preceded that the missions of our Navy, since the defeat of the Japanese Navy in World War II, have been oriented shoreward. Opposing fleets have simply been obstacles to overcome. All the anti-air warfare and anti-submarine warfare capabilities of the fleet, representing by a rough estimate well over half the total cost of the Navy, exist for the purpose of guarding against interference with its land-oriented missions. The Soviet Navy, on the other hand, appears to have been oriented primarily toward preventing shore-oriented U.S. operations by defeating the U.S. fleet.[14] The differing naval concepts of the two countries were both reasonable during the decade or so after World War II, given the relative positions and strengths of the two countries. Since then the capabilities have changed, and there have been clear indications of change in Soviet naval concepts as well.[15]

As we saw in Chapter 5, except for the submarines' torpedoes, all of the immediate threat against ships of a U.S. naval force can be considered an air threat in view of the Soviets' heavy reliance on various forms of cruise missiles for attack. Thus far, the Soviets have been using the long-range, subsonic Bear turboprop aircraft for targeting and midcourse guidance. These aircraft are thus prime targets in case our own fleet has to defend itself; the picture of a Bear being intercepted by an F-4 as it observes NATO maneuvers is a familiar one.[16] Eventually the Soviets may be able to substitute more advanced technology for this vulnerable link in their naval-attack system. (Of course, if the Soviet naval forces are designed to deliver a crushing first strike, as many writers, including their own Adm. S. G. Gorshkov, have suggested,[17] the prestrike vulnerability of these aircraft may not be so critical for them. However, naval history from Philip II's Armada to Pearl Harbor is replete with failures of the irresistible first strike to force a decisive outcome in a longer war. Benjamin F. Tracy, secretary of the Navy in 1889, said, in relation to the new class of battleships he wanted built, that "naval wars in the future will be short and sharp. . . . The nation that is ready to strike the first blow will gain an advantage which its antagonist can never offset, and inflict an injury from which . . . he can never recover.")[18]

Neither the attack nor the defense have options for action that are independent of geography. As E. Wegener, and Mahan before him, pointed out, sea power not only requires a fleet (or, in the modern age, aircraft that can dominate the sea) and an orientation by the naval power towards the sea, but a strategic position from which to operate.[19] The United States, in attempting to protect its maritime power and the shore bases it supports, is favored by the fact that Soviet ships and submarines must enter the open oceans through relatively narrow passages where surveillance and barrier operations can be conducted: the so-called Greenland–Iceland–United Kingdom (GIUK) Gap; the Mediterranean or Red Sea; the Sea of Japan (see Figure 9–2). The advantages for the USSR of having established bases outside its boundaries, in areas such as Cuba, the coasts of Africa or India, or the coast of Vietnam, would be enormous in case of war and are sufficient to explain prima facie any apparent Soviet drives in such directions.[20] On the other hand, we noted earlier the experience of World War II in such areas as the Mediterranean and on the convoy route to Murmansk through the Norwegian Sea, that surface naval forces alone would find it difficult to survive against a sustained land-based aircraft assault.[21] The problem for the United States in protecting the sea lanes would be compounded today and would be extended to include the sea approaches to Northwest Europe, Japan, Korea, and China, since the assault could be mounted by the long-range Backfires of Soviet naval aviation as well as Soviet nuclear attack submarines. If the Soviets were willing to risk perhaps severe attrition to remove the main striking power of the U.S. fleet in such waters, they could probably do so. (We explored in chapter 5 the changes in the structure of our maritime power that would be needed to reduce this vulnerability.)

Soviet air power would have trouble reaching beyond the areas listed above without crossing hostile territory from which their aircraft would be vulnerable to land-based defenses. (This vulnerability exists in varying degrees even in the eastern Mediterranean.) However, if their long-range naval aviation could be transferred rapidly to bases near the coasts of Africa, key areas of the Central and South Atlantic and the approaches to the Middle East and south Asia through the western Indian Ocean could be covered by those aircraft as well as by submarines and made very dangerous for U.S. and other Western shipping and sea power. This furnishes an additional reason for the Soviets to covet and attempt to establish an African base structure. Such a structure would also be needed to support the growing Soviet surface fleet if it is to extend its reach beyond close-in defense of the homeland.

More recently, it has appeared that the Soviet navy will assume some of the overseas tasks that have characterized our own. This was suggested, for example, by its covering of the sealift into Egypt and Syria during the 1973

214

FIGURE 9-2: Restricted Soviet Access to Major Oceans

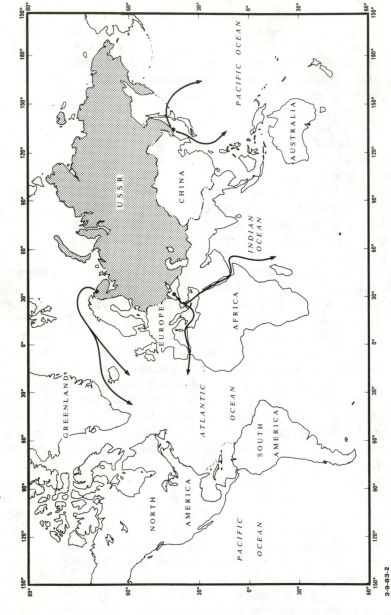

3-9-83-2

Middle East war,[22] by its demonstration at the time of the Soviet lift of Cuban troops into Angola, and by support of its sealift of supplies (and probably Cuban troops) to Ethiopia.[23] At the same time, we cannot in the case of either country fully separate the general purpose navy from the strategic navy—the SSBNs on both sides. In the event of imminent or actual all-out war, all the maritime forces of both sides might be used against opposing SSBNs, as necessary and feasible,[24] in addition to their participation in other, tactical, operations.

The large investment we are currently making in a naval buildup joins that being set aside to tailor and support the Rapid Deployment Force in shifting the orientation of our military power from Europe toward other parts of the world. The naval buildup as well as the RDF are demanding resources that would otherwise be available to support forces in Europe. (Whether a naval buildup of the kind and magnitude we have undertaken is actually needed, rather than a shifting of forces and procurement of less expensive and less vulnerable forces to exercise maritime power in the ocean areas under greatest Soviet threat, is a question that was examined in Chapter 5.) The gradual tailoring of the divisions designated to be part of the RDF for areas outside Europe will eventually mean that those forces couldn't easily be used in Europe without reequipment and some retraining. Thus the shift in strategic emphasis away from Europe that we have been examining entails a different balancing of risks and needs from the one that has dominated our military strategy for the past decade.

It has often been stated in popular writing about national security strategy that we are planning for "one and a half wars." The scale of effort underlying such concepts is rarely considered in these discussions. It is of interest to note that from the U.S. point of view we were also engaged in "one and a half wars" during World War II: the combined Army and Navy personnel strength (including respective air forces) in the Pacific ran between 40 and 50 percent of that in the Atlantic and Europe for the entire period from early 1943 through 1945.[25] And, of course, the "beat Hitler first" strategy of the war was consistent with this distribution, since Japan surrendered before there could be substantial force transfers from Europe to the Pacific after the defeat of Germany.

Today, despite the great and visible increase of emphasis on the Navy and RDF as compared with Europe, the forces and budget reflect a similar picture. The Navy budget in fiscal year 1984 is about 35 percent of the total budgets of the three Services taken together (this includes strategic naval and air forces, but they are only a small part of the total—just over 10 percent). Some uncertain part of the Navy budget applies to Europe. The four and two-thirds Army and Marine divisions designated for the RDF represent about one-quarter of our active combat divisions. The seven Air Force tactical fighter wings are about one-quarter of the total active Air Force fighter and attack unit strength.[26]

By these rough numbers an argument can be made that our current strategic emphasis has not deviated far from the general balance we have maintained since World War II, even though the current orientation and that of the late 1970s appear at first glance to be far apart. By constraining the forces that may be available for Europe we are shifting the balance of deterrence from the war we are less likely to fight toward the potential wars that history since World War II has shown are more likely. There is some added risk that a reduction of apparent military strength and commitment in Europe can make a conflict there more likely. But this is a difficult argument to make as long as the "deterrent triad" described in the previous chapter is maintained at some reasonable level. A change in the level of the conventional force deterrent aimed at "elsewhere" could, in light of the history just cited, make a much bigger difference in deterring war "elsewhere."

None of this is to argue that we should simply throw money at these force and deterrence problems. It is still necessary to build our forces as efficiently as possible and to adapt them to the realities of advancing military technology. We will be reviewing some of those realities more specifically from the defense management and planning point of view in the next section.

Part 3
Absorbing Technological Change

10
Frustrated Expectations

The first edition of this book[1] went into extensive detail at this point about the management problems of creating and sustaining the general purpose forces. The discussion dealt, among other things, with the costs of defense manpower; the problems of managing defense system acquisition to control frustrating and pervasive growth of system costs; and the possible extent of budget increases that might be needed to build up to the general purpose military strength being demanded by the evolution of world events that was described earlier. Two important conclusions of that discussion were that between 3 and 12 percent per year real budget increase might be needed to meet our commitments satisfactorily and that despite a sequence of management approaches to the problem of controlling cost growth over the years, that problem was proving rather intractable. Over a long period of years (1965–77), the average growth of military system costs over initial estimates was between about 50 and 80 percent, according to figures from congressional hearings and the General Accounting Office. Recent experience shows that this pattern continues,[2] bearing out the observation that in this area we are bound to follow the Red Queen's dictum: We must run as hard as we can to stay in the same place.

Since the earlier volume was written there has been the change in defense budget that many observers thought was necessary. While reducing the rate of spending increase on social programs, the Reagan administration added an average of 7 percent per year of real growth to the defense budget. With the pain of a deep economic recession and the impact of large budget deficits there has been a consequent clamor to reduce defense spending to lower levels. As we have seen, much of the issue comes down to questions of risk in the face of a threat that is feared but whose form is not very specific even though we feel strongly that it is associated with Soviet expansionism. But an underlying problem is that of defense technology and how it is absorbed by the military society and the civilian society that supports it.

Since the early 1950s there has been enormous technological change in the armed forces. Major elements of this change have included intercontinental ballistic missiles (ICBMs) and long-range sea-launched ballistic missiles (SLBMs); supersonic combat aircraft; long-range jet aircraft able to carry tens or hundreds of thousands of pounds of cargo across the oceans; nuclear-powered submarines; spacecraft to aid in observation, navigation, and communications; guided weapons for all purposes; the new computers of the computer revolution. The civilian economy has shared the benefits of many of these advances and others like them. Some of them, like the use of spacecraft and the advance of computer technology and application, have only begun to run their course. With this much technological change in but a quarter of a century, dislocations and imperfect adaptations are inevitable. Thus, we are faced with the problem that the cost of the change itself, which has obviously been great, is increased by the inefficiencies these poor adjustments cause.

At the same time, the accompanying technological revolution in the civilian economy has led to a rise in living standards reflected in social programs that we consider essential to our national well-being. The result is reflected in the decline of defense expenditure from about 9 percent of GNP to under 6 percent over a twenty-year period, and this is accompanied by disappointment that the technological revolution in defense matters doesn't get us more for our money. As a nation, we don't want to return to the days of 9 percent of GNP invested in defense, and in our frustration we are turning against the technology that we thought would help us.

The gradual replacement of the technologies of the 1940s and 1950s by entirely new means for carrying out military tasks raised many hopes that, after the Vietnam war subsided, we would be able to reduce the amount of money we would have to spend on defense. Many of these hopes focused on the quality of advanced ships and airplanes and the smart weapons they would launch against the enemy. On a one-target, one-weapon basis, it was felt, we would not have to buy weapons in enormous numbers or have forces of enormous size to defeat larger but cruder opposition.

The realities, of course, have proven to be very different from these expectations. As the previous chapters have demonstrated, about all that has emerged with certainty is that rates of destruction of the machinery of war, when engagements take place, will be much higher than ever before in history and that the great sophistication that makes weapons smart is also, in most cases, making them expensive. (Some, like the original laser-guided bomb, are not very expensive, but such instances are rare.) The problems of managing the acquisition and operation of the general purpose forces are consequently becoming more difficult and complex, rather than simpler and more tractable.

As we noted in chapters 3, 4, and 5, the costs of major defense systems and weapons in each of the three Services are increasing faster than their budgets. Defense planners have not been unaware of these trends, although they may not have perceived how persistent the trends have been through the years. As a consequence, however, cost considerations have come in large measure to dominate the creation of our own armed forces and, even more, those of most of our allies. There have been many changes in both theory and practice in an attempt to come to grips with these adverse cost trends. Unfortunately, every measure has generated its own problems, essentially frustrating progress.

1. For a long time we were telling ourselves that since the technology of the Western allies is so much better than that of their major opponents east of the Iron Curtain, the higher quality of our systems will make up for the Soviet bloc's greater numbers. But as we saw in discussing the problems of a conventional war in Europe, this is only partly true. Size of forces does count, especially when the other side's quality may not be very far behind our own after all.* In an attempt to come to grips with this realization, the so-called high-low force mix, discussed in Chapter 3 and described indirectly in Chapter 5, was proposed. But as we saw there, it is necessary to interweave the sophisticated and the simple force elements to achieve an effective operating capability for any military purpose. Moreover, the sophistication of potential adversaries does not reside in one place where they can be opposed by the numerically small, high-quality, expensive parts of our forces. As a result of our efforts, those of our allies, and those of the Soviet Union, advanced military technology is being spread worldwide. There are few places in the world now where a simple military force without advanced technical capabilities can prevail over determined and effective opposition. Thus,

---

*We might remind ourselves of the equations of F. W. Lanchester.[3] They show that, depending on the circumstances of battle, if technical capability is the same on both sides, the ratio of relative combat strengths of opposing forces is somewhere between the ratio of the numbers fighting and the ratio of the squares of the numbers fighting. This simply means that if the other side outnumbers us by two to one, our weapons have to be somewhere between two and four times better than his for the two sides to be considered equally strong. It would be difficult to prove that this much disparity would exist between U.S. and Soviet weapons systems if they were used equally well. This is because, even though in most cases our basic technology may be far advanced over that of the USSR, it is able to compensate for much of this lag by the way its systems are designed and used. Its air defense systems and airplanes are examples of such compensation for inferior technology.

increasingly, the quality-versus-quantity argument as a rationale for reducing the numbers of expensive military systems we must purchase is proving to be evanescent.

2. Reasons of a political and operational character have also been advanced to justify reductions in the size of our general purpose forces. Senator Mike Mansfield argued in 1970 that it was no longer necessary to keep forces in Europe.[4] Recent articulations of the reasons for a "naval strategy" or even complete withdrawal from overseas positions show that the desire for a return to pre–World War II isolationism is not far from the surface.[5] Others argued that we could reduce the size of our forces because we would avoid further involvements like Vietnam, leaving a need for forces in Europe only; since the Europeans are providing a large part of their own defense, the United States could reduce the total size of its armed forces.[6] Another approach has been to say that there are forces we do not need. The arguments about the missions and composition of the Navy and about large aircraft carriers, described in Chapter 5, are in this category. We have found, however, that the Defense Department's warnings of prior years about the growth of Soviet military strength were not simply scare tactics to pressure Congress into increasing defense budgets. The claimed growth of Soviet strength has become much more visible and seems to continue apace (regardless of Soviet reasons or objectives for such growth). Thus, the logic of arguments for reducing our armed forces evaporated, and the arguments now are about how much it is necessary to increase them.

3. It has been hoped that we could reduce our own defense budget by sharing costs and responsibilities with the Europeans, by standardizing equipment and taking more pains to ensure that their systems and ours could operate together. But we found that, although such steps are necessary to help knit NATO together as an economic and military unit, it is costing *more*, not less, to achieve such integration. This is because multinational production of systems like aircraft involves costs of coordination and integration of diverse national capabilities that don't exist within a single economy. In the case of the German-French Roland anti-aircraft missile system, the problems of Americanization (whether justified by program management considerations or not) doubled the cost of the weapon over the original estimates, and the program was cancelled by Congress. Finally, we have found that competition for technological advantage in the civilian economy, competition for third-country arms sales, and concerns about the health of defense industries for national economic reasons have all worked against close arms cooperation with our allies, regardless of the possibilities for saving by sharing.

4. Recognizing the potentially high rates of destruction that are likely to characterize war using modern weapons (and that were demonstrated in 1973 Middle East war), we argued for a time that a major conventional war in Europe would be short and that large inventories of the most expensive weapon systems were therefore not needed.[7] This argument, as we have seen, is vulnerable to the uncertainties that historically have bedeviled the predictive aspects of military planning. It is vulnerable, also, to the other side's option, if it wishes to make the commitment, to put by enough to prevail when our side, having been more frugal, runs out of weapons or ammunition. As a consequence, we have in recent years heard defense planners say that we must plan for more sustained fighting capabilities than had been thought necessary just a short time previously.[8]

5. As noted above, there have been strenuous attempts to reduce the costs of defense systems by better management of their acquisition and operation. The Congress has continually urged the Defense Department to use better and more careful management techniques to reduce the costs of defense systems, and it has reinforced its exhortations with legislation.[9] Yet these costs keep rising.

These cascading contradictions and frustrations have engendered argument, uncertainty, and indecision about the value of major elements of the general purpose forces. The arguments have come increasingly to be focused by what has come to be called the "reform movement" in defense. Its proponents are drawn in part from defense circles, including men such as Franklin Spinney of the Office of the Secretary of Defense,[10] and they have found a champion in Senator Gary Hart and spokesmen such as James Fallows in the media.[11] Although their message often takes a long time to convey (Spinney's briefing is said to require three hours of listening), it is basically simple:

1. Technology for its own sake has been allowed to dominate weapon system design. This has made weapon systems excessively complex, costly, unreliable, and difficult to use.
2. Thus in our search for quality we have given up the chance to acquire weapon systems in sufficient quantity within budgets we can afford, while we have failed to achieve the desired quality as well.
3. By backing away from the search for the most advanced technology, we can make weapons simpler, cheaper, and easier to use and thereby make our general purpose forces larger and sturdier.

The tone of the arguments engendered by these views can become strident as the press, in its current mode of emphasizing critical commentary on government activity, picks them up and amplifies them. But the situations being described are far more complex than the simple arguments sketched above imply.

First, there is the assumption that the simpler weapons called for will be much less expensive than the ones they would replace. Engineering cost estimates for alternative systems are rarely given. The assertions of lower cost usually neglect the complexity of the military tasks to be performed; when such complexity is accounted for the systems prove to be neither simple nor inexpensive once development starts. The experiences with the F-16 and the F-18 fighter aircraft provide useful analogies. Both started out to be "lightweight fighters," and both have become complex combat aircraft in the $20 million or more "per copy" class. Some would argue that the changes in these aircraft that caused them to grow in sophistication and cost from their initial "lightweight fighter" concepts are really the fault of the military Services, because they kept dressing up the "requirements." Without completely absolving the Services of responsibility for such behavior, we must nevertheless remember that the first requirement for any combat aircraft is to carry out useful missions in the face of enemy defenses, *not* simply to be an economical aircraft to procure and operate in peacetime. The true cost drivers of any design are these mission needs, one of the most important of which is the ability to "swing" the aircraft force between offense and defense. The most successful combat aircraft, from the P-51 Mustang of World War II to the F-4 Phantom, have been used for both types of mission. Given limited force sizes and the vagaries of war, a commander needs flexibility, sometimes requiring air-to-air and sometimes air-to-ground operations. Suitable basic designs are not cheap, even today, as both the F-16 and the F-18 illustrate very well. Training and support requirements are correspondingly costly.

Second, the "reformers" point to the fact that modern military systems seem more difficult and costly to maintain in a state of high combat readiness. But a recent report of the Defense Science Board[12] showed that this reflects at least in part a decline in the budgets allocated to spare parts and other support for new systems, in relation to their purchase costs. This was in turn a result of deliberate policy that said, in effect, that in a time of declining budget it is better to buy the major system and to worry about supporting it later. Part of the Reagan defense budget increase is designed to rectify this imbalance (as was the Carter budget before it). Since spares are easier to buy than total systems, this outcome suggests that from the long-term planner's point of view the policy was correct. In addition the study showed that, at least in the electronics area, systems of similar *functional* complexity have, in general, tended to become more, not less, reliable as they have progressed from the transistor to the integrated circuit technology. This trend is far from running its course.

Third, those who argue for larger forces of simpler systems (tanks, airplanes, ships) tend to neglect the manpower implications of increasing force size. We have shown great reluctance, as a nation, to increase our armed forces. The All Volunteer Force was having trouble meeting its recruiting requirements before the country went into recession in the late 1970s. And it has yet to be shown that, with manpower costs taking up over half the budget and "simpler" weapon systems not becoming as inexpensive as might be hoped, the net cost of the armed forces would indeed be less than it is now.

Fourth, the reform movement argues that we cannot afford a sufficient number of advanced, modern fighter aircraft (or tanks, or ships, etc.) to meet our military needs. It is of interest to consider this assumption in light of actual experience with the F-4, mentioned above. Over 4000 of these aircraft were procured for U.S. forces, including the Air Force, the Navy, and the Marines. In its day the F-4 was viewed in the United States and the world as the most advanced tactical aircraft that could be acquired for anybody's air force. It is still, and will remain for some time to come, a first-line combat aircraft of many nations, including our NATO allies. There was never any argument about the airplane's being too sophisticated or too expensive. In view of the unknown effects of great differences in production rates and methods, and great uncertainties about what have been the real inflation rates and "learning curve" effects in the aircraft industry over the respective time periods, the costs of the F-4 and the F-15 have been roughly the same fraction of the GNP—of the resources available to the nation. They may differ by up to a factor of two in these terms, but they do not differ by an order of magnitude. Such differences appear to be accepted with relative equanimity in the civilian economy for products varying from cars to quartz watches when significant differences in performance, quality, or simple style are involved. What really *has* changed, however, is our view of "affordability" in military systems—not our ability to *buy* the aircraft, but the criteria by which we *judge* that ability. As we have noted at several points, there are now many more demands for the money for both defense and nondefense purposes than there were in the days when the F-4 was our main tactical combat aircraft.

Another reason for the arguments against more expensive systems like the F-15 air superiority fighter lies in the realization that the potential combat situations have changed and these very expensive aircraft may not have it all their own way over enemy airspace, as was more nearly true in the day of F-4 dominance. The "reform" arguments tend to assume that problems of this kind will be solved by more of the same kinds of system we have now, albeit in a somewhat different form, rather than by making some more drastic changes in the form and machinery of tactical air warfare. For example, they support the idea of simpler fighters than the F-15 for air defense. But if air defense were the only concern, why must there be a fighter aircraft for the purpose? It might prove to be much more economical for the same effect to buy a variety of SAM systems with associated countermeasures-resistant and attack-resistant command and control systems for purely air-defense purposes. If our offensive aircraft would have trouble trying to penetrate opposing defenses, both air- and ground-based, then we might have to concentrate more on standoff attack systems, including weapons, target acquisition means, command and control networks, basing, and logistics quite different from those we use now. In that case the type, sophistication, and detailed designs for relevant aircraft would become wholly different from the fighters and attack aircraft we know today. Similar needs to change force philosophy, rather than simply change to cheaper systems, can be demonstrated in the areas of land and naval warfare, as chapters 4 and 5 showed.

None of this is to say that there isn't some validity in the arguments being made against excesses in technological application and its attending costs. But the solutions being proposed—to give up technological advance in favor of cheaper and less capable versions of the same tanks, airplanes, guns, and ships that have already been found wanting in the face of the improving opposition—display a lack of recognition of the real problem they are trying to address. To gain some insight into that problem, we need to look elsewhere, namely, at the ways the armed forces manage technological change and at their relationships with the civilian technological community that supports them.

Uses and Misuses of Technology

All applications of technology reach performance limits imposed by strengths of materials, efficiency of energy conversion, or other physical phenomena.[13] The essence of new applications of technology is the extension of such limits. But whatever the technology permits, the closer its technical limits are approached the more costly will be the achievement of the resulting performance. Figure 10-1 and Table 10-1 illustrate this cost-performance phenomenon for two typical aircraft subsystems.

The interaction of performance—cost variation with system acquisition management is illustrated in a more general way by the hypothetical curves in Figure 10-2. The solid line represents current technology (e.g., the upper of the two curves in Figure 10-1). Typically, the designer will select an operating point just before the steep part of the cost rise. In moving to new technology (dashed line), he may try to maintain this relationship. Although

FIGURE 10–1: Cost-Performance Curves for Airborne Inertial Navigation Systems

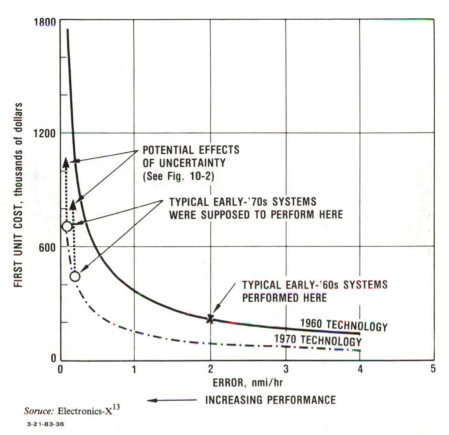

Soruce: Electronics-X[13]

3-21-83-36

he expects his costs to be somewhat higher, he looks for greatly increased performance. Characteristically, the technological advance will be marked by uncertainty and will probably have been projected over-optimistically. If the designer continues to seek the same performance increase while the technology actually follows the intermediate (dot-dash) curve, he is obviously in trouble.

He could, of course, have tried to use the new technology to reduce cost while keeping performance constant. As an example, the small, four-function hand-held calculator that now costs between ten and twenty dollars is a replacement for the massive electromechanical desk calculators that, as recently as the mid-1960s, were the accepted available tool for the purpose at a cost of about a thousand dollars. Once the achievement of the cost

Table 10–1: COST-PERFORMANCE RELATIONSHIPS FOR FIGHTER AIRCRAFT RADARS

Technical Features	Approximate Maximum Range (Nautical Miles)	Approximate Cost of "n"h", unit of a "buy" (1978 Dollars)
Basic radar with mapping[a] and moving target indication, usable for air-to-air and air-to-ground	15	100,000
Above, with weapon guidance capability, wide angle scan, high range accuracy, and resistance to countermeasures	20	225,000
Same as above, with higher power	40	300,000
Same as above, with high-resolution mapping and data link to remote ground station	40	450,000
Long-range air-to-air, with high range accuracy, high counter-measures resistance, and weapon guidance	100	600,000

Source: Compiled and simplified from various company brochures.

[a] "Mapping" permits observation on a screen of the scene "painted" by the scanning radar beam and of manmade objects therein. The higher the "resolution," the smaller the natural and manmade objects that can be distinguished in the scene.

FIGURE 10–2: Effect of Uncertainty on Advancing Technology to Improve Performance: A Hypothetical Case

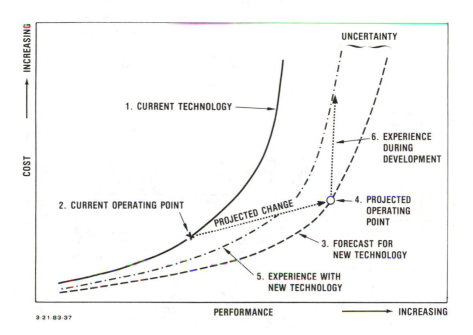

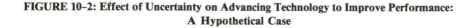

reduction is assured, the designer might decide that it is worth spending several times the basic amount of money—e.g., to go from twenty to fifty dollars—to acquire a calculator that can do much more than the four-function calculator. A typical example is shown in Figure 10–3, which indicates that, at least in the civilian world, this approach often pays handsomely. But in defense systems, with one's adversaries breathing down one's neck, it always appears necessary to shoot farther, fly higher and faster, perform more calculations per second, confound electronic countermeasures—and, indeed, very often it *is*. The risk of the denouement of Figure 10–2 must then be accepted. If the program manager could recognize soon enough when the shift from the dashed to the dot-dash curve begins, and if he could then decide to back away from the initial performance requirements, he might still save the situation. This has been the philosophical basis of many of the management steps taken by the Defense Department during the 1970s to hold cost overruns to a minimum.

By the time the program manager might see the need for such a step, however, the prestige of the Service will likely have been committed by the

FIGURE 10–3: Example of Successful Performance Advance with
Large Cost Reduction

	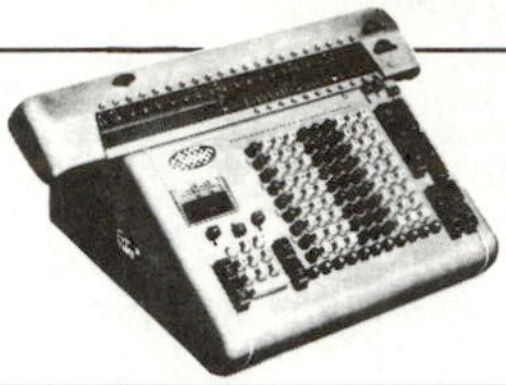	
SIZE & WEIGHT	LIKE A TYPEWRITER	2'' x 3½'' x ¼'' -- ∿2 oz
PARTS COUNT	MORE THAN 6000 (ELECTROMECHANICAL)	LESS THAN 100 (MECHANICAL); ORDER OF 100,000 ELECTRONIC SWITCHES
PERFORMANCE	4 FUNCTIONS (11-PLACE) (WITH VARIATIONS IN MANIPULATION)	24-60 FUNCTIONS (DEPENDS ON HOW COUNTED) (8-PLACE)
PROCUREMENT COST	$1000 IN 1965	$40 IN 1978
OPERATION & SUPPORT COST	$73/YR IN 1965 (MAINTENANCE CONTRACT)	$3.00 EACH 2-4 YEARS (BATTERIES)

Source: Compiled by author.

7-22-81-8

very case it has made to the Congress to justify the money for the new system. The performance requirement will have been approved by the Service secretary and chief of staff, and perhaps by the secretary of defense through the formal defense system acquisition process. The attempt to achieve the requirement is managed at a far lower level, probably by an officer who sees his future involved in the achievement. All this inertia simply means that an excessively high performance requirement may well be difficult to change, and the Service will continue to spend money trying to achieve it even though it can never do so within the designated budget limit.

An example can serve to highlight the nature of the problem as a Service tries to integrate a new technical capability. In a military battlefield data system intended to control the operation of a particular set of weapon systems—artillery battery fire, perhaps—extensive research and development resources might be devoted to devising what amounts to the bookkeeping and computational part of the system. Its purpose is to keep records of the firing status of all batteries; to accept and integrate target information from many different sources; and to allocate fire efficiently, telling each battery commander what to fire at, how much to fire, and when to do so. Extensive and expensive communications equipment would also be needed to transfer the necessary information among the nodes of the system, which would be designed to make the most of limited artillery resources. Development of such a system and distribution of the complex equipment to the field may cost many hundreds of millions of dollars. Annual operating and maintenance cost and manpower requirements will have been increased. In addition to more effective use of a set of weapon systems, we will have also acquired a new vulnerability, in that once the artillery comes to depend on the new system, it will be in worse than its original condition if a computation and communication center is knocked out by enemy fire.

An alternate approach to the task might say that, since artillery ammunition is used liberally in any case and since the direct effects of artillery fire are often difficult to quantify, we could tolerate less efficiency in the distribution of fire in order to gain the advantage of lower vulnerability, more rapid response at the battery level, and lower cost in the command and control part of the system. We could then simplify the system for allocating fire by eschewing the centralized targeting and computation center in favor of a simpler, distributed tallying and mapping system that could be maintained by small groups of men. These groups would have standard military radios for communications. Each battery commander would be given a version of a commercial hand-held calculator, preprogrammed for most of the book-keeping and fire-control equations he would have to solve. The distribution of fire would then not be optimal, but perhaps it would be satisfactory. The money saved by this much simpler approach could be used to acquire more ammunition and perhaps more cannon. If the money saved were not sufficient to have much impact in this alternate use, we would at least have acquired a simpler system, one that would be less likely to fail at critical times or be taken out of action by a lucky enemy hit. But if the Service had started down the first track, above, then after a few years, regardless of the problems encountered, it would be thought impossible to shift to the second track. It is easier to spend money to try to fix the burgeoning problems than to start over.

To avoid some of these difficulties, those at the highest management levels may establish a few, flexible performance specifications, with the intent that these will describe performance boundaries within which the program manager at a much lower level has the freedom to operate. But for all the reasons just noted and because of the simple need to specify what each component of a system must be like and what it must do, a much greater number of specifications tends to grow at the implementation level, as illustrated in Table 10–2. If at this point the program manager decides he wants to reduce a performance requirement to save cost, it would no longer be obvious to him what the effect would be. Most likely he would now be operating on one of the small elements of this very great structure, and he would not always know whether changing that element would have a modest or a large effect, would bring the whole structure down, or would never be

Table 10–2: THE "REQUIREMENTS PYRAMID"
(Based on a current major system acquisition)

Management Level	Number of "Requirements" or Specifications Explicitly Expressed	Remarks
Highest service acquisition tion decision level	About 10	Major-system speed, endurance, weapon load, crew size, kill probability, etc.
Formal service "requirement" statement, service staff level	About 100	As above, specified for all important subsystems as well.
Request for proposals, from system project office with higher-level approval	Several hundred	Tells contractors what will be expected in all important elements and how they should perform.
Detailed implementation, system project office	About 1,000	All significant system and subsystem parts and elements

Source: Service documents for the procurement action.

noticed. Even if he were given the freedom to make the change, it might no longer be obvious whether he could or should make it. If he *could* put his finger on the key to the Chinese puzzle, he would trigger the ponderous and politically charged workings of the upper-management structure.

   The need and desire to improve performance also create the temptation to ignore the difficulty of bringing new technology into being. The development of a wholly new technology requires a high initial investment.[14] The simple demonstration of a technical principle in the laboratory does not mean that this principle can easily be made to work in a piece of operating hardware. Very often, individual technical capabilities may have been demonstrated, but severe technical problems may still be involved in making them work together, integrated into a system. Neglect of such factors can cause very difficult and extensive development delays and add to development costs. Many illustrations are possible, but perhaps two factual cases will suffice. Although the examples date from many years ago, the phenomena have changed but little.

Mark II Advanced Avionics* for the F-111 Aircraft. Table 10–3 shows, for the interested reader, the course of this complex procurement of the mid-1960s, in terms of the technical detail of the system. In simpler terms, there was a difference of opinion on the requirement. Many in the Service R&D senior headquarters staff believed that with modest changes and additions to the existing system, well within the state of the art, it would be possible to achieve attack avionics improvements that would be useful and necessary and to add a relatively modest air-to-air capability. However, requirements and technical staffs and the aspiring avionics contractors pressed for an integrated system with a centralized digital processor that was later found to be pressing the state of the art. Key components of the integrated display had barely been demonstrated in the laboratory. The secretary of defense decided in favor of the advanced system. Later reviews did not lead to a decision to reduce performance specifications when it was found that costs were becoming excessive. Ultimately, the specifications for the display did have to be changed to permit it to function at all, and the full Mark II avionics system was installed on only about 100 aircraft (labeled the F-111Ds).

Main Battle Tank. Figure 10–4 shows the cost of a succession of tanks and the division of costs between the fire-control system and the remainder of the tank for each one. The added fire-control functions that led to increased costs are also shown. The figure indicates that electronic system costs grew much faster than those of tank armament, armor, suspension, and propulsion, despite significant changes in all these other components. A significant illustration of how performance requirements can be changed by arbitrary circumstances is given by the canceled XM-803 tank and the M-1 main battle tank currently being acquired. Virtually the same information was available in both cases, on infantry anti-tank weapons that would exist, on anti-tank helicopters in development, on tactical aircraft anti-tank weapons available or in development, and on projected Soviet tank numbers and characteristics. Yet it was decided that the XM-803 needed a missile for the anti-tank defense role, while the M-1 did not need it. The rationale at the time was that the M-1 would operate in an offensive role only and that other anti-tank systems would defend it against tank attack. The driving force in this change of outlook was a congressional instruction on how much the tank should cost. Of course, the change was all in the realm of rationalization. Now that it is being fielded, the tank is considered the best in the world, and it will be used for all tank missions. In another technical area, the earlier approach to the day-night sight, which was an important factor in XM-803 fire-control system cost, was expensive. This cost is lower in the M-1, since

---

*"Avionics" is the term for electronic subsystems aboard an aircraft.

**Table 10–3: AN EXAMPLE OF COST GROWTH: MARK II AVIONICS
FOR THE F-111 AIRCRAFT**

Original Package in F-111A	Original Concept of Improvements	Final Requirement
Ground-mapping, weapon-delivery, terrain-avoidance radar (15 mi)	Continuously computed impact point (digital)	30-mi, high-resolution radar
Standard radar display	Aided visual display	Integrated multisensor, multi-capability display
Inertial navigation with analog computer (2 nmi/hr)	Loran C/D	Improved inertial navigation (0.5 nmi/hr)
Standard bombsight: no continuously computed impact point (analog computer)	Air to Air Missile Capability	Central analog-digital converter

Cost Growth			
Estimate	Ultimate	Sources	Reasons
∿$1 million per set	∿$3 million per set	**Technical** Display	Pressed technology beyond capability or need, based on laboratory devices never developed, integrated, or tested
		Radar	Pressed state of the art, cooling problems necessitated changes in aircraft
		Analog-digital system	New component development and system integration, across the board
		Inertial navigation system	Pressed state of the art, underbid
		Management Disagreements on requirements	Uncertainty not allowed for
		Contract structure	Prime-sub-sub compounded overhead and fees, increasing cost 40 percent in management alone

Source: Data compiled by the author from interviews.

FIGURE 10-4: Costs and Characteristics of Several Tanks

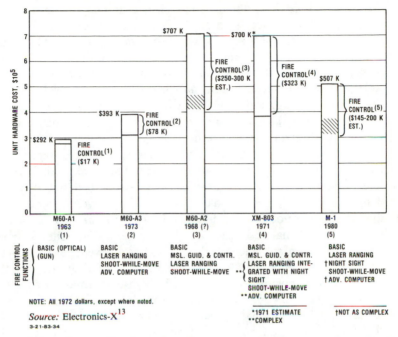

	M60-A1 1963 (1)	M60-A3 1973 (2)	M60-A2 1968 (?) (3)	XM-803 1971 (4)	M-1 1980 (5)
FIRE CONTROL FUNCTIONS	BASIC (OPTICAL) (GUN)	BASIC LASER RANGING SHOOT-WHILE-MOVE ADV. COMPUTER	BASIC MSL. GUID. & CONTR. LASER RANGING SHOOT-WHILE-MOVE	BASIC MSL. GUID. & CONTR. **{ LASER RANGING INTE- GRATED WITH NIGHT SIGHT SHOOT-WHILE-MOVE **ADV. COMPUTER	BASIC LASER RANGING †NIGHT SIGHT SHOOT-WHILE-MOVE †ADV. COMPUTER

NOTE: All 1972 dollars, except where noted.

Source: Electronics-X[13]

3-21-83-34

*1971 ESTIMATE
**COMPLEX

†NOT AS COMPLEX

thermal imaging technology has become available to replace the laser technology initially pursued. It can be supposed that if the earlier tank had been developed using fire-control technology then available, with the intention of incorporating more advanced technology after it was *proven,* the overall costs would have been lower.

These examples illustrate the tendency to press ahead with technology on many fronts all at once, each one requiring extensive research, development, and learning costs. Each system element involves problems different from those of the others; and yet the insistence on integrating all the elements into a complex system, all of whose parts must meet a single operational date, distorts the development process and increases costs. Finally, by the time all such problems are solved, some of the basic technologies may have changed sufficiently to warrant incorporating the alternate capabilities in the system—the tank night sights afford an example. If undertaken during development, the mid-course changes in development of subsystems and components all affect the total development time and cost, and they can lead to exceedingly expensive systems that are not purchased. The Service must then retreat, simplify, and start over, after having spent a good deal of time (which is not recoverable) and a good deal of money (only some of which is recoverable) for the system in its earlier form.

Usually, the system evolves continuously with mounting cost, as did the Mark II avionics illustrated above. Some clear examples of the stop-and-restart history exist in a succession of Army systems, where the Army, the secretary of defense, or the Congress found that the systems were becoming too expensive and decided to cancel the developments and start again. One of these was the main battle tank acquisitions just described. Another was the Mauler low-altitude surface-to-air missile system, under development in the early 1960s.[15] After cancellation, it was not replaced in the development process until, in the early 1970s, the decision was made to acquire the German Roland SAM system. Since then the latter system also came to be viewed as too expensive and was also canceled by Congress. A third example is contained in the Army's attack-helicopter program. The Lockheed Cheyenne helicopter, which the Army hoped (by using a new rotor design principle) to push up to a very high speed for a helicopter, suffered from rotor dynamic instability that could not be solved expeditiously without significant cost, schedule, and performance impact on the program. The Cheyenne was canceled, and the Army subsequently decided to buy a lower-speed helicopter, the advanced attack helicopter (AH-64) that is now in acquisition. Even that machine has come to cost nearly as much as a high-performance fixed-wing combat aircraft—to which it is quite analogous. In a more recent example, the secretary of defense, in making his presentation to Congress on the fiscal year 1979 budget, indicated that the new mechanized infantry combat vehicle (MICV) had become too expensive. (It had been in development for many years and was supposed to be the U.S. Army's analog to the Russian BMP armored combat vehicle). The Army was asked to examine how the system could be simplified and made less expensive.[16] However, that system (the Bradley) is now (in 1983) being identified as one of the systems that may be too complex and expensive to be worth acquiring.[17]

To show that all the Services suffer from the same difficulties, we might round out this succession of illustrations of the traps facing the unwary in attempting to advance the performance of weapon systems by mentioning the Navy's SSN-688 class nuclear attack submarine. This development exploded in a major imbroglio between the General Dynamics Corporation and the Navy over more than $500 million worth of cost claims for the lead submarine.[18] The Navy claimed that the excessive costs resulted from the contractor's inefficiency, and the contractor claimed that the costs were generated by hundreds of change orders during the construction of the submarine. Clearly, this was another illustration of the familiar phenomenon. Although it is tempting to assess blame, all this really arises from the pressure to achieve and maintain system performance better than that of the opposition we expect to encounter. It bespeaks also a price entailed in the pursuit of technical advance under circumstances where total system development takes several times longer than the turnover of subordinate technical capabilities.

It is also true that when we buy very advanced technology in defense systems we may, at least initially, tend to commit ourselves to more, rather than less, operating and maintenance costs, thereby increasing system life-cycle costs. Spare parts for more expensive systems are more costly, and the systems may be more difficult to maintain. If the technology changes in a revolutionary way, however, this trend can be reversed. Aircraft avionics systems afford the best-documented examples of these occurrences. Until very recently the weight of electronics equipment on combat aircraft has grown steadily through the years. Higher weight means more functions, more complexity, and higher cost, as Table 10–1 illustrates. Since electronics equipment was becoming increasingly miniaturized during this period, functional complexity was increasing exponentially with this growth in weight. For a given technology—e.g., transistorized systems—and for similar approaches to development and acquisition, the more expensive (and, by implication, the more complex) an avionic system is, the less reliable it tends to become— that is, it requires more maintenance and, therefore, generates increased operating costs. It is important to stress that the phenomena have not been unique to U.S. systems. Perusal of the characterictics, design, and avionics weights of successive generations of Western European and Soviet ships and aircraft (in *Jane's,* for example) would show similar trends, with a few years' lag. More recently, fighter aircraft such as the F-16 and the F-18 have come to use integrated circuit technology for their avionics. Although it remains true that the more expensive and complex a system is the less reliable it becomes, the entire level of avionic reliability is higher with the newer technology than it was with the older technology. On the whole, accounting for this increase of reliability as well as the higher cost of maintenance for the more advanced equipment, avionic system support costs with the new technology have *decreased* to between one-half and one-third of what they were with the transistor technology, for a given level of complexity or per- formance. Thus, as in the case of calculators (Figure 10–3), advancing technology can save money if we don't push it too hard.

Finally, economic forces beyond the Defense Department's control often affect its cost of doing business. Figure 10–5 shows the value of new-ship construction at U.S. shipyards for the years 1963 to 1974.[19] The large in- crease beginning in 1972 was stimulated by the Merchant Marine Act of 1970, designed to stimulate the construction of U.S. commercial hulls. The shipyards' much bigger workloads, of course, made it more difficult for the Navy to get its work done in private yards and drove its costs up, while at the same time the Navy has been prohibited from undertaking new ship construction in its own shipyards.[20] Since 1974 the decline in demand for

FIGURE 10–5: Value of Ships Under Construction in Private U.S. Shipyards

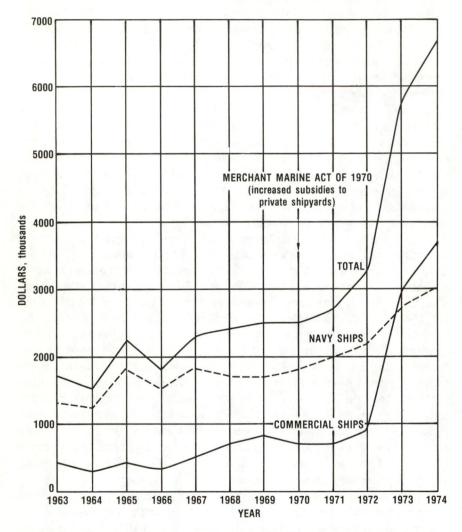

Source: Figures given in J. D. Morgan et al., *Accomplishing Shipyard Work for the United States Navy: Institutions, Systems and Operations,* Institute for Defense Analyses Paper P-1132, August 1975, vol. 1, p. 302.

3-21-83-33

FIGURE 10–6: Defense Share of the Monolithic Microcircuit Market

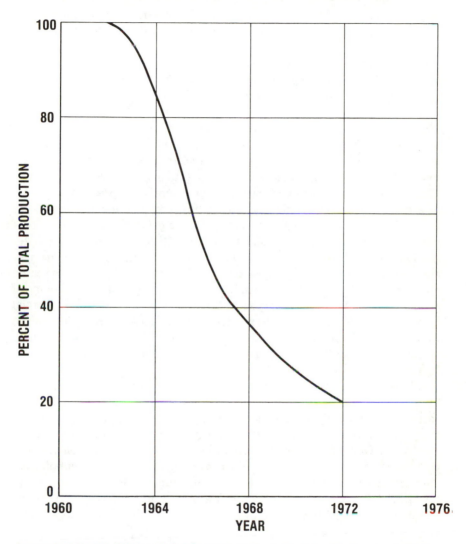

Sources: Data for 1962–1968 from N. J. Asher and L. D. Strom, *The Role of the Department of Defense in the Development of Integrated Circuits,* Institute for Defense Analyses Paper P-1271, May 1977. Data for 1972 from H. P. Gates, Jr., et al., *Electronics-X: A Study of Military Electronics with Particular Reference to Cost and Reliability,* vol. 2, Complete Report, Institute for Defense Analyses Report R-195, January 1974, Chap. III-B and Appendix C.

3-21-83-32

tankers has made excess private shipyard capacity available, changing the shipbuilding supply, demand, and cost relationships again. A similar phenomenon occurred when there was a boom in sales of commercial transport aircraft from 1965 through 1970, coincident with the aircraft-production peak of the Vietnam War. This was followed by a great slackening in demand as the air transport industry felt the effects of recession and over-capacity. These phenomena follow time cycles that are not compatible with typical military system planning and acquisition times.

In a wholly different area, Figure 10–6 shows the fraction that the Defense Department purchased of the industry output of electronic monolithic microcircuits (integrated circuits on single "chips")[21] over the ten-year period from 1962 to 1972. Whereas in 1962 the department was that industry's sole support, after 1972 it came to represent less than 20 percent of the market. Thus, although the Defense Department, by its initial support, paid the cost of achieving this new technical capability, it is now at the mercy of market forces that it cannot control in trying to use the capability for its own purposes. It does not purchase enough to be able to influence the market substantially. Where it cannot use the commercial output, the department must therefore pay the high cost of special designs, captive or dedicated production lines, small production runs, and special quality-control arrangements. As a secondary consequence, the fact that commercial technology is turning over every three to five years in microelectronics, whereas military development takes seven to ten years from inception to inventory, suggests that some portions of military electronics are obsolescent by the time they are deployed.

All the factors cited above show that while it is quite possible to go wrong by pressing technology too hard, it is also possible to make great gains in cost and capability by advancing to new generations of technology. It is no exaggeration to suggest that a technological revolution that is half digested may be far worse than one pursued without surcease. The problem is not with advanced technology but with unwise management of technological advance. Another, major aspect of this problem lies in the decision about how fast, and in which forms, to press the changing technology in decisions about system aquisition and improvement.

11
What Systems to Buy

No technique of managing defense system acquisitions to try to control costs more tightly is likely to have as great an effect on defense expenditure as the simple decision to acquire or not to acquire a major new system. The Commission on Government Procurement recognized this when it stressed the importance of mission definition and selection of the appropriate means to meet military-mission needs.[1] The importance of this decision is illustrated by the variation of system costs as technological advance progresses from one decade to the next. For a large variety of systems, the cost of successive generations of systems—from the F-100 to the F-4 to the F-15, or from Polaris to Poseidon to Trident—has increased by about a factor of five per decade. However, the progression for a succession of what might be called product-improved systems of one generation has increased by about a factor of two per decade. These systems are generally based on the same vehicle or "platform," but they incorporate a sequence of improved or new electronic subsystems, power plants, control systems, and so forth. Examples are the successive models of the A-7 attack aircraft with improved bombing systems or successive models of the Sidewinder air-to-air missile with improved seekers and controls. The average difference between these two kinds of technology progression is about a factor of two and a half. That is, over a given period of time, by a comparison in which the effects of inflation are about the same for the two cases, it is less than half as expensive to improve the capabilities of major systems by continually improving their subsystems as it is to buy wholly new systems incorporating new technology in all their parts. Another drastic cost difference in system acquisition derives from the difference between "weapons" and "platforms"—the guided missiles, sensors, and other subsystems that perform modern weapon delivery tasks, and the airplanes, ships, and fighting vehicles that launch the weapons. Extensive data show that total acquisition costs of guided missile systems for various missions such as air defense or attack are on the average from a fifth to a seventh as great as the costs of total new ship and airplane systems.[2] This includes the costs of development and the total "buys" of missiles, airplanes, or other platforms, which can vary. It must also be noted that the platforms include parts of weapon systems, such as radars, needed to make the systems function. However, since the data describe many actual cases, the average cost differences noted can be taken to represent factors useful for general planning purposes.

The significance of the cost differentials outlined above will become apparent in a moment.

Extending the Utility of Systems

Obviously, the more time one can spend improving a system before the cost of a wholly new system is incurred, the more money will be made available to buy other capabilities if they are needed. With the current directions of development of advanced technology, we have come increasingly to provide platforms for sophisticated weapon, control, and guidance systems that do the real work. For example, airplanes of many types carry air-to-air missiles that are guided to their targets, in some cases with the help of radars on the aircraft. Precision-guided air-to-surface munitions can be carried by various kinds of aircraft; they are guided either from the aircraft or by self-contained seekers to targets on land or sea. Especially if these are standoff weapons, the launching aircraft has, mainly, to carry the weight and to reach its launch position on time. Vehicles that are specialized trucks and trailers, or many kinds of ships, fire surface-to-air missiles at attacking aircraft; the platforms need but carry the weight of missiles, launchers, sensors (e.g., radars), and guidance computers.

New electronic developments of various kinds, in sensing, guidance, and control, can make complete systems viable after they may have been losing capability relative to enemy technical advances. Suppose an older-generation fighter has a good enough radar to acquire a target from a few miles away while it is pointing at the target, but not good enough to be able to search large areas to find targets. The AWACS airplane can direct that fighter to the right place and give it a bearing, to enable its radar to acquire an opposing enemy aircraft. It would then not be necessary to purchase a new air-to-air radar system and, probably, a new, more capable airplane to carry it. This would remain true as long as the AWACS survives. In extending the system, a vulnerability was added. That can be remedied by putting a better radar in the fighter aircraft, as well. That step by itself would be cheaper than buying a whole new aircraft system. In addition, the entire system could be made more capable by developing a new missile to launch from the aircraft. This, too, would cost far less than an entire new aircraft program.

The argument is often made that a platform, whether it be an aircraft, a ship, or a vehicle, is becoming over age and must be replaced. Once we are doing that, why not replace it with new-generation technology? This argument is attractive, but it is not always valid. One can buy more of the same platforms over a longer period of time, and thus the *units* do not become over age. As examples, the Air Force through the early and mid-1970s was developing a short-takeoff-and-landing jet aircraft to replace the turboprop-powered C-130 Hercules short- and medium-haul cargo airplane. A case could be made that the new aircraft would be more cost-effective, but it was decided that the air and ground forces could live with the older design and the capability provided, for some time.[3] Relative capability, in this case, depended on how the job was defined. Similarly, the Army did acquire a new cargo helicopter (the UH-60 Blackhawk)[4] when it might, for a longer time than planned, have continued to use the UH-1 (the "Huey" of Vietnam fame) even though a using unit would have had to distribute its loads differently, the older machine would be more vulnerable to enemy fire, and there would have been some tasks that could not be done with the older aircraft. In this case it was decided that the gains were worth the added cost. In both cases, judgment played an important role.

But we must distinguish between the age of a vehicle and the age of its technology. Eventually, the need to carry new and improved weapons and electronic gear may require so loading up an existing aircraft, ship, or vehicle that it can no longer perform its task with that load; it will not be able to carry enough or go where it can be effective in a short enough time. Then, of course, a change in platform performance is called for. The question always is, however, to determine when such a change is absolutely needed. In part, this depends on our perception of the threat and, specifically in the real world of today, on what developments the Soviet Union is seen to be pursuing. For example, if the Soviets change a generation of aircraft, as they have been doing, they may approach the capability of our own current generation of aircraft. The Soviet Flogger will have given them essentially the capability of an F-4; but if the weapons carried by the F-4 are much better than those of the USSR, or new and improved weapons can be fitted to the F-4, it may be that the differences between the aircraft per se do not matter very much. On the other hand, it may be found that to carry weapons that would ensure superiority over the Flogger and *its* weapons requires an airplane with higher performance than an F-4. For example, the need to carry a number of large, long-range missiles (the Phoenix) with a long-range radar that can control several of them simultaneously required a more capable aircraft than the F-4, and this led to the Navy's acquisition of the F-14 for fleet air defense. Clearly, though, it was not purely a matter of need, but one of opportunity as well. The threat, the technical capability, and the solution converged at a particular time.

Thus, it sometimes becomes apparent that a host of new capabilities has become available, and an entire type of system can be advanced in all its parts. Always, current capability will have to be compared with the threat as it is seen *now,* and with estimates of what it may be at the time when the new system will have been developed. The possibilities for improving the existing systems by improving their major subsystems will also have to be examined. Almost invariably, in such comparisons, the advocates for acquiring a new system can show that it will be more cost-effective than the existing system. This will be especially true if, because it is new, the expected performance is overstated and the cost is underestimated, as illustrated in the discussion of the previous chapter. Usually, the outcome is driven by the assumptions about cost, performance, threat, and scenario that enter the analysis; the effects can be discerned by a perspicacious observer. If it can be demonstrated (with the help of alternative assumptions and judgments) that the change to a wholly new-generation system can be deferred, good management to save defense expenditures (in *one* area) will have been exercised in a way different from that usually conceived under this rubric. It will work *if* the acquisition of a wholly new generation of systems can legitimately be deferred by improving the systems of the existing generation. The Defense Department has recognized this in its current policy of planned product improvement. This policy has attempted to formalize the process that the above data show has been in existence for many years.

Changing Institutional Patterns

It is almost impossible for responsible officials and members of the public to be completely unbiased about when system generations should be changed. Partly, there is the competitive pressure, already noted, which urges that we stay as far ahead of a potential enemy as possible in the technical sense. Partly, this is reinforced by the modern industrial pattern of working on new-generation developments almost before the existing generation has emerged from development. Although the pattern can be dismissed glibly as evidence of the nefarious workings of the "military-industrial complex," the situation is much more complicated than that. It interacts strongly with the civilian economy and with our view of the long-range security of the country.

We might illustrate the nature of the problem with an example from the past.[5] In 1868 the United States commissioned a warship started during the Civil War, the *Wampanoag,* that was far ahead of her time. She was the first steam-powered ship that could sustain a speed of over 16 knots for over 24 hours. A large ship with a sleek, propeller-driven hull designed for speed, she mounted ten eight-inch guns and several smaller ones. She was the most advanced warship in the world. Yet, the U.S. Navy decided a year later to decommission her. The reason, when one digs through the bureaucratic rhetoric and carping criticism of the ship that were intended to justify the decision, was that the United States was then at peace and did not need such a ship. From the related discussions it becomes clear that there was a related concern that lumbering, commercial sailing, and many secondary industries would all be threatened if shipbuilding technology were allowed to advance very rapidly. It was considered to be better to maintain the existing technology and capability, in the absence of some crisis that would force a change, than to disrupt the existing order to no apparent avail. That is, the Navy was, consciously or unconsciously, seeking to maintain stability and to arrest change that would be too sudden and would entail too much dislocation of both its own bureaucracy and the civilian economy with which it was intertwined.

The current situation is similar in the large but exactly opposite in detail. Our defense now depends on high-technology industry that is built on the concept of continuous change. The problem is to maintain the pace of change as a means of improving productivity and staying ahead of the competition—whether the competition is another company or another country, such as the USSR or even one of our own NATO allies. Stability in today's economy means continuing innovation and the advance of the next-generation system while the current generation is becoming fully operational. Planned obsolescence to maintain a given rate of sales of automobiles or appliances, and avoidance of obsolescence in the interest of national security, are both children of the same industrial culture. And with good reason in the area of national security: World War II was won by superior technology as well as by greater productive capacity and by valor.

The fact that our military and civilian economies and cultures are based on continual change of their technical machinery doesn't mean that there isn't resistance to drastic technological change in certain directions. Each branch of the military Services, each related branch of industry, and the adjacent or interacting parts of the civilian economy all have vested economic and career interests in the products they use—the weapons, ships, airplanes, vehicles—and in the forces that operate them.[6] The entire system is in balance, and it attempts to control change so as to maintain that balance. Although military technology has changed extensively in the past decades, and the cost relationships among the different elements of that technology have changed also (as we saw in chapters 3 through 5), there has been remarkable stability in the relative expenditures for diverse kinds of military systems. Table 11–1 shows the relative long-term average expenditures on combat systems (weapons, combat aircraft, and combat ships) and supporting systems (command, control, communications, target acquisition, and logistics) for the Air Force and the Navy. Table 11–2 shows the relative long-

Table 11-1: ACQUISITION BUDGET ALLOCATION TO COMBAT AND SUPPORT FORCES AND SYSTEMS[a]

Service	Years Covered	Percent to Combat	Percent to Support
Air Force[b]	1962–85 (1984–85 projected)	Average is 72 percent Variation from average line is up to ± 12 percent	Average is 28 percent
Navy[b]	1962–88 (1984–88 projected)	Average line slopes from 60 percent in 1962 to 72 percent in 1988 Variation from average line is up to ± 10 percent	Average line slopes from 40 percent in 1962 to 28 percent in 1988

[a] "Acquisition" includes research, development, test, evaluation, and procurement. "Combat" includes ships, airplanes, guns, ammunition, missiles, and the using forces. "Support" includes target acquisition, electronic warfare, command, control, communications, navigation, logistic systems, and the using forces.

[b] Tactical forces only. Marine Corps not included with Navy.

Table 11-2: AVERAGE FRACTION OF ACQUISITION BUDGETS DEVOTED TO "WEAPONS" AND "PLATFORMS"

Service	Years Covered	Average Percentage Breakdown
Air Force	1962–80	Aircraft—94 percent Missiles—6 percent
	1980–88 (1984–88 projected)	Aircraft—83 percent Missiles—17 percent
Navy[a]	1962–73	Ship construction and conversion—37 percent Aircraft and missiles—63 percent
	1974–83	Ship construction and conversion—45 percent Aircraft—44 percent Missiles—11 percent
	1984–88 (projected)	Ship construction and conversion—45 percent Aircraft—39 percent Missiles—16 percent
Army[b]	1976–88 (1984–88 projected)	Weapons and tracked vehicles—43 percent Aircraft—27 percent Missiles—70 percent

Source: Based on data in the five-year defense programs for years shown, compiled by J. Stahl of IDA Cost Analysis Group.

[a] Navy budget categories changed between 1973 and 1974.

[b] Army program stable only in the years shown.

term average expenditures on weapons and platforms for the Army, Navy, and Air Force. Figures 11–1a through 11–1c show the data on which the tables are based, giving a more graphic illustration of the stability in division of resources among systems despite the inflationary cost and budget increases of the 1970s.[7]

**FIGURE 11–1: Allocation of Expenditures to Systems
by the Military Services**

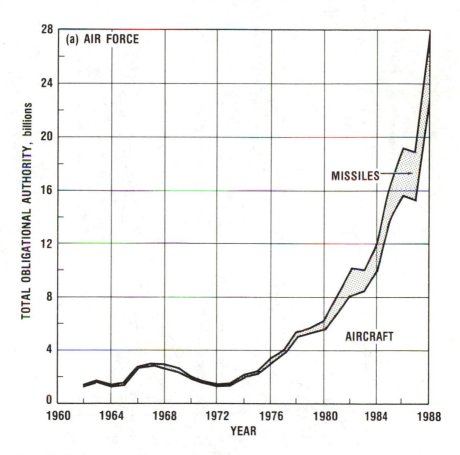

Source: Based on data in the five-year defense programs for years shown, compiled by J. Stahl of IDA Cost Analysis Group.

3-21-83-28   *(Cont'd)*

FIGURE 11–1: Allocation of Expenditures to Systems by the Military Services *(Cont'd)*

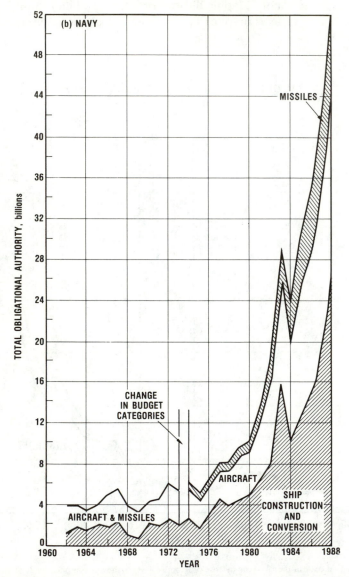

Source: Based on data in the five-year defense programs for years shown, compiled by J. Stahl of IDA Cost Analysis Group.

3-21-83-29

(Cont'd)

**FIGURE 11–1: Allocation of Expenditures to Systems
by the Military Services** *(Cont'd)*

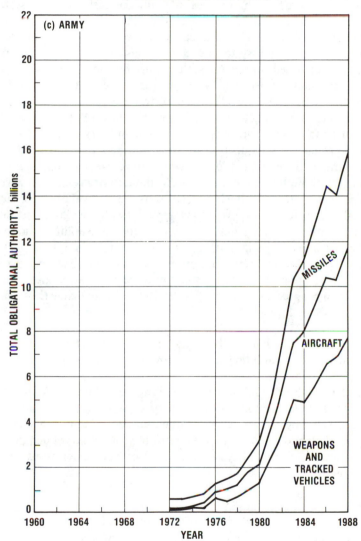

Source: Based on data in the five-year defense programs for years shown, compiled by J. Stahl of IDA Cost Analysis Group.

3-21-83-30

Although as noted in the tables there have been fluctuations in the averages, and there has been some shift toward greater expenditure on weapons in the Navy and the Air Force, the data do not show changes of a magnitude that would reflect shifting importance of military tasks among systems or adaptation to the evolution of a drastically changed cost and force structure among them. In fact, the Navy's allocations have been drifting toward greater expenditure for combat systems even as target acquisition and denial, and essential space-based supporting systems, are becoming relatively more important and more expensive. When the nation decided to modernize its military strength after the decline of that strength during the Vietnam years, the investment attending that growth was (and has been) devoted mainly to ships, aircraft, tanks, and other symbols of military strength. It was not devoted primarily to acquisition of large numbers of tactical missiles and to accelerated development of what we have been calling "supporting systems," although in the modern world the latter two may very well have as much or more to do with winning a war as the renewal of ships, airplanes, and tanks in the force. The symbolism remains with the platforms, however.

Thus, we must conclude that the various parts of the military and industrial system have been adapting to the great recent changes in military technology in such a way as to maintain the rough balances described above. Changes in force structure and associated weapon acquisition strategies of the kind described in chapters 3–5 and in Chapter 10 would challenge those balances. For example, changes such as

1. reducing the share of the budget that goes to tactical combat aviation in favor of building up the ground forces, as air defenses keep improving, or
2. building up the submarine force, long-range land-based aviation, and missiles for sea control instead of expanding the surface navy, or
3. developing and purchasing large numbers of long-range air defense and standoff attack missiles, with associated target acquisition and command/control systems, instead of new generations of combat aircraft

could change the spending patterns shown in tables 11–1 and 11–2 significantly. The balance among missions and professional specialties in the military forces would also change. Such changes would in many respects be greater and different in kind than those described at the beginning of Chapter 10. Many of the latter, such as the adoption of jet transport aircraft, supersonic fighters, nuclear-powered submarines, and the products of advances in electronic technology were supportive of, rather than challenging to, the existing mission and career patterns of the military forces. Where those patterns have been challenged to the extent that new kinds of missions and forces have had to be defined and created, such as those using ballistic missiles of intercontinental range or (currently) the use of space-based systems for related missions that have to be carried out by more than one Service, there has been institutional turmoil while the issues were (or are) being resolved. We could expect such turmoil to exist while changes such as those described immediately above are reviewed and absorbed. Technological change of this character won't come easily or quickly or necessarily in the directions noted as all the attending issues are painfully resolved.

The problems of absorbing technological change of this magnitude are, moreover, not limited to the military. They interact strongly with the civilian economy as well. As we showed in Chapter 10 in discussing the example of the microcircuit industry, we may come to depend on government funding— from the Defense Department, NASA, or even the National Science Foundation—to get over the initial hurdle of large investments with uncertain futures when entering a period of new technological application. Once we are in such a period, commercial applications may take over. Then, the only way the Defense Department can keep its share of the output at reasonable cost is to keep buying. Once it is shut out of this marketplace by deciding to forgo purchases for a substantial period of time, it may not be able to reenter it when necessary. As we observed in considering the defense of Europe, if we think any serious conflict in which advanced technology may be decisive will end in a matter of days or a few weeks, there is no need to maintain industrial capacity to generate new technical capability in a hurry. The war will be fought with the existing weapon inventories. But if we want to hedge our bets against the possibility that we may have to fight longer, we must maintain the capability to improve existing systems or to develop new ones in an emergency. For example, in electronic warfare we may not know all that we are up against until after a war starts.

It may be unrealistic to anticipate, in any future emergency, the kind of major retooling and production buildups that took place in World War II. They actually began during the late 1930s in response to the crises in Europe and proceeded for a full two years into our part of the war (to 1943 and 1944) before we hit our stride. But we do need some capacity to respond industrially between the two extremes. Some research and development, technology, and production base needs to be kept warm for a response to a crisis whose development may occur over a period of several months or two or three years. In the modern technological era such a base cannot function on a boom-and-bust basis. If trained technical manpower is lost to an industry, it is not likely to be recovered very soon. This was illustrated during the large layoffs of technical personnel in the aerospace industry during the period 1969 through 1972. As shown in Figure 11–2, once these people entered other areas, the most technically qualified element of the industry simply remained at a lower level for a long time.[8]

Thus, stability and some smoothing of the employment ups and downs are needed in high-technology industry, especially that devoted heavily to defense. The problem is to adjust the scope and directions of change to be consistent with any new defense system acquisition policy that might be

FIGURE 11–2: History of Technical Manpower in a Key Defense Industry (Engineers and Scientists in Aerospace Research and Development)

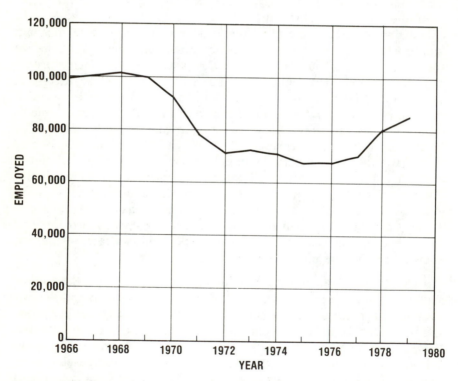

Source: *Aerospace Facts and Figures* for years shown. Published by *Aviation Week and Space Technology,* 1978 and 1982.

3-21-83-31

adopted. There is considerable overlap as successive system generations are developed and operated. Heretofore the time from one generation of major systems of the "platform" variety to the next has been on the order of ten to fifteen years. Suppose we want to extend this time to twenty or more years—that is, we want to halve the rate of growth of major system costs. In parallel, we would increase the performance of subsystems, such as means for target acquisition, weapon guidance, data processing and control systems, and so forth, and we would acquire more guided missiles with their essential supporting systems. Such changes are more rapid, occurring perhaps each three to eight years. Moreover, from the relative cost figures given in the previous chapter, we could acquire many more such systems than new major platforms within the budgets we are willing to spend. In time, defense industry could adapt to such a change of emphasis. But we would have to recognize and accept that we might need, say, fewer airframe manufacturers and more electronics manufacturers. Once committed to such a course, we would find it hard to change. The implications affect patterns of commerce, politics, demography, and culture. Such a step should not be made by happenstance but should be undertaken as the result of a considered decision. The need for such a decision underlies many of the arguments described in the previous chapter, about defense technology and the general purpose forces' budgets today.

We could also maintain a high rate of innovation together with a slower rate of procurement of the most expensive systems by adjusting research and development against procurement expenditure—developing more systems than we produce. This would lead to some adjusted cost-time progression, perhaps between the extremes we have been considering. But then, the development of new systems tends to increase the pressure to buy them in quantity. This pressure is felt through industrial proposals for new systems; through industry lobbying with the Services and the Congress; through the desire of the entire defense community to have the latest, most up-to-date equipment; through fear of enemy progress; through the expressed need to maintain employment; and so on. It also seems wasteful in the public view to develop but not to use systems, as in the case of the initial version of the B-1 bomber or the advanced medium transport aircraft mentioned earlier. Very strong management and a sustainable rationale would be required to withstand these pressures. But the approach would have advantages.

The value of undertaking development is, of course, that having the prototypes on the shelf increases flexibility. Suppose we were to tailor our defense industry to a slower rate of system turnover. Then it would be more difficult to increase our military strength on demand. But if we were to maintain a higher rate of development and then decide for each case whether to buy the new system or not, the lag wouldn't be as great because several years of development time would have been gained. We could then start the procurement buildup with more advanced systems than if we hadn't undertaken the "excess" developments. This course is, however, politically much more difficult than simply developing and buying individual systems, each in turn. There is no way to decide the issue firmly, except by judgment and willingness to foster and to deal with the controversies individual decisions will raise. The problem will become more severe as systems continue to become more expensive, as we compete more with our European allies for the acquisition of defense systems and as Soviet capability keeps growing. The Europeans have attempted to solve the problem in part by integrating their system acquisitions cross-nationally. The Soviets must also eventually come to face the same problem, but we do not know where their saturation point will be.

* * *

How to manage all these aspects of the march of military technology is one of the most difficult of all defense policy issues. It can never be solved for all time but will have to be taken up anew every few years for the indefinite future. It is apparent, however, that the complexities of the military and industrial problems that we have explored very briefly here far transcend the simple arguments of those who call for a return to simpler military technology so that we can buy more systems and operate them less expensively.

We need to separate concerns that deal with how well or badly system design and acquisition are managed from considerations of what military technology can and should do for us. The armed forces are still in a state of very rapid technological change, as indeed is our whole society. Attempting to arrest that trend in our own armed forces while both our allies and the USSR pursue it, as they are doing, will leave us with inferior military capability vis-a-vis our opponents and far less able to lead our friends in our collective defense. We must devote our energies to the difficult decisions about *which* advanced military systems we should develop and procure and which ones we should forgo or defer. We must devote attention to insuring sound management of the military-industrial collaboration on the systems we do decide to acquire, in order to avoid the waste and dislocations that have resulted from conflict over the value of the technology itself.

The problem is to understand the nature of the technological change that is profoundly affecting our armed forces and our ability to exercise military power in our national interest and to manage that change wisely for our benefit. This book will have served its purpose if it has contributed to that understanding.

Notes

Chapter 1

1. For descriptions of the evolution of military technology, see McNeill, W. H., *The Rise of the West* (Chicago: University of Chicago Press, 1963); L. White, Jr., *Medieval Technology and Social Change* (London: Oxford University Press, 1962); T. Wintringham and J. N. Blashford-Snell, *Weapons and Tactics* (London: Penguin Books, 1973); and S. E. Morison, *The Two-Ocean War* (Boston: Atlantic Monthly-Little, Brown, 1963).

2. Lt. Col. J. B. Mitchell and Sir Edward S. Creasy, *Twenty Decisive Battles of the World* (New York: Macmillan Co., 1964), pp. 224–242.

3. R. G. Ruppenthal, *Logistical Support of the Armies, United States Army in World War II: European Theatre of Operations* (Washington, D.C.: Office of the Chief of Military History, Department of the Army, 1953).

4. W. Craig, *Enemy at the Gates: The Battle for Stalingrad* (New York: Ballantine Books, 1973), pp. 169–191.

5. For an appreciation of the place of the ship of the line, see E. E. Morison, *From Know-How to Nowhere: The Development of American Technology* (New York: Basic Books, 1974), pp. 147–151.

6. S. E. Morison, *The Two-Ocean War,* pp. 161–162, 339, and 406.

7. See P. Stanford, "The Automated Battlefield," the *New York Times Magazine,* February 23, 1975; and P. Dickson, *The Electronic Battlefield* (Bloomington: Indiana University Press, 1976).

8. J. Fallows, *National Defense* (New York: Random House, 1981).

9. E. E. Morison, *From Know-How to Nowhere,* pp. 155–157.

Chapter 2

1. *Hearing* before the Subcommittee on Military Applications, Joint Committee on Atomic Energy, U. S. Congress, 93rd Congress, 1st Session, 1971, pt. I, pp. 36–37.

2. S. Glasstone (ed.), *The Effects of Nuclear Weapons* (Washington, D.C.: U.S. Atomic Energy Commission, April 1962).

3. See, for example, Michelin road map numbr 987 of Benelux, Germany, and Austria, 1974.

4. *Operations,* U.S. Army Field Manual, FM 100–5, Headquarters, Department of the Army, Washington, D.C., July 1976, p. 2–29.

5. The following discussion draws heavily upon my earlier work, S. J. Deitchman, *Limited War and American Defense Policy* (Cambridge, Mass. MIT Press, 1964 and 1969). Chapters 3 and 7 have been suitably modified to account for developments since then, although the basic situations and their implications have not changed greatly since the earlier discussion.

6. R. G. Ruppenthal, *Logistical Support of the Armies, United States Army in World War II: European Theatre of Operations* (Washington, D.C.: Office of the Chief of Military History, Department of the Army, 1953), pp. 490–491.

7. B. Catton, *A Stillness at Appomatox* (Garden City, N.Y.: Doubleday & Co., 1954), pp. 237–246.

8. F. O. Miksche, *Atomic Weapons and Armies* (New York: Praeger, 1955).

9. Capt. G. S. Patton, "Operation Crusader," *Armor,* vol. 67 (May-June 1958): 6–19.

10. S. E. Morison, *The Two-Ocean War* (Boston: Atlantic Monthly–Little, Brown, 1963), p. 394.

11. See, for example, Col. Gen. N. A. Lomov (ed.), *The Revolution in Military Affairs.* Translated and published under the auspices of the U.S. Air Force; (Washington, D.C.: U.S. Government Printing Office, 1974); and A. A. Sidorenko, *The Offensive.* Translated and published under the auspices of the U.S. Air Force; (Washington, D.C.: U.S. Government Printing Office, 1973).

12. Col. Gen. N. A. Lomov, *The Revolution in Military Affairs,* pp. 150–151.

13. A. A. Sidorenko, *The Offensive,* p. 82; and Col. Gen. N. A. Lomov, *The Revolution in Military Affairs,* p. 145.

14. Col. Gen. N. A. Lomov, *The Revolution in Military Affairs,* pp. 122–128.

15. McG. Bundy, G. Kennan, R. McNamara, G. Smith, "Nuclear Weapons and the Atlantic Alliance," *Foreign Affairs (Spring 1982).*

16. V. D. Sokolovskii (ed.), *Soviet Military Strategy,* translated by H. Dinerstein, L. Gouré, and T. E. Wolfe (Englewood Cliffs, N.J.: Prentice-Hall, 1963), pp. 343–344 and 410–417.

17. K. F. Spielman, *Prospects for a Soviet Strategy of Controlled Nuclear War: An Assessment of Some Key Indicators,* Institute for Defense Analyses Paper P-1236, March 1976. See also J. D. Douglass, Jr., and A. M. Hoeber, *Soviet Strategy for Nuclear War* (Stanford, Calif.: Hoover Institution Press, 1979).

18. See *Jane's Weapon Systems,* 7th Edition (New York: Franklin Watts, 1976).

19. Characteristics described in *Aviation Week and Space Technology,* vol. 104 (March 15, 1976):83–84.

20. *Soviet Military Power* (Washington, D.C.: U.S. Government Printing Office, 1981), p. 25–51, esp. 30-34.

21. Ibid, p. 26-27.

22. Ibid, p. 37-38.

23. See, for example, Department of State *Bulletin,* vol. 66, no. 1719 (June 5, 1972):792–801.

Chapter 3

1. See Maj. A. P. DeSeversky, *Victory Through Air Power* (New York: Simon & Schuster, 1942; C. Bekker, *The Luftwaffe War Diaries*, translated and edited by F. Zeigler (Garden City, N.Y.: Doubleday & Co., 1968), pp. 148–151, R. Leckie, *Conflict: The History of the Korean War, 1950–53* (New York: G. P. Putnam's Sons, 1962), pp. 53 and 318; *The Pentagon Papers* (New York: Bantam Books, 1971), pp. 307–344.

2. S. E. Morison, *The Two-Ocean War* (Boston: Atlantic Monthly–Little, Brown, 1963, pp. 359–360.

3. A. C. Brown, *Bodyguard of Lies* (New York: Bantam Books, 1976), pp. 773–775.

4. H. M. Cole, *The Ardennes: Battle of the Bulge, United States Army in World War II: European Theatre of Operations* (Washington, D.C.: Office of the Chief of Military History, Department of the Army, 1965).

5. From a personal conversation with Israeli Air Force personnel.

6. Lt. Gen. W. Pearson, *The War in the Northern Provinces*, Vietnam Studies Series (Washington, D.C.: Department of the Army, 1975).

7. C. Bekker, *The Luftwaffe War Diaries*, p. 142.

8. S. E. Morison, *The Two-Ocean War*, p. 387.

9. F. M. Sallager, *Operation STRANGLE (Italy, Spring 1944): A Case Study of Tactical Air Interdiction*, Project RAND Report R-851-PR. Prepared for the U.S. Air Force, February 1972.

10. *Tactical Air Operations,* Tactical Air Command TACM 2-1, 1978, p. 4–36.

11. R. Leckie, *Conflict*, pp. 318–321.

12. *The Pentagon Papers*, loc. cit.

13. *The Washington Post*, May 30, 1976.

14. *Command and Employment of Air Power*, War Department Field Manual FM 100–20, July 21, 1943.

15. *Tactical Air Operations*, Chapter 4.

16. *Tactical Air Operations*.

17. *Aviation Week and Space Technology*, vol. 103 (July 14, 1975):49; *Jane's Weapon Systems*, (New York: Franklin Watts, 1981–82), p. 211.

18. See *Close Air Support*, Hearings before the Special Subcommittee on Close Air Support of the Preparedness Investigating Subcommittee, Committee on Armed Services, U.S. Senate, 93rd Congress, 1st Session, October-November 1971.

19. See, for example, *Accuracy Demonstrations for Delivery of Iron Bombs*, Litton Systems, Inc., Guidance and Control Systems Division, Publication No. 13396, September 1975.

20. S. E. Morison, *The Two-Ocean War*, pp. 356 and 359.

21. *Guided Missiles and Techniques*, Summary Technical Report of Division 5, National Defense Research Committee (Washington, D.C.: Office of Scientific Research and Development, 1946), pp. 27–47.

22. I. A. Getting, "The SCR-584 Radar Mark 56 Naval Gunfire Control System," *IEEE Transactions on Aerospace and Electronic Systems*, vol. AES-11, no. 5 (September 1975):921–939.

23. *Aviation Week and Space Technology*, vol. 99 (December 3, 1973):18–21.

24. For a complete discussion of electronic warfare, see *Aviation Week and Space Technology*, Special Report on Electronic Warfare (January 27, 1975):41–144.

25. *The Washington Post*, June 11, 1982, p. A-19; *Aviation Week and Space Technology* (July 5, 1982):16–17.

26. See my article, S. J. Deitchman, "The Future of Tactical Air Power in Land Warfare," *Astronautics and Aeronautics*, vol. 18, no. 7/8 (July-August 1980).

27. K. Tsipis, "Cruise Missiles," *Scientific American*, vol. 234, no. 2 (February 1977).

28. See the *New York Times*, September 22, 1976, on technology in the MiG-25 (Foxbat) fighter.

29. *Aviation Week and Space Technology* (May 25, 1970):19; and (December 3, 1973):21.

30. See *Soviet Military Power* (Washington, D.C.: U.S. Government Printing Office, 1981).

31. *Report* of the Subcommittee on Defense Appropriations, Department of Defense Appropriation Bill, Committee on Appropriations, U.S. House, 94th Congress, 2nd Session, 1976, p. 152. The discussion of the 1977 defense appropriation has been corrected to 1982 dollars in this text.

32. P. Stanford, "The Automated Battlefield," the *New York Times Magazine*, February 23, 1975.

33. S. J. Deitchman, *Limited War and American Defense Policy* (Cambridge, Mass.: MIT Press, 1964 and 1969), chapters 2 and 12.

Chapter 4

1. J. Weeks, *Men Against Tanks* (New York: Mason/Charter, 1975).

2. See discussion in J. Digby, *Precision-Guided Weapons*, Adelphi Papers No. 118 (London: The International Institute for Strategic Studies, 1975); and P. F. Walker, "Precision Guided Weapons," *Scientific American*, vol. 245, no. 2 (August 1981).

3. Further information can be found in selected quotations from Armor Operations, U.S. Army Field Manual, FM 17-1, Headquarters, Department of the Army, Washington, D.C., October 1966; A. A. Sidorenko, *The Offensive*. Translated and published under the auspices of the U.S. Air Force (Washington, D.C.: U.S. Government Printing Office, 1973); and V. Ye. Savkin, *The Basic Principles of Operational Art and Tactics*, translated and published under the auspices of the U.S. Air Force (Washington, D.C.: U.S. Government Printing Office, 1974).

4. Gen. M. Dayan, *Diary of the Sinai Campaign* (New York: Schocken Books, 1967), p. 83.

5. R. G. Ruppenthal, *Logistical Support of the Armies, United States Army in World War II: European Theatre of Operations* (Washington, D.C.: Office of the Chief of Military History, Department of the Army, 1953).

6. V. Ye. Savkin, *The Basic Principles*, p. 102; A. A. Sidorenko, *The Offensive*, p. 160.

7. *Armor Operations*, p. 90.

8. C. Ryan, *A Bridge Too Far* (New York: Popular Library, 1974), pp. 488–508.

9. B. B. Fall, *Street Without Joy* (Harrisburg, Pa.: Stackpole Co., 1961), Chapter 9.

10. *The Washington Post*, June 8, 1976.

11. J. Digby, *Precision-Guided Weapons*, p. 2.

12. H. P. Gates, Jr., et al., *Electronics-X: A Study of Military Electronics with Particular Reference to Cost and Reliability*, vol. 2, Complete Report, Institute for Defense Analyses Report R-195, January 1974, Appendix C, p. 397.

13. See H. M. Cole, *The Ardennes: Battle of the Bulge, United States Army in World War II: European Theatre of Operations* (Washington, D.C.: Office of the Chief of Military History, Department of the Army, 1965); and W. Craig, *Enemy at the Gates: The Battle for Stalingrad* (New York: Ballantine Books, 1973) for typical development of large-scale actions. See also M. Caidin, *The Tigers Are Burning* (New York: Hawthorne Books, 1974).

14. For a brief description of the German breakthrough in the Ardennes that led to the fall of France in 1940, see the *Encyclopedia Americana*, International Edition, 1974, vol. 29:387–395. This coverage was written by C. B. McDonald, Chief, World War II Branch, Office of the Chief of Military History, Department of the Army.

15. *Aviation Week and Space Technology*, vol. 99 (December 3, 1973):21 and (December 17, 1973):16–17.

Chapter 5

1. A. T. Mahan, *The Influence of Sea Power Upon History: 1660–1783* (Boston: Little, Brown, 1890), especially pp. 505–541. Mahan's ideas are elaborated on and related to modern times, through World War II, in essays by H. Rosinski, *The Development of Naval Thought*, edited and with an introduction by B. M. Simpson, III (Newport, R.I.: Naval War College Press, 1977).

2. See *Soviet Military Power* (Washington, D.C.: U.S. Government Printing Office, 1981), pp. 39–51.

3. S. G. Gorshkov, *The Sea Power of the State* (Oxford: Pergamon Press, 1979). Translated from the Russian.

4. S. G. Gorshkov, *The Sea Power of the State*; B. W. Watson, *Red Navy at Sea: Soviet Naval Operations on the High Seas, 1956–1980* (Boulder, Colo.: Westview Press, 1982); and *Soviet Military Power*.

5. See *U.S. Naval Force Alternatives*, Congressional Budget Office, Staff Working Paper, March 26, 1976; *Planning U.S. General Purpose Forces: The Navy*, Congressional Budget Office, Budget Issue Paper, December 1976; D. B. Kassing, "General Purpose Forces: Navy and Marine Corps," in F. P. Hoeber and W. Schneider, Jr. (eds.), *Arms, Men, and Military Budgets: Issues for Fiscal Year 1978* (New York: Crane, Russak, 1977); *Full Committee Consideration of the CVV Program*, Committee on Armed Services, U.S. House of Representatives, May 24, 1977, Report No. 95-25.

6. *Authorizing Appropriations for Fiscal Year 1978 for Military Procurement*

. . ., Committee on Armed Services, U.S. Senate, May 10, 1977, Report No. 95–125, p. 53.

7. C. W. Weinberger, Secretary of Defense, *Annual Report to the Congress for Fiscal Year 1983*, February 8, 1982.

8. These developments are summarized in S. E. Morison, *The Two-Ocean War* (Boston: Atlantic Monthly–Little, Brown, 1963).

9. These data are taken from S. E. Morison, *The Two-Ocean War*, pp. 333 and 336; from *Jane's Fighting Ships* and *Jane's All the World's Aircraft* for the years shown in the tables (New York: Franklin Watts, various years); and from N. Polmar, *Aircraft Carrier* (Garden City, N.Y.: Doubleday & Co., 1969).

10. S. E. Morison, *The Two-Ocean War*, indicates that there were 90 cruisers and destroyers in Task Force 58; there were about 195 cruisers, destroyers, and frigates in the Navy as of 1979.

11. The missiles and their ranges are described briefly in *Soviet Military Power* and in various editions of *Jane's Weapon Systems*.

12. These missiles and their ranges are described in *Jane's Weapon Systems*, 8th Edition (New York: Franklin Watts, 1976), pp. 24, 68, 69, and 157.

13. For a complete discussion of underwater sound phenomena as related to the problem of finding submarines, see J. W. Horton, *Fundamentals of Sonar* (Annapolis: U.S. Naval Institute, 1959). The Swedish submarine incident is described in *Science*, vol. 218, no. 4571 (October 29, 1982):450–451.

14. S. E. Morison, *History of United States Naval Operations in World War II*, Vol. 1, *The Battle of the Atlantic, September 1939–May 1943*, and Vol. 10, *The Battle of the Atlantic Won, May 1943–May 1945* (Boston: Little, Brown, 1947 and 1956, respectively).

15. See *U.S. Naval Force Alternatives*, pp. 33–42.

16. S. E. Morison, *The Two-Ocean War*.

17. *Soviet Military Power*, p. 40.

18. S. E. Morison, *History of United States Naval Operations in World War II*, Vol. 14, *Victory in the Pacific: 1945* (Boston: Little, Brown, 1960).

19. *CVAN-70 Aircraft Carrier*, Hearings before the Joint Senate-House Armed Services Subcommittee of the Senate and House Armed Services Committees, April 7, 8, 10, 13, 15, and 16, 1970, p. 230.

20. *CVAN-70 Aircraft Carrier*, pp. 229, 230; also S. E. Morison, *The Two-Ocean War*.

21. C. W. Weinberger, *Annual Report to the Congress for Fiscal Year 1983*, PI-30.

22. *Hearings on Military Posture, Fiscal Year 1973*, Committee on Armed Services, Report 92–1, p. I, pp. 9687 and 9724.

23. D. H. Rumsfeld, Secretary of Defense, *Annual Defense Department Report for Fiscal Year 1978*, January 17, 1977, pp. 112 and 194.

24. *Planning U.S. General Purpose Forces: The Navy*, p. 35.

25. Described briefly in *The Washington Post*, October 9, 1976, and in *Aviation Week and Space Technology*, vol. 105 (October 18, 1976). Described in detail by W. D. O'Neil, "Land-Based Aircraft Options for Naval Missions," paper presented at Society of Automotive Engineers Aerospace Meeting, Los Angeles, November 14–17, 1977.

26. Congressional Budget Office, Budget Issue Report, *Planning General Purpose Forces: The Navy*, pp. 59–62.

27. D. B. Kassing, "General Purpose Forces," pp. 129–137.

28. *Jane's Weapon Systems*, 8th Edition, p. 15; also *Aerospace Daily*, November 14, 1974, p. 14-F.

29. S. T. DeLa Mater, "The Carrier," *United States Naval Institute Proceedings*, vol. 102/10/884 (October 1976):66.

30. P. S. Dull, *A Battle History of the Imperial Japanese Navy (1914–1945)* (Annapolis: United States Naval Institute, 1978); and S. E. Morison, *The Two-Ocean War*.

31. Contemporary news accounts; J. F. Dunnigan, "New Weapons, Old Truths," *Forbes*, June 21, 1982. Also *Aviation Week and Space Technology* (July 19, 1982):18–22 and (July 26, 1982):24–25.

32. J. W. Abellera and R. Clark, "Forces of Habit: Budgeting for Tomorrow's Fleets," *AEI Foreign Policy and Defense Review*, vol. 3, nos. 2 and 3 (especially 36 ff).

33. J. H. Grotte, "Alternative Surface Navy Force Structures for the Future," unpublished manuscript, Institute for Defense Analyses, 1982.

34. For a realistic appraisal of the future of V/STOL in the Navy, see D. C. Hazen, "V/STOL and the Naval Planner's Dilemma," *Astronautics and Aeronautics*, vol. 15, no. 6 (June 1977).

35. For more detailed discussion of these possibilities, see "The Implications of Advancing Technology for Naval Aviation," Naval Studies Board, National Research Council, National Academy of Sciences, Washington, D.C., 1982.

36. J. H. Grotte, "Alternative Surface Navy Force Structures."

37. S. J. Deitchman, "Turning Point for Tactical Naval Forces?" *Astronautics and Aeronautics*, vol. 20, no. 11 (November 1982).

38. J. W. Finney, "Dreadnaught or Dinosaur?" the *New York Times Magazine*, January 18, 1976, p. 6.

Chapter 6

1. If specific sources are not given, the discussion of political and military events and popular attitudes in this chapter is based on contemporary news accounts, primarily in *The Washington Post* and the *New York Times*, but also in other newspapers, journals, and news magazines. All such accounts are shaded and interpreted according to the views of the writer, and you must also allow for the biased filter of this reader.

2. L. F. Richardson, *Statistics of Deadly Quarrels* (Pittsburgh: Boxwood Press and Chicago: Quadrangle Books, 1960).

3. *U.S. Statistical Abstract* (Washington, D.C.: U.S. Government Printing Office, various years and scattered relevant tables—by index.)

4. *Soviet Economic Problems and Prospects*, study prepared for the use of the Subcommittee on Priorities and Economy in Government, Joint Economic Committee, U.S. Congress, 1977. Also, *USSR: Measures of Economic Growth and Development, 1950–80*, study prepared for the use of the Joint Economic Committee, U.S. Congress, December 8, 1982.

5. S. J. Deitchman, *Limited War and American Defense Policy* (Cambridge, Mass.: MIT Press, 1964 and 1969), Chapter 2.

6. W. H. McNeill, *The Rise of the West* (Chicago: University of Chicago Press, 1963).

7. M. T. Kaufman, "A Reign of War in the Land of Sheba," the *New York Times Magazine*, January 8, 1978.

8. See Che Guevara *On Guerrilla Warfare* (New York: Praeger, 1961), pp. 81–85; R. Debray, *Revolution in the Revolution?* (New York: MR Press, 1967).

9. L. Dash, a series of articles in *The Washington Post*, August 7–13, 1977, and subsequent news reports. In 1981–1982 the United States made it a matter of policy that the improvement of relations with Cuba and a South African settlement in Namibia depend on Cuban withdrawal from Angola. Cuba has just as staunchly refused to discuss such a step.

10. M. T. Kaufman, "A Reign of War," loc. cit.

11. For example, the concept runs through the *Hearings on Proposed Expansion of U.S. Military Facilities in the Indian Ocean*, Subcommittee on the Near East and South Asia, U.S. House of Representatives, February–March 1974.

12. S. J. Deitchman, *Limited War*, Chapter 18. See also S. J. Deitchman, "A Lanchester Model of Guerrilla Warfare," *Operations Research*, vol. 10, no. 6 (November–December 1962):818–827.

13. A concise review of the extent and nature of these commitments is given in S. J. Deitchman, *Limited War*, pp. 56–57.

Chapter 7

1. The North Atlantic Treaty was signed by Belgium, Canada, Denmark, France, Iceland, Luxembourg, the Netherlands, Norway, Portugal, the United Kingdom, and the United States on April 4. 1949, in Washington, D.C.; it was extended to Greece and Turkey in 1952 and to the Federal Republic of Germany in 1955.

2. See, for example, *Pravda*, November 25, 1982, second edition, p. 6, as reported in U.S. Foreign Broadcast Information Service, FBIS-SOV-82-228, November 26, 1982, p. AA3.

3. *The Security of the Federal Republic of Germany and the Development of the Federal Armed Forces*, Federal Republic of Germany White Paper 1975/1976, Bonn, January 20, 1976, p. 89.

4. Remarks by Secretary General Leonid Brezhnev at the 25th Congress of the Communist Part of the Soviet Union, as reported in FBIS-SOV-76-38, February 28, 1976, p. 16.

5. See, for example, P. H. Vigor, "Doubts and Difficulties Confronting a Would-be Soviet Attacker," *Journal of the Royal United Services Institute for Defence Studies* (June 1980):32–38.

6. See V. D. Sokolovskii (ed.), *Soviet Military Strategy*, translated by H. Dinerstein, L. Gouré, and T. E. Wolfe (Englewood Cliffs, N.J.: Prentice-Hall, 1963), for references to and implications of Soviet offensive strategy and the destruction of the "aggressor's"—referring to U.S.—home territory. Also, Soviet force designs

for possible war in Europe as set forth in C. N. Donnelly, "The Soviet Operational Manoeuvre Group: A New Challenge for NATO," *International Defense Review*, vol. 9 (1982):1177–1186.

7. The *New York Times*, July 17, 1976; *The Washington Post*, April 17, 1976, and January 12 and 13, 1978.

8. See A. Ye. Yefremov, *Europe and Nuclear Weapons*, U.S. Department of Commerce, Joint Publications Research Service (JPRS) 58481, March 14, 1973, Chapter 4.

9. Quoted in A. L. Horelick, *The Strategic Mind-Set of the Soviet Military: An Essay-Review*, RAND Paper Series P-5813, February 1977, Santa Monica, Calif.: p. 7.

10. As reported in FBIS-SOV-76-38, February 28, 1976.

11. Speech given on November 15, 1982, as reported in FBIS-SOV-82-220, vol. III, no. 220, p. 10.

12. See, for example, V. Zorza, "The Kremlin Defense Debate," *The Washington Post*, May 14, 1976.

13. As reported in FBIS-SOV-76-38, February 28, 1976.

14. *Understanding Soviet Naval Developments*, Office of the Chief of Naval Operations, Department of the Navy, NAVSO P-3560, April 1975. Also *Soviet Military Power* (Washington, D.C.: U.S. Government Printing Office, 1981), and B. W. Watson, *Red Navy at Sea: Soviet Naval Operations on the High Seas, 1956–1980* (Boulder, Colo.: Westview Press, 1982).

15. C. N. Donnelly, "The Soviet Operational Manoeuvre Group."

16. For elaboration of this idea, see R. Rosecrance, *Strategic Deterrence Reconsidered*, Adelphi Papers no. 116 (London: International Institute for Strategic Studies, Spring 1975), p. 25.

17. *NATO and the Warsaw Pact: Force Comparisons*, published in 1982 by Joseph Luns, the Secretary General of NATO.

Chapter 8

1. C. W. Weinberger, Secretary of Defense, *Annual Report to the Congress for Fiscal Year 1983*, February 8, 1982.

2. Discussed in detail in a letter from A. M. Rivlin, Congressional Budget Office, to Hon. B. Adams, Chairman, Committee on the Budget, U.S. House of Representatives, July 21, 1976.

3. Force numbers are from *NATO and the Warsaw Pact: Force Comparisons*, published by Joseph Luns, the Secretary General of NATO, in 1982.

4. See, for example, article by Lord Chalfont in the London *Times*, March 15, 1976, p. 12; see also the report of the NATO study on p. 9 of the London *Times* of the same date.

5. *NATO and the Warsaw Pact: Force Comparisons*.

6. Estimated from *NATO and the Warsaw Pact: Force Comparisons* and from *The Military Balance*, published by the International Institute for Strategic Studies in London (1982–83).

7. See, for example, P. H. Vigor, "Doubts and Difficulties Confronting a Would-be Soviet Attacker," *Journal of the Royal United Services Institute for Defence Studies* (June 1980):32–38.

8. These techniques are discussed in some detail in the original edition of this book, S. J. Deitchman, *New Technology and Military Power* (Boulder, Colo.: Westview Press, 1979), pp. 172–175.

9. B. Catton, *A Stillness at Appomatox* (Garden City, N.Y.: Doubleday & Co., 1954).

10. T. Wintringham and J. N. Blashford-Snell, *Weapons and Tactics* (London: Penguin, 1973).

11. See S. J. Deitchman, "A Lanchester Model of Guerrilla Warfare," *Operations Research*, vol. 10, no. 6 (November-December 1962):818–827.

12. R. Leckie, *Conflict: The History of the Korean War, 1950–53* (New York: G. P. Putnam's Sons, 1962), pp. 193–228.

13. C. N. Donnelly, "The Soviet Operational Manoeuvre Group: A New Challenge for NATO," *International Defense Review*, vol. 9 (1982):1177–1186.

14. C. Ryan, *A Bridge Too Far* (New York: Popular Library, 1974).

15. "Alliance Defense Policy, Ministerial Guidance 1975, and Annex to Final Communique DPC Ministerial Meeting," May 1975, pars. 4 and 11.

16. See the *New York Times*, September 24, 1976; also H. Owen and C. L. Schultze (eds.), *Setting National Priorities: The Next Ten Years* (Washington, D.C.: Brookings Institution, 1976), pp. 67–70.

17. *Setting National Priorities*, pp. 67–70.

18. A. A. Sidorenko, *The Offensive*, p. 98. Translated and published under the auspices of the U.S. Air Force (Washington, D.C.: U.S. Government Printing Office, 1973).

19. Col. Gen. N. A. Lomov (ed.), *The Revolution in Military Affairs*, pp. 123–124. Translated and published under the auspices of the U.S. Air Force (Washington, D.C.: U.S. Government Printing Office, 1974).

20. B. Tuchman, *The Guns of August* (New York: Dell, 1962), pp. 42 and 219.

21. See C. Bekker, *The Luftwaffe War Diaries*, translated and edited by F. Zeigler (Garden City, N.Y.: Doubleday & Col, 1968), pp. 150–151; also H. Guderian, *Panzer Leader* (New York: Ballantine Books, 1957), pp. 117 and 125.

22. P. H. Vigor, "Doubts and Difficulties Confronting a Would-be Soviet Attacker."

23. W. Churchill, *Their Finest Hour* (Boston: Houghton Mifflin, 1949), App. C.

24. C. Bekker, *The Luftwaffe War Diaries*, p. 143 and Appendices 1, 13, and 14.

25. See A. A. Sidorenko, *The Offensive*; also V. Ye. Savkin, *The Basic Principles of Operational Art and Tactics*. Translated and published under the auspices of the U.S. Air Force (Washington, D.C.: U.S. Government Printing Office, 1974).

26. J. R. Schlesinger, Secretary of Defense, *Annual Defense Department Report for Fiscal Year 1975*, pp. 8 and 82–91.

27. For a statement of the concerns on both sides, see, for example, H. A. Kissinger, "Strains on the Alliance," *Foreign Affairs*, vol. 41, no. 42 (January 1963):271–281.

28. R. S. McNamara, "Defense Arrangements of the North Atlantic Community," address at the University of Michigan, June 16, 1962; reprinted in Department of State *Bulletin* (July 9, 1962):64–69.

29. N. Leites, *French Ideas on American Domination and Withdrawal*, RAND Corporation Memorandum RM-4521-1 SA, June 1965, Santa Monica, Calif., pp. 51–54.

30. See *The Washington Post*, December 22, 1977.

31. J. Joffe, "Euromissile Myths," the *New York Times*, December 28, 1982.

32. McG. Bundy, G. Kennan, R. McNamara, G. Smith, "Nuclear Weapons and the Atlantic Alliance," *Foreign Affairs* (Spring 1982).

33. S. J. Deitchman, *New Technology and Military Power*, p. 204.

34. Gen. B. W. Rogers, "The Atlantic Alliance: Prescriptions for a Difficult Decade," *Foreign Affairs*, vol. 60, no. 5 (Summer 1982):1145–1156.

Chapter 9

1. W. Manchester, *American Caesar: Douglas MacArthur, 1880–1964* (New York: Dell, 1978), parts IX–XI.

2. F. Butterfield, "The New Vietnam Scholarship," the *New York Times Magazine*, February 13, 1983.

3. C. W. Weinberger, Secretary of Defense, *Annual Report to the Congress for Fiscal Year 1984* (known in defense circles as the "Posture Statement"), p. 36.

4. R. Halloran, "U.S. Warns Europe on Military Needs," the *New York Times*, May 16, 1982, p. 19.

5. C. W. Weinberger, *Annual Report to the Congress for Fiscal Year 1984*, pp. 46 and 139.

6. For continuity in such a view, see H. Salisbury, the *New York Times*, May 7, 1969, and H. A. Kissinger, *The Washington Post*, December 21, 1981.

7. J. E. Carter, President of the United States, *State of the Union Address*, January 23, 1980.

8. *Rapid Deployment Forces: Policy and Budget Implications*, A CBO Study, Congressional Budget Office, February 1983.

9. Ibid.

10. W. Manchester, *American Caesar*.

11. *Rapid Deployment Forces*.

12. Report of the Special Operations Review Group regarding the mission to rescue the U.S. hostages held in Iran, April 1980, published in *Aviation Week and Space Technology* (September 15, 1980):61–71, (September 22, 1980):140–144, and (September 29, 1980):84–91.

13. See R. Wohlstetter, *Pearl Harbor: Warning and Decision* (Stanford: Stanford University Press, 1962); H. M. Cole, *The Ardennes: Battle of the Bulge, United States Army in World War II: European Theatre of Operations* (Washington, D.C.: Office of the Chief of Military History, Department of the Army, 1965), pp. 56–74; and B. Wholey, *Codeword BARBAROSSA* (Cambridge, Mass.: MIT Press, 1973).

14. S. G. Gorshkov, *The Sea Power of the State* (Oxford: Pergamon Press, 1979. Translated from the Russian.

15. B. W. Watson, *Red Navy at Sea: Soviet Naval Operations on the High Seas, 1956–1980* (Boulder, Colo.: Westview Press, 1982).

16. *Understanding Soviet Naval Developments*, Office of the Chief of Naval Operations, Department of the Navy, NAVSO P-3560, 4th Edition, revised January 1981, p. 82.

17. D. J. Kenney, "A Primer on S. G. Gorshkov's 'Sea Power of the State,' " *Naval War College Review* (Spring 1977):99.

18. Quoted in W. Millis, *Arms and Men: A Study in American Military History* (New York: G. P. Putnam's Sons, 1956), p. 157.

19. E. Wegener, *The Soviet Naval Offensive* (Annapolis: U.S. Naval Institute Press, 1975). Translated by H. Wegener.

20. An article in *The Washington Post*, October 27, 1977, described a Soviet attempt to purchase base rights in the Maldive Islands near Diego Garcia.

21. Described by W. Churchill in *Their Finest Hour*, Bk. 2, Chapter 7, "The Mediterranean Passage"; and in *The Hinge of Fate*, Bk. 1, Chapter 15, "The Arctic Convoys," and Chapter 17, "Malta and the Desert" (Boston: Houghton Mifflin, 1949 and 1950, respectively).

22. B. W. Watson, *Red Navy at Sea*.

23. The *New York Times*, January 7, 1976; *The Washington Post*, January 20, 1978.

24. See *The Washington Post*, July 29, 1977, p. 3, on a relevant Soviet submarine warfare exercise. Also, see S. G. Gorshkov, *The Sea Power of the State*.

25. *Strengths of the Army and Navy*, monthly reports published by the Office of the Adjutant General during World War II, made available by the U.S. Army and U.S. Navy libraries.

26. Budget and force size comparisons based on data in C. W. Weinberger, *Annual Report to the Congress for Fiscal Year 1984* and in *Rapid Deployment Forces*.

Chapter 10

1. S. J. Deitchman, *New Technology and Military Power* (Boulder, Colo.: Westview Press, 1979).

2. *Status of Major Acquisitions as of September 30, 1981: Better Reporting Essential to Controlling Cost Growth* (Washington, D.C.: General Accounting Office, April 22, 1982).

3. F. W. Lanchester, *Aircraft in Warfare: The Dawn of the Fourth Arm* (London: Constable, 1916).

4. See discussion of the Mansfield Sense-of-the Senate Resolution in the *New York Times*, January 16, 21, 24, and 25, 1970.

5. J. Record and R. J. Hanks, *U.S. Strategy at the Crossroads: Two Views* (Cambridge, Mass., and Washington, D.C.: Institute for Foreign Policy Analysis, Inc., 1982); and E. C. Ravenal, "The Case for Withdrawal of Our Forces," the *New York Times Magazine*, March 6, 1983.

6. See frequent news items in the *New York Times*, April–June 1970; see also *Setting National Priorities: The 1975 Budget* (Washington, D.C.: Brookings Institution, 1974), p. 128; and Senator McGovern's proposal for a 5–10 billion dollar defense budget reduction, reported in *Defense / Space Daily*, March 24, 1978, p. 139.

7. The concept, although not argued publicly, emerged in several discussions with some of my NATO colleagues in relation to inventories of sophisticated weaponry. See also the *New York Times*, January 10, 1977.

8. Private discussions. See also H. Brown, Secretary of Defense, *Annual Defense Department Report for Fiscal Year 1979*, p. 85, and all subsequent Posture Statements.

9. See *Department of Defense Authorization Act, 1983*, reported in U.S. House, August 16, 1982, Report No. 97-749, Sect. 139b, p. 26.

10. See "The Winds of Reform," *Time* magazine, March 7, 1983.

11. See, for example, J. Fallows, *National Defense* (New York: Random House, 1981); and G. Hart, "What's Wrong With the Military?", the *New York Times Magazine*, February 14, 1982. Articles and newspaper reports on the theme have been appearing with great regularity for the past two to three years.

12. *Report of the Defense Science Board 1981 Summer Study Panel on Operational Readiness with High Performance Systems* (Washington, D.C.: Office of the Under Secretary of Defense for Research and Engineering, April 1982).

13. Unless otherwise noted, the factual material in this section is taken from H. P. Gates, Jr., et al., *Electronics - X: A Study of Military Electronics with Particular Reference to Cost and Reliability*, vol. 2, Complete Report, Institute for Defense Analyses Report R-195, January 1974, Chapter III-B and Appendix C. This material was originally compiled and analyzed by me.

14. A. H. Flax, "Aeronautics: A Study in Technological Growth and Form," 63rd Wilbur and Orville Wright Memorial Lecture given before the Royal Aeronautical Society on December 5, 1974. Published in *Aeronautical Journal* (December 1974).

15. The Record on cancellation of the Mauler is obscure. See, however, *Hearings on Department of Defense Appropriations for 1964*, Appropriations Subcommittee, U.S. House of Representatives, 1964, pt. 5, p. 355; *Hearings on Department of Defense Appropriations for 1965*, Appropriations and Armed Services Committees, U.S. House of Representatives, 1965, pt. 1, pp. 856-857; *Hearings on Department of Defense Approprations for 1966*, Appropriations and Armed Services Committees, U.S. House of Representatives, 1966, pt. 1, pp. 163 and 510. Respectively, these hearings show: a planned production buy; technical problems that caused the systems to be returned to development; no funds requested; and continuing technical problems.

16. H. Brown, *Annual Defense Department Report for Fiscal Year 1979*, p. 145.

17. See "The Winds of Reform," *Time* magazine, March 7, 1983.

18. *The Washington Post*, March 15, 1978.

19. Office of Management and Budget figures given in J. D. Morgan et al., *Accomplishing Shipyard Work for the United States Navy: Institutions, Systems and Operations*, Institute for Defense Analyses Paper P-1132, August 1975, vol. 1, p. 302.

20. By presidential directive, since about 1967.

21. Data for 1962-1968 from N. J. Asher and L. D. Strom, *The Role of the Department of Defense in the Development of Integrated Circuits*, Institute for Defense Analyses Paper P-1271, May 1977; data for 1972 from Gates et al., *Electronics-X*.

Chapter 11

1. *Report of the Commission on Government Procurement* (Washington, D.C.: U.S. Government Printing Office, 1972).

2. S. J. Deitchman, "The Future of Tactical Air Power in Land Warfare," *Astronautics and Aeronautics*, vol. 18, no. 7/8 (July/August 1980); S. J. Deitchman, "Turning Point for Tactical Naval Forces?", *Astronautics and Aeronautics*, vol. 20, no. 11 (November 1982).

3. H. Brown, Secretary of Defense, *Annual Defense Department Report for Fiscal Year 1979*, p. 233.

4. For a description of Blackhawk, see *Jane's All the World's Aircraft, 1977–78* (New York: Franklin Watts, 197), p. 407.

5. E. E. Morison, *Men, Machines, and Modern Times* (Cambridge, Mass.: MIT Press, 1966), pp. 98–122.

6. For a more extensive discussion of this point, see S. J. Deitchman, "Turning Point for Tactical Naval Forces?".

7. These data have been compiled by J. Stahl, Institute for Defense Analyses, Cost Analysis Group, from the *Five Year Defense Programs, 1962–1988*.

8. *Aerospace Facts and Figures, 1976–77*, compiled by Aerospace Industries Association of America, Inc., and published by *Aviation Week and Space Technology* (New York: McGraw Hill, 1978), p. 120; and *Aerospace Facts and Figures, 1980–81* , p. 132.

Index

Specific weapons systems are entered under the heading for their general type—e.g., Aircraft types; Helicopters; Missile systems; Tanks. Entries designated "*p.*" refer to the photograph section that follows page 65.

Afghanistan, 139, 156–157, 160
Africa, 204, 262n
Airborne warning and control
    systems (AWACS), 59, 115, 242
Aircraft carriers
  as air bases, 88, 91
  aircraft complement of, 97(table),
    103, 106, 118, 119
  attack, 94(fig.)
  objectives of, 110
  vulnerability of, 115
  in World War II, 95(fig.)
  See also Carrier forces; Naval
    forces
Aircraft shelters, 57
Aircraft types
  A-4F Skyhawk, *p.*
  A-10, 37, 63, *p.*
  B-1, 115
  B-52, 115
  C-5, 208, 209
  C-17, 209
  C-130 Hercules, 243
  E-2C Hawkeye, 118
  F-4 Phantom, 56, 225, 243
  F-14, 115, 243
  F-15 fighter, 56, 60, 225

F-16 fighter, 56, 60, 224
F-18, 224
F-111, 115, 233, 234(table)
long-range, 209
Mirage fighters (Fr.), 56, 60
P-3C Orion, *p.*
remotely piloted vehicles (RPVs),
    37
S-3 Viking, 118
V/STOL aircraft, 117–118, 118n,
    243
See also Forward air controller
    aircraft; Helicopters;
    Interceptors
Aircraft types—Soviet
  Backfire bombers, 88
  Bear turboprop, 212
  Fencer (SU-24), 57
  Fitter-C (SU-17), 57
  Flogger (MiG-23D), 57, 243
  MiG-21, 55
Air defenses, 47–53, 59–60,
    61(table), 62, 226
  basing of, 115
  cost-effectiveness of, 52
  missile systems, 47–49, 48(table),
    51, 52, 56, 58–59, *p.*, 99, 222, 236

multistage systems, 48–49,
50(fig.), 58
precision-guided munitions and,
52, 53
Roland SAM system (Ger.), 222,
236
SAM systems, 47–49, 51, 52, 56,
58–59, *p.,* 99, 222, 236
sea-based, 99, 100(fig.), 212
suppression tactics, 49, 51–52, 118
Air forces, 114, 177, 179(fig.), 180
cost-effectiveness and, 64–65, 224
cost of, 64–65, 120, 224
defense budget and, 62–63
high-low mix, 63–64
land-based, 115, 116, 117, 120
sea-based. *See* Aircraft carriers;
Carrier forces
structure of, 5–6
uses of, 31–40
Air operatio.s, 31–40
air-to-ground, 39
in Korean war, 33
loss rates, 62
nighttime, 40, 43
performance indicators, 40,
42(table)
tactical attacks, 32–33, 34–40,
41(fig.)
target identification, 36–39
in Vietnam war, 33–34
weapon delivery accuracy, 40,
42(table), 43–47
in World War II, 31, 33
See also Air-to-air warfare
Air-to-air warfare, 55–59, *p.*
Alliances, 142–143. *See also* Proxies
All Volunteer Force, 225
Andropov, Yuri, 165
Anti-submarine warfare (ASW),
101–103, 104(fig.), 107, 115
Anti-tank guided missiles (ATGMs),
67, 77–85
accuracy of, 79
armored warfare and, 81–84
SS-10/SS-11 (Fr.), 85

vulnerability of, 79–80
wire-guided, 85
See also Anti-tank weapons
Anti-tank weapons, 44, *p.,* 67, 74,
76–85. *See also* Anti-tank
guided missiles
APCs. *See* Armored personnel
carriers
Armored personnel carriers (APCs),
69. *See also* Armored vehicles;
Tanks
Armored vehicles, 69, 178–179(figs.),
236. *See also* Tanks
Armored warfare, 68–69, 70–71,
72–73(table), 81–85
anti-tank, 75–81
defense, 74–75
logistics, 71, 74
mobility in, 74
See also Tanks
Arms control, 163
Artillery, 178–179(figs.)
ASW. *See* Anti-submarine warfare
ATGMs. *See* Anti-tank guided
missiles
Avionics systems, 233, 234(table),
237
AWACS. *See* Airborne warning and
control system

Ballistic missiles. *See* Missile
systems
Bazookas, 77
Berlin Agreements (1971), 156
Biological weapons. *See* Chemical
warfare
Bonesteel, Gen. Charles, 139
Bradley fighting vehicle, *p.,* 84
Brandt, Willy, 162
Brezhnev, Leonid, 23–24, 165
Brezhnev Doctrine, 163
Bundy, McGeorge, 196

Caribbean basin, 202–203
Carrier forces, 117–118
cost of, 120

Carter, Jimmy
  defense spending, 128–129, 224
  Eurocommunism and, 162
  force deployment by, 204, 205
  Iran crisis and, 205
  Latin America and, 202, 203
  NATO and, 158
  naval forces and, 90
  synfuels program, 210–211
Carter Doctrine, 151, 153
Castro, Fidel, 143
Central America, 203
Chemical warfare
  binary-munitions, 28–29
  deterrence of, 29
  in World War II, 24
China. *See* People's Republic of
  China
Churchill, Sir Winston, 160, 161
Clausewitz, Karl von, 131
Cluster weapons, 44
Communications
  command pyramid and, 39
  in theater of operations, 17, 36
Communism
  spread of, 139, 162, 165–166. *See
  also* People's Republic of China,
  expansionism; Soviet Union,
  expansionism
Computers
  simulation techniques, 183
  weapons delivery and, 44
Concentration principles. *See*
  Nuclear weapons, concentration
  principles and
Conventional forces
  deterrence value of, 167, 194,
  195–196, 197–198
  in Europe, 184–192
  modernization of, 201
Conventional war, 23–24, 129,
  130(table), 132–133
  deterrence of, 188, 192–195
  duration of, 189, 190–192
  in Europe, 184–187, 188–192
  potential areas of, 202(fig.)

See also Escalation
Coral Sea, 111
"Counterair," 57
Cruise missiles, *p.,* 195
  cost-effectiveness of, 53–54
  deterrence value of, 55
  sea-based, 99, 101, 118–119
Cruisers, 94(fig.). *See also* Naval
  forces
Cuba, 203
  Africa and, 262n
  as Soviet proxy, 143, 160

Defense Science Board, 224
deGaulle, Charles, 194
Delivery systems, 19, 25. *See also*
  Missile systems; Platforms
Deterred war. *See* War, deterred
Deterrence, 170, 192–198
  of chemical warfare, 29
  conventional forces and, 167,
  194, 195–196, 197–198
  of conventional war, 188, 192–195
  cruise missiles and, 55
  effective uses of, 146(table),
  146–148
  escalation and, 147–148, 149–150
  failures of, 147
  focus of efforts, 216
  force imbalance and, 196
  in Korea, 205
  NATO efforts, 166–167
  political, 167
  RDF and, 206
  triad of, 194–197, 216

Eastern Europe
  stability of, 162–163
  See also Warsaw Pact
East Germany, 163
Electronics
  advances in, 6–7, 51–52
  air defense suppression and,
  51–52
  nighttime air operations and, 40,
  43–44

reconnaissance and, 36–37, 38–39
  See also Technology
El Salvador, 203
Enhanced-radiation weapons, 12,
  23
  in Europe, 195
  tactical war and, 13–14
Enterprise, 108
Escalation, 23–27, 136
  deterrence and, 147–148, 149–150
  justifiable, 150
Escorts, 94(fig.). *See also* Naval
  forces
Eurocommunism, 162
Europe. *See* Conventional forces, in
  Europe; Eastern Europe;
  "Eurostrategic" attack; North
  Atlantic Treaty Organization;
  Nuclear weapons, in Europe;
  Soviet Union, European
  strategy; War, European scenario
"Eurostrategic" attack, 27, 195
Exchange ratio, 60

FACs. *See* Forward air controller
  aircraft
Fallows, James, 223
FEBA (forward edge of the battle
  area), 15–17
First use policy, 22
Flexible response strategy
  in Europe, 187
Ford, Gerald R., 90
Forrestal, 111
Forward air controller aircraft
  (FACs), 36–37
Forward edge of the battle area.
  See FEBA
France, 161, 181–182

GCI. *See* Interceptors, ground-
  controlled
General Dynamics Corporation,
  236
German Territorial Forces, 182

Germany. *See* East Germany; West
  Germany
Goering, Hermann, 190
Gorshkov, Adm. S. G., 212
Grant, U. S., 183
Great Britain, 140
Grechko, A. A., 164
Guerrilla war. *See* War,
  unconventional
Guidance systems, 6–7, 45–47
  anti-aircraft, 47–49, 50
  on ATGMs, 78–79

Harrier, 117, 118n
Hart, Gary, 223
HEAT. *See* High-explosive anti-
  tank rounds
Helicopters, 8
  AH-64 Apache, 84, 236
  air support from, 37
  in anti-tank warfare, 78
  Cheyenne, 236
  UH-1 (Huey), 243
  UH-60 Blackhawk, 243
Helsinki accord (1975), 156
High-explosive anti-tank rounds
  (HEAT), 77. *See also* Anti-tank
  weapons
High-low force mix, 63–64, 221
Hitler, Adolf, 190
Hugging tactic, 15, 192

ICBMs. *See* Missile systems,
  intercontinental
Imports
  U.S. dependence on, 137–138
Improved TOW Vehicle (ITV), 84
Industry—private
  defense spending and, 245–254
  technology advances and,
    244–245, 251
INF. *See* Intermediate-range nuclear
  force
Intelligence gathering. *See*
  Reconnaissance; War, tactical
  surprise in

Interceptors, 55–56, 115
 ground-controlled (GCI), 56, 58
Intermediate-range nuclear force
 (INF), 195. *See also* Missile
 systems, intermediate-range
International Institute of Strategic
 Studies, 175n
Iran, 205
IRBMs. *See* Missile systems,
 intermediate-range
Israel, 32, 48
ITV. *See* Improved TOW Vehicle

Japan, 200
 China and, 204
 defense spending, 177(fig.)
 Korea and, 205
 national security, 26, 137,
 204–205
Johnson, Lyndon B., 150

Kamikazes, 45, 107–108
Kennan, George, 196
Kesselring, Albert, 33
Kiev (Soviet), 88
Kim Il Sung, 204–205
Kissinger, Henry, 162
Kohl, Helmut, 162
Korea
 instability of, 204–205
Korean war, 26, 138–139, 200
 air operations in, 33
 escalation of, 149–150

Lanchester, F. W., 221n
Latin America, 202
LAW. *See* Light anti-tank weapon
Lebanon, 205
Lee, Robert E., 183
Leninism, 157
Light anti-tank weapon (LAW), 77.
 See also Anti-tank weapons
Limited war. *See* Escalation; War,
 limited

MacArthur, Gen. Douglas, 149, 185

McNamara, Robert, 22, 194, 196
Mahan, Capt. A. T., 87–88, 213
Mansfield, Mike, 221
Mark II Avionics, 233, 234(table)
Mechanized infantry combat vehicle
 (MICV), 236
Merchant Marine Act (1970), 237,
 238(fig.)
Microcircuits, 239, 240, 251
MICV. *See* Mechanized infantry
 combat vehicle
Midway, 106, 111
Military Balance, The, 175n
Mines, 76, 85. *See also* Anti-tank
 weapons
Missile systems, *p.,* 166
 for air defense, 47–49, 48(table),
 51, 52, 56, 58–59, *p.,* 99, 222,
 236
 air-to-air, 56, *p.*
 anti-tank. *See* Anti-tank guided
 missiles
 Assault Breaker, 51–52
 in Europe, 163–164
 Harpoon, 115
 intercontinental (ICBMs), 25
 intermediate-range (IRBMs), 25,
 195
 Lance, 25
 Mauler, 236
 Maverick anti-tank, *p. See also*
 Anti-tank weapons
 medium-range (MRBMs), 25
 medium-range air-to-surface
 (MRASMs), 55
 Pershing II, 195
 Phoenix, 115
 Shrike, *p.*
 Sidewinder, 56, *p.*
 submarine-launched, 8
 Tomahawk, 115
 TOW anti-tank, *p. See also* Anti-
 tank weapons
 See also Cruise missiles;
 Precision-guided munitions;
 Surface-to-air missile systems

Mitscher, Marc A., 92
Mitterand, François, 162
Monroe Doctrine, 203
Montgomery, Gen. Sir Bernard, 75,
    186
Morison, E. E., 8, 87
Moving target indication (MTI), 43
Moving target tracking (MTT), 43
MRASMs. *See* Missile systems,
    medium-range air-to-surface
MRBMs. *See* Missile systems,
    medium-range
MTI. *See* Moving target indication
MTT. *See* Moving target tracking

National security, 125–126,
    137–138, 151–152, 211
  Caribbean basin and, 203
  Europe and, 173
  strategy orientation, 199, 201,
    215–216
NATO. *See* North Atlantic Treaty
    Organization
Naval aviation. *See* Aircraft carriers;
    Carrier forces
Naval forces
  amphibious landing capacity, 98
  attack capability, 92, 95,
    96(table), 112–113
  attrition of, 107
  changes in, 91–98, 93–94(figs.),
    95–98(tables), 119–121
  cost of, 105, 237, 238(table), 240
  defense budget and, 120
  defense systems, 99, 100(fig.)
  expansion of, 90, 111, 114
  firepower, 92, 95, 96(table)
  force expansion, 201
  purpose of, 87, 91, 212, 213
  RDF and, 211–213, 215–216
  Soviet. *See* Soviet navy
  structure of, 119
  vulnerability of, 107–111
  See also Aircraft carriers; Carrier
    forces; Cruisers; Escorts;
    Submarines

Naval operations, 98–99, 101–103
  amphibious landing capacity,
    98(table), 210
  cruise missiles in, 118–119
  objectives of, 112–113
  projection, 112–113
  rapid deployment, 210
  reconnaissance, 88, 101
  sea-control, 112–113, 116
  ship detection, 106
  in World War II, 107–108, 116
Naval warfare, 87–121, 169–170
  changes in, 4–5, 87–91
  in 19th century, 8–9
  See also Naval operations
Navigation systems, 227(fig.)
  satellite, 44
Navstar, 44
Neutron bomb. *See* Enhanced-
    radiation weapons
Nicaragua, 202–203
Nimitz, 90, 106
Nixon Doctrine, 145
No-first-use policy, 196, 197
North Atlantic Treaty, 154
North Atlantic Treaty Organization
    (NATO)
  air defense suppression
    requirements, 49, 51–53
  boundaries, 174(fig.)
  defense regions, 174, 180, 181,
    181(fig.)
  defense spending, 128(fig.),
    128–129, 166, 175, 176(fig.),
    196–197, 198
  defense strategies, 184–192, 196
  deterrence efforts, 166–167
  force distribution, 169
  force modernization, 184
  founding of, 154
  priorities of, 155, 156
  relative strength of, 175, 177,
    178(fig.), 179(fig.), 180, 181(fig.),
    181–183
  reserve forces, 182
  SAM systems, 56

social spending, 128(fig.), 128–129
Soviet Union and, 155–158,
    161, 167, 186–187, 193–194, 195
unity of, 161, 164, 167, 194
Warsaw Pact and, 193–194, 195
Nuclear battlefield, 14–22
logistics of, 16–17, 18–19
Nuclear weapons
air tactics and, 15
concentration principles and,
    14–18, 21–22
as conventional war deterrent,
    192–195
in Europe, 156, 163–164, 192–197
first-use policy, 22
flexible response strategy and,
    187
at sea, 19–20
Soviet use theory, 20–22, 23–24
strategic war and, 6
tactical war and, 11–22

Oil, 142, 151, 211
Operation Market-Garden (1944),
    38n, 75
Operation Strangle (1944), 33, 45,
    46(table)
Operation Strangle (1951), 33
"Overpressure," 12n, 13

Panama Canal, 202, 203
Patriot system, 56
Patton, Gen. George, 4, 70, 74
People's Republic of China,
    153–154, 200
expansionism, 138–139
Japan and, 204
national security, 138
Soviet Union and, 204
Vietnam and, 149
Personnel
competition for, 251–252, 252(fig.)
See also Technology, manpower
    and
PGMs. See Precision-guided
    munitions

Platforms, 84, 241, 242, 243, 253
defense budget and, 246(table),
    247–249(figs.)
symbolic value of, 250
Poland
1981 crisis, 148, 163
Precision-guided munitions (PGMs),
    45, 46–47, p., 110
air defenses and, 52, 53. See also
    Surface-to-air missile systems
cost-effectiveness of, 65
dependency of, 208
at sea, 101
See also Anti-tank guided
    missiles; Cruise missiles;
    Guidance systems; Missile
    systems
Private sector. See Industry—private
Projection, 112–113
Proxies, 137, 138, 200, 205,
    Soviet, 143, 156, 160

Radar, 43–44, 51
cost-performance relationships,
    228(table)
low-altitude gaps, 58–59
Rapid Deployment Force (RDF),
    205–211
basing of, 208, 209, 210
deterrence value of, 206
intelligence and, 209
jurisdiction of, 206, 207
strength of, 206
structure of, 209–210, 215–216
RDF. See Rapid Deployment Force
Reagan, Ronald
defense spending, 127, 129, 219,
    224
force expansion and, 153, 154
Latin America and, 203
naval forces and, 90, 111, 153
and perception of U.S., 156
synfuels program, 210–211
war in Europe and, 189
Reconnaissance, 38–39
in naval warfare, 88, 101

technology of, 36–37, 38–39
  in World War II, 38n
  See also Air operations, target
    identification
"Reform movement," 223–226
Richardson, Lewis, 135
Rockeye anti-armor munition, 44.
    See also Anti-tank weapons
Rogers, Gen. Bernard W., 158, 196
RPG-7 rocket (Soviet), 77. *See
    also* Anti-tank weapons
RPVs. *See* Aircraft types, remotely
  piloted vehicles

SAM. *See* Surface-to-air missile
  systems
Satellites. *See* Navigation systems,
  satellite
Schlieffen plan, 190
Schmidt, Helmut, 162
Sea control, 112–113
  land-based, 115–117
  submarines and, 115–116, 117
  in World War II, 116
Sheridan armored reconnaissance
    vehicle, 80. *See also* Armored
    vehicles; Tanks
Short takeoff and landing aircraft.
    See Aircraft types, V/STOL
    aircraft
"Showing the flag." *See* Deterrence
Slessor, Sir John, 33
Smith, Gerard, 196
Sonar, 101–103
Sonobuoys, 102–103
Soviet bloc. *See* Warsaw Pact
Soviet navy
  air power of, 213
  defense against, 115–116
  force expansion, 169
  mission of, 212, 213, 214
  ocean access, 213, 214(fig.)
  strategies, 99, 101
  structure of, 88, 89(table), 90
Soviet Union

air defenses, 49, 51, 59–60,
    61(table)
air power, 213
armored warfare strategies,
    72–73(table)
base structure, 140, 168, 204,
    213
chemical weapons, 28, 29
China and, 204
defense spending, 175, 176(fig.),
    177(fig.)
defense strategy, 164–165
deterrence and, 148
European strategy, 189–190
expansionism, 134, 138–139,
    154–155, 156–157, 158–161,
    167, 201
force expansion, 157, 164, 171
in foreign conflicts, 142–143, 155
global presence of, 141(table),
    142–143, 151, 155
military exports, 141(table)
national security, 138, 161–162,
    170–171
NATO and, 155–158, 161, 167,
    186–187, 193–194, 195
nuclear weapons use theory,
    20–22, 23–24
proxies, 143, 156, 160
sphere of influence, 142–143,
    158, 159(fig.), 160. *See also*
    Warsaw Pact
tactical aviation policy, 57–58
tactical theory in, 20–22, 57–58
U.S. force expansion and,
    153–154
weapons quality, 182
Spinney, Franklin, 223
Spotter planes. *See* Forward air
  controller aircraft
SSBNs, 88
"Strike packages," 41(fig.), 64
Submarines, 5, 101
  attack, 103, 236
  cost of, 236
  nuclear, 7–8, 92

radii of operation, 106–107
sea control and, 115–116, 117
SSBNs, 88
SSN-688, 236
in World War II, 106
See also Anti-submarine warfare
"Superstates," 136
"Supporting systems," 250
Surface-to-air missile (SAM)
systems, 47–49, 51, 52, 56,
58–59, *p.*, 99, 222, 236
Surgical strikes, 209
Synfuels, 210–211
Syria, 205

Tanks, 67–75, 178–179(fig.)
cost of, 233, 235, 235(fig.)
development of, 68
M-1, 233
M-60A2, 80
mobility of, 71, 74
performance requirements, 233,
235
XM-803, 233
See also Anti-tank weapons;
Armored vehicles
Task Force 58, 92, 95(fig.)
Technology
advances in, 3–9, 44–45, 220,
244–245, 250–251, 252, 254
air operations and, 44–45
application of, 226–240
appropriate, 226
compatibility of, 222, 232–235,
234(table), 235(table)
cost-effectiveness of, 220–221,
237
cost-performance phenomenon,
226–227, 227(fig.), 228(table),
229–230, 229(fig.), 230(fig.)
cost progression, 241–242
dependency on, 208
high-low force mix, 63–64, 221
manpower and, 225
nighttime operations and, 40,
43–44

reconnaissance, 36–37, 38–39
reform movement and, 223
See also Computers; Delivery
systems; Electronics; Guidance
systems
"Teeth-to-tail ratio," 189
Theater of operations. *See* FEBA;
Nuclear battlefield
Tito, Marshal, 168
TOW anti-tank missile, 84. *See
also* Anti-tank weapons
Tracy, Benjamin F., 212
Troop concentration. *See* FEBA
Truman, Harry S, 149

Unconventional war. *See* War,
unconventional
United States
base structure, 140, 205, 208,
209
defense spending, 62, 63, 126(fig.),
127, 129, 175, 176(fig.), 177,
198, 201, 219, 220–221, 222,
223–226, 245, 246(tables), 247,
247–249(figs.), 250
force expansion, 153–154
in foreign conflicts, 143–145, 204
military commitments, 150–152
social spending, 126(fig.), 127
space exploration, 126(fig.), 127
USSR. *See* Soviet Union

Vertical takeoff and landing aircraft.
See Aircraft types, V/STOL
aircraft
Vietnam war, 200, 203
air defense suppression in, 49, 51
air operations in, 33–34, 37
escalation of, 149–150
Viper, 77. *See also* Anti-tank
weapons

Wampanoag, 244–245
War
causes of, 131, 132–133(table),
134, 161–168

constraints upon, 136, 137(table),
    138, 139, 142, 143–145
deterred, 129, 130(table),
    132–133(table)
duration of, 188, 189, 190–192,
    195, 209, 223, 251
European scenario, 184–186, 189
force imbalance in, 184, 191,
    221, 221n
limited, 131. *See also* Escalation
magnitude of, 135(fig.), 135–136
potential conflicts, 201–207,
    202(fig.)
by proxy. *See* Proxies
recent history of, 129–134
scenarios, 184–186, 189, 201–207,
    202(fig.)
tactical surprise in, 209
unconventional, 129, 130(table),
    132–133, 148–149
See also Air-to-air warfare; Anti-
    submarine warfare; Armored
    warfare; Chemical warfare;
    Conventional war
War Powers Act (1973), 143
Warsaw Pact, 154
    air defenses, 49, 51
    boundaries, 174(fig.)
    defense spending, 128(fig.),
        128–129, 175, 176(fig.), 177(fig.)
    force modernization, 188
    NATO and, 193–194, 195
    ready forces, 180, 181(fig.),
        181–182
    relative strength of, 175, 177,
        178(fig.), 179(figs.), 180, 181(fig.),
        181–183
    reserve forces, 182
    social spending, 128(fig.), 128–129
Waterloo

battle of, 4
Weapons systems
    "affordability," 225
    applicability, 208, 209–210
    combat readiness requirements,
        224
    defense budget and, 246(table),
        247–249(figs.)
    development rate, 253–254
    evolution of, 230–236
    mission changes, 250–251
    performance requirements,
        229–232, 232(table), 233,
        234(table)
    utility extension, 242–244, 253
Weather
    air operations and, 40, 43
Wegener, E., 213
West Germany
    defense of, 184–188
    East Germany and, 162, 163
    NATO and, 156
    reunification efforts in, 162
    Soviet Union and, 154, 156, 167,
        168
World War II
    air operations in, 31, 33, 34–35,
        39, 45–46, 46(table)
    armored warfare in, 68–69, 70–71
    chemical weapons in, 24
    force depletion in, 191
    naval forces in, 92, 93(fig.),
        95(fig.)
    naval operations in, 107–108,
        116
    reconnaissance in, 38n
    strategy in, 215
    submarines in, 106
    technology development in, 5–7

Yugoslavia, 168